South View of Whitehaven 1815

WHITEHAVEN

AN ILLUSTRATED HISTORY

WHITEHAVEN
AN ILLUSTRATED HISTORY

DANIEL HAY, F.R.S.A., F.Ph.S., A.L.A.

Michael Moon at the Beckermet Bookshop, Beckermet, Cumbria
and also at
Michael Moon's Bookshop, 41–42 Roper Street, Whitehaven, Cumbria

1979

© Daniel Hay, 1966

Second impression 1968

New edition, revised and enlarged, 1979

ISBN 0-904131-21-1

Designed by Ron Holmes, M.S.I.A.D.

Text set in I.B.M. Baskerville by Typewright Beverley East Yorkshire

Printed and bound in Great Britain by The Scolar Press Ilkley West Yorkshire

Frontispiece: Aerial view of Whitehaven, 1978. Crosthwaite School and new multi-storey car park are in the foreground. *Photograph by Roger Savage.*

To Stella

Publisher's Foreword

This new book on Whitehaven is the result of several years close co-operation between the author and the publisher. Within its pages will be found a wealth of historical and factual material gathered by Daniel Hay over a period of nearly fifty years.

My brief, as publisher, to Mr Hay was to ask him to rewrite his 1966 History of the town, recheck the information, correct where necessary and to add several new chapters to bring the story up to date and make it more complete. I particularly requested that a complete list be drawn up of all victims of local mine disasters which would act as a reminder to us all of the sacrifice that these men and boys made in laying down their lives for the town and of the loss suffered by their families and the entire community on far too many occasions in the past.

Over the last decade much has happened in the reshaping of the town's future, and many avenues of research have been explored yielding much interesting material. During this time a revolution in the techniques of printing has taken place which allow new freedoms in typesetting and greater flexibility in the use of illustrations. I have made use of all these technical advances in this book. The author and I went through the text many times and decided to include relevant illustrations where these could be found. Initially we found seventy-five illustrations, a goodly number in itself but, as we checked the proofs and re-read the manuscript, ably assisted by my managers, Mary Kipling and Ruth Eversley, we found more and more, and, like Topsy, it just grew and grew. So now we have found over one hundred and fifty illustrations of varying kinds: photographs, engravings, maps, portraits, coats of arms, caricatures and title pages with which to illuminate the text.

This book is our twenty-first local history publication and I feel it is a fitting and entirely suitable volume with which to come of age and to house safely between its covers the patient notetaking and literary detective work of a man's working lifetime — that of Daniel Hay, the town's former borough librarian. I must point out that though this book is definitely the latest word on Whitehaven, it is certainly not the last. The past is still being explored and new material is constantly turning up, the present is still being written and the future has still to be determined.

The constant support of my wife, Sylvia, over the last few years has helped me to achieve this small literary milestone — our twenty-first book — and her practical proof reading has speeded up the passage of this particular volume through the presses.

I feel special mention should also be made of Ron Holmes, my designer, who has nurtured a pile of typed sheets and many scribbled broadsides into a book which we think the reader will enjoy now and which his family will cherish in years to come.

Michael Moon
Whitehaven, 1979

Contents

Publisher's Foreword   6

Preface   7

Chapter 1   Origin of the name Whitehaven   11

Chapter 2   Medieval Whitehaven   13

Chapter 3   Whitehaven before the Reformation   18

Chapter 4   The Lowthers   20

Chapter 5   The seventeenth and eighteenth centuries   27

Chapter 6   John Paul Jones   33

Chapter 7   The fortifications at Whitehaven   36

Chapter 8   Coal mining   39

Chapter 9   The nineteenth century   61

Chapter 10   Shipbuilding   64

Chapter 11   The building of the harbour   74

Chapter 12   Railways   80

Chapter 13   Local government: Trustee Board to Town Council   82

Chapter 14   Council achievement   91

Chapter 15   Churches   102

Chapter 16   The Theatre   121

Chapter 17   Education   123

Chapter 18   Whitehaven potteries   125

Chapter 19   The twentieth century including local industries   128

Chapter 20   Famous personalities   151

Chapter 21   Whitehaven artists   171

Chapter 22   The Hospital Service   179

Chapter 23   Booksellers and Printers   184

Appendices I-VIII   189

Where to look for more information   208

Index   212

Preface

This history of Whitehaven owes its genesis to a suggestion made by my friend Councillor Thompson Reed at a Town Council meeting some thirteen years ago.

It was primarily meant to provide some general information on Whitehaven's development for those who had grown up in the town and for those who had come to live here and wanted to know more about its history, for pupils doing school projects and for students wanting background reading for training college or university theses.

For my own basic knowledge I owe a great deal to the late Mr W. Stewart Rees, of Liverpool, whose requests for data on the early history of the Brocklebank shipping company laid the foundation of my interest in maritime history, to Mr Oliver Wood who when working for his Ph.D. thesis provided me with more information than I ever gave him, and to the late Mr William Watson whose knowledge of Whitehaven history was surpassed only by his willingness to share what he knew.

I am grateful to the Editor of the *Whitehaven News* for permission to reproduce what has appeared in his paper, to the Editor of *Sea Breezes* for the chapter on shipbuilding, to the Editor of *Nucleus* for that on the theatres, to the Editor of the *Transactions of the Cumberland and Westmorland Antiquarian and Archaeological Society* for that on the fortifications, and to the Earl of Lonsdale for permission to reproduce the street map of 1714.

The present revision has only been possible by the kindness and co-operation of many people. I should like particularly to thank Mrs C. Baudrand for help in updating the account of the Silk Mills; Mr M. J. Clay, Mr A. W. Routledge and Miss Kathryn Black for the Marchon story; Mr D. Edgard for information on H. Edgard & Sons (London) Ltd; Mr Tom Stout for that on Egremont Tubes Ltd; and Mr George Crichton for that on Smith Brothers (Whitehaven) Ltd. Mr Dalton Leslie has been most helpful in providing information about his family's building record, and Mr J. E. S. Swift and the Technical and Planning Department of Copeland Borough Council have helped to clarify the achievements of the former Whitehaven Borough Council. Mr J. L. Bartholomew, of Border Engineering Contractors Ltd. has provided up-to-date information on the activities of that firm, while Mr Tom Milburn has made available background information on his.

Mr Robert Crosby and Mrs Ida Parrish have contributed data on the harbour, and Mr William Foster, Mr Andrew Young and Mr D. Hoten have helped with information and pictures relating to the mining industry.

Mr David Andrews and members of the Whitehaven Library staff, Mr Harry Fancy and Mrs Lyn Purnell at the Whitehaven Museum, and Mr Bruce Jones and the staff of the County Record Office have all been extremely helpful in innumerable ways. I am particularly grateful to Mrs Beryl McAllister for clerical help in the preparation of the text.

My thanks must also go to Mr P. J. Pollitt, Mrs Wise and Mr C. Turner at the West Cumberland Hospital, and to Mr H. Jefferson for information on his firm.

This book cannot tell the whole Whitehaven story; I can only hope that it will encourage those who read it to explore some of the avenues it opens up. For example, since the first edition appeared my friend Mrs Elizabeth Lawrence-Dow has done a great deal to explore the fascinating story of Whitehaven's trading links with Virginia and Maryland.

Above all, I hope that it will help its younger readers to develop a pride in their native town, so that they are prepared to echo the words of St Paul who in his day proclaimed himself 'a citizen of no mean city'.

Chapter 1

Origin of the name Whitehaven

The origin of the name WHITEHAVEN has intrigued scholars for many years. One of the earliest attempts to elucidate the problem was made by Parson and White's *History, Directory and Gazetteer of Cumberland and Westmorland* (1829). They state: 'The rocky headlands on each side of the haven have a whitish appearance when contrasted with the dark red sandstone of the conspicuous promontory of St Bees Head, which is conjectured by some to have given name to the port but others, perhaps with plausibility, assert that it was originally called *White's Haven*, owing to a person whose surname was *White* being the first fisherman that frequented the bay, and built a thatched cottage in 1502 – this, the only thatched house of late date in the town, was situated near Old Town, and fell down about fifteen years ago.'

Samuel Jefferson, in his *History of Allerdale-Above-Derwent* disagrees with this derivation and says 'This latter supposition cannot be correct, as in the *Register of the Priory of St Bees* the place is very frequently mentioned, at a much older period, as Witofhaven, Quitofhaven, sufficient evidence to prove the fallacy of the latter etymology.'

The Register supplies an interesting number of variants of the name of Whitehaven: Whitofthavene, Witehavedhafne, Qwytofthavene, Wittofthavene, Witofthaven, Quithaven, Wytofhaven, Quithofthaven, Qwittofthaven, Withofthaven, Whitythaven, Whithofthaven, Hwithothaven.

The constancy of the three elements in the name has led to the compilers of the English Place Names Society's *The place-names of Cumberland* to say: 'The origin of this name is correctly stated by Denton: "Whitehaven or Whit-toft-haven is a creek in the sea at the north end of a great bergh or rising hill there which is washed with the flood on the west side where there is a great rock or quarry of white hard stone which gives name to the village and haven." This rock was known as "white headland" (O N *hvit hofud*). Before 1150 a harbour had come into being under the headland and had given rise to the triple compound *hvithofud-hafn*, of which the second element was early lost. The word "haven" is of Scandinavian origin (Bjorkman, *Scandinavian Loan-words in Middle English*, 242). It is not recorded in England before the 11th century, and Whitehaven is a remarkably early example of its appearance in an English place-name.'

Mannix and Whellan (1847) preferred to look elsewhere for the origin of the name and aver: 'That Whitehaven was anciently a place of resort for shipping appears from some particulars respecting it mentioned in those remarkable Irish documents called the *Annals of the Four Masters*, in the County of Louth – nearby, opposite on the Irish shore. In the account of the domestic habits and manufactures of the Irish, it is stated that their *Coracles*, or *Wicker Boats*, their *Noggins*, and other domestic utensils, were made of wood called *Wythe* or *Withey* brought from the opposite shore or *Barach* (i.e. rocky coast), and that a small colony was placed there for the purpose of collecting this wood.'

The author of a *Visitors' Guide to St Bees, Whitehaven, etc*, scoffs at this as childish and says: 'We may observe that Sandwith is very near. Now Gwyth, in composition Wyth, in the ancient British signifies a channel or gutter or watercourse, and Wythoven might be corrupted for Wyth and dofen or doven, deep; signifying the deep gut or gutter.'

Interesting as this attempt at a Celtic derivation for the name 'Whitehaven' must be, it must be set against the fact that the early form of 'Sandwith', from 1260 onwards to 1607 is 'Sandwath', meaning 'the sandy ford' so that there is little doubt that the origin of the name 'Whitehaven' is from the Old Norse meaning 'the haven by the white head.'

Two Anglo-Saxon cross fragments at St Bees Priory.

Anglo Saxon Impost built into Nave Wall in St Bees Priory.

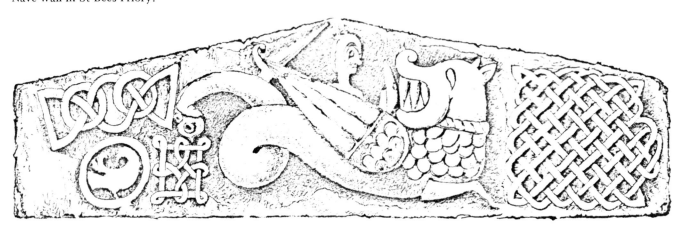

Chapter 2   Medieval Whitehaven

Remains of an anglo-saxon churchyard cross at St Bees.

For two and a half centuries after the Romans left Britain the Romano-Britons, the Cymru or Cumbri, living south of Hadrian's Wall, managed to maintain some sort of independence, but between A.D.670 and 680 the Angles of Northumbria forced their way through the Tyne gap and overcame them. In A.D.876 the Danes burnt Carlisle and for more than two centuries following that date they and a mixed multitude of Celto-Scandinavians, Vikings from Ireland and the Isles continued to settle in Cumberland. Their movement over the district is recorded in our place names.

The Anglo-Saxon Chronicle records that in A.D.945 the English king, Edmund, harried all Cumbria but goes on to say that he 'let it all to Malcolm, King of the Scots, on condition that he be his helper on sea and on land'. For the next century and a half the Kingdom of Scotland embraced both sides of the Solway. Despite the quotation from the *Chronicon Cumbria* quoted in the St Bees and Wetherall registers, it is fairly obvious that Cumbria remained outside the England of William the Conqueror.

In the confusion following the Norman invasion Malcolm of Scotland seized possession of it, but Gospatric of Northumberland harried Cumbria in 1070. Two years later William deprived Gospatric of his earldom and forced him to seek refuge in Scotland.

Events in Cumbria are confused until 1092 when William Rufus marched north with a great army and took Carlisle. He restored the town and built the castle. What became known as the 'Power of Carlisle' was given to Ranulf Meschin, son of Ranulf Meschin, sheriff of Bayeux in Normandy. About 1122 Ranulf succeeded to the earldom of Chester and the 'Power of Carlisle' was resumed by the Crown. About the time he departed Henry I came to Carlisle and ordered the city to be fortified. Instead of appointing another great vassal in Ranulf's place, the king created the baronies of Allerdale, Wigton, Levington, Greystoke and Coupland. Coupland stretched from the Derwent to the Duddon and was given to William, Ranulf's brother.

Thurstin, Archbishop of York, like William Meschin, was also a native of Bayeux, and it was at his suggestion that William founded the Priory of St Bees about 1125. This was a development rather than an innovation, because the name of the place – Kirkby Becoc – indicates that a church going back at least to Anglican times was already in existence.

The advent of the Normans and the establishment of the Priory saw the inauguration of an era of record keeping which enables us to form a fair idea of what the Whitehaven of the period between the Conquest and the Reformation was like. It formed part of a scattered rural community which raised horses, cattle, sheep and pigs, and maintained one or two minor industries.

The Barony of Coupland was split down into manors and townships, and the lord of each manor had to render certain feudal services to the baron. Whitehaven was a township the boundaries of which were early defined in the Priory records.

The township extended from the mouth of the Pow Beck, along the east bank of the beck as far as to the present goods station, across to Midgey Ghyll, along the front of the present hospital site and thence by what is now George Street and Wellington Row to the mouth of Bransty

13

Beck. Along the west side of the beck and covering what is roughly the present Kells and Sandwith electoral wards was the manor of Arrow-thwaite. Flanking the north-eastern boundary of Whitehaven lay the township of Hothwaite, which stretched up into the moorland above. It was bounded on one side by the great ghyll (now the New Road) and on the other by Midgey Ghyll.

William Meschin's first gift to the projected prior of St Bees was six carucates of land in Kirkby as well as the manor held by William the Bowman and he confirmed gifts promised by others who witnessed the deed – Waldeve, Reinar, Godard, Ketel, William the chaplain, Coremac and Gillebecoc. Waldeve, lord of Allerdale-below-Derwent, granted the manor of Stainburn; Ketel gave Preston. Reiner, two oxgangs of land in Rottington with the native who dwelt there. Godard, lord of Millom, gave the churches of Whicham and Bootle, with two manses, and their whole parishes and titles.

William Meschin supplemented his previous gift by adding the church of Kirkby and its parish which was defined as everything contained within a line from Whitehaven up to Bransty Beck, over Harras Moor to Keekle Beck, then down its course to Egremont, and thence down the Ehen to the sea at Sellafield. He also gave the chapel of Egremont and the tithes of his domain and all his men, as well as the tithes of his fisheries and the skins of his venison.

The monastic establishment St Bees was to consist of a prior and six monks.

Ranulf, son of William Meschin, confirmed his father's gifts and added to them the Manor of Ennerdale. Ranulf died without a son to succeed him and the barony passed to his sister, Alice de Rumelly, who was married to William Fitz Duncan, the nephew of David, King of Scotland. On the death of her husband she confirmed the gifts made by her father and brother and added substantially to them. Amongst other things she gave Hothwaite to the Priory with power to cultivate and rebuilt Hothwaite, rights over salt-making, and control of the fisheries in the port of Whitehaven.

Upon the death of Alice, for which no records exist, the inheritance fell to three heiresses, Cecily is supposed to have had Skipton; Annabel, Allerdale-above-Derwent, and Alice, Allerdale-below-Derwent. Cecily, the eldest daughter, married firstly, Alexander Fitz-Gerald, and secondly, William le Gros, Earl of Albemarle, who died in 1179, leaving a daughter, Hawise, who in 1180, married William de Mandeville, Earl of Essex.

The Priory Church, St Bees. Drawn by W. Kinnebrook, engraved by W. H. Lizars.

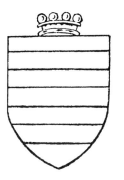

Thomas de Multan of Egremand
Arms:— Argent, 3 bars, Gules.

Although the landed possessions of Fitz Duncan and his wife were ultimately divided there seems to have been some usurpation, particularly on the part of Cecily and her daughter. Both William le Gros and his wife made gifts to the Priory.

Annabel married Reginald de Lucy but it seems that it was not until 1200 that their son Richard, succeeded to the Barony of Coupland.

Thomas de Multon who obtained the wardship of the daughters and the lands of Richard de Lucy in 1213 married the widow and gave his wards in marriage to his two sons, Annabel to Lambert de Multon and Alice to Alan de Multon, between whom the Lucy inheritance was divided in 1230. The manor of Egremont and the bulk of the lordship of Coupland was apportioned to Lambert and Annabel.

The Chronicles have little good to say of Lambert, who died in 1246, Matthew Paris says that by not a few presents to the Pope he obtained the singular privilege that nobody could excommunicate him for any fault except by special mandate of the Pontiff himself, as if he might be allowed to sin with impunity. It is in the charters of the Priory of St Bees relating to the period of Thomas and Lambert de Multon that we get information about Hothwaite.

About 1220, Adam of Harras gave his daughter Matilda six acres of arable land next to Hothwaite 'as the stream descends from the malt-kiln of Hothwaite through the orchard, and flows into the ghyll, and thence to the moor; and thence across to the aforementioned stream next to the malt-kiln' on payment of 12 pence annually.

About 1250, Thomas, son of Richard Collan gave to the monks of St Bees a road 20 feet wide from Hothwaite through his middle land of Whillimoor. He also gave them a similar roadway from Hothwaite to the moor of Hensingham. Both of these gifts were confirmed by Hugh of Harras, his feudal superior.

About the same date Robert of Hothwaite gave six acres of land to his son, Gilbert, in the township of Hothwaite. The boundaries of the grant are described as 'the house that was Adam's son of Whok (i.e. Hulkill) with toft, which contains one acre and half acre which lies by the thorn on the south part, and four acres and a half lying next to the land of Henry of Hothwaite, my brother.'

This charter is most interesting because when linked with a later charter by Gilbert and his wife, Christian, giving the land to the priory and referring to it as 'our whole land in the flat of Hothwaite', it indicates that this is the site on which Whitehaven Castle was later built and that it is the oldest inhabited site in the vicinity. The earliest charter relating to Arrowthwaite is one in which Clement, who was abbot of St Mary's, York, from 1161-84, granted Arrowthwaite to Reginald, son of Dermot. It sets out the boundaries of the manor.

The next charter is dated about 1230. In it Maurice of Man grants to the monks of Wetherel a place in the territory of Arrowthwaite for the construction of a salt-pan, with free entrance and exit by the way which he had given to the Monks of St Bees, and the right to take such firewood as is necessary.

Sometime during the period (1256-82) when Nicholas de Langton was prior of St Bees, Reginald son of Maurice of Arrowthwaite, was confirmed in possession of the manor. The abbot makes the following reservation: 'Saving to us and our successors the way to our salt-pans and seacoals in the bank and under the bank for salt-making where we are accustomed to take coals ...' This reservation, taken in conjunction with Maurice of Man's grant to the monks of Wetherel, indicates that coal mining had been going on at Arrowthwaite from the early years of the thirteenth-century.

Another charter of Reginald, son of Maurice, contains a reference to Reginald the quarryman, indicating that quarrying was another local industry.

From Reginald the Arrowthwaite estates passed to Nigel of Arrowthwaite but the relationship between the two is not clear. On Nigel's death the estate passed to his daughter Margaret, who was married to Thomas Wymondham. The Wymondham charters relate to the period 1315-31. Margaret conveyed the manor to Roger of Sutton in Galtres and in 1335 Roger bequeathed his lands and tenements in Arrowthwaite and Whitehaven to the Abbot of St Mary's, York, and to the monks of St Bees. His holdings in these places included fourteen messuages and six tofts, 124 acres of land, eight acres of meadow, one acre of wood, forty acres of waste, ten acres of moor, four acres of marsh, and twelve pence rent, the term 'messuages' implying dwelling houses with lands, 'tofts' houses with rights of common.

Owing to the Statute of Mortmain consent had to be obtained for the gift, and on 5 December 1334, an inquisition was taken at Egremont in the presence of William of Clapham, escheator of the king in the counties of York, Northumberland and Westmorland at which a jury of twelve say on oath that there will be no danger or prejudice to the king or others if Roger de Sutton conveyed the property to the abbot. The annual value of the estate is set at twenty six shillings and eight pence.

A most interesting charter of this period is one dated 1 July 1324, in which Roger de Sutton 'let for rent to Simon Crump, of Ireland, one vault (drift) in Whitehaven with free entrance and exit to the same to obtain coal and stone within the solitary part of Arrowthwaite next to the seashore'.

Another, even more interesting charter is the one in which Hugh Fleming and Christina, his wife, gave to 'Sir John, rector of the church of Lamplugh, and Sir Richard, of Whitehaven, chaplain, the half manor of Walton, with all meadows, buildings, woods, turbaries, and all their other appurtenances in the township of Kirkebibecoc'. It is dated 26 April 1359. It is not clear where Sir Richard was chaplain. If it was at Whitehaven the date is most significant.

The South-East Prospect of Whitehaven, 1642.

Regulations as to the toll by land and sea were in force, but it is curious that although Richard de Lucy had granted a weekly market and a yearly fair to Ravenglass in 1208, and in the same century grants of a similar nature were given to Cockermouth (1227), Millom (1234), Egremont (1267), Keswick (1276), and Seaton near Workington (1280), Whitehaven did not receive the privilege until 1654.

Information about the effect of Border feuds and the wars between England and Scotland on West Cumberland is not always easy to come by; but in the year 1315 Robert Bruce invaded England and ravaged the northern counties. Sir James Douglas did much damage at Egremont and despoiled the Priory of St Bees. It was probably in this invasion, or that of 1322, that injuries were inflicted on Calder Abbey which were never repaired.

After 1359 there is no further mention of Whitehaven in the St Bees registers.

Whitehaven appears to have been called upon to furnish shipping in 1172, when the Nevilles, of Raby Castle, accompanied Henry II to Ireland; and again in 1299 in the reign of Edward I we find that Alexander Scot, master of the *Mariote*, of Whitehaven, and his five sailors, were paid 14*s* for eight days work in carrying corn to Whitehaven to be ground at the mill there. From the document in which this is recorded it is clear that the standard rate of pay was 3*d* per day for sailors and 6*d* per day for ship-masters. In this latter document there is reference to two other Whitehaven ship-masters, Alexander Stute and his son, Alan; but these are the only records of Whitehaven as a port in the medieval period.

Chapter 3

Whitehaven before the Reformation

By the middle of the fourteenth century the priory of St Bees had received all the land that was likely to be ceded to it. The Statute of Mortmain of 1279 had severely restricted the transfer of land to religious houses, nevertheless although St Bees was not as richly endowed as some institutions, it possessed all the land now covered by the parish of St Bees and other pieces further afield.

The clear income of the priory as set out in 1535 at the time of the dissolution was £143 17s 2d.

There were nineteen priors up to the middle of the fourteenth century, and in their way they must have wielded as much influence on Whitehaven as the lords of the Barony of Egremont.

Their successors and the dates of their priorates as far as can be ascertained, are as follows:

William de Seynesbury	1360
Thomas de Brignal	1370-71
Thomas de Cotingham	1379
Nicholas de Warthill	1387
Roger Kirkeby	1434-37
Doctor Stanlaw	1465
John Ward	1473-74
Roger Armyn	1485
Edmund Thornton	1496
Thomas Barwyke, custos.	1498
Edmund Whalley	1517
Robert Alanby	1523
John Matthew	1533
John Poule, incumbens.	1535
Robert Paddy, last prior	1537-38

Not very much is known about them except the latter ones. Robert Alanby was prior of Wetheral about 1494. In 1523 he reported ships off the coast of Cumberland. He is said to have retired to 'Harmless Hill,' Whitehaven. This place-name is said to be a corruption of his name.

John Matthew was removed from his priorate, 1533, on account of complaints against him by tenants and inhabitants of St Bees. At the dissolution of St Mary's, York, in 1539, he received a pension of £6 13s 4d.

Robert Paddy was sent to St Bees in January, 1537, when the northern counties were in a rebellious state. At the dissolution of the Priory, a yearly pension of £40 was assigned to him on 3 June 1538.

Some incorrect ideas are held with regard to the treatment of the monks when the monastic establishments were dissolved. Not all were harshly treated. Some leading men became bishops and deans, others became parochial clergy, and the others were pensioned. The pension of £40 granted to the last prior of St Bees would be equal to £2,000 or more today.

Those who did not accept the new regime were driven from their former homes, and forced to wear secular apparel, and forbidden to exercise their sacred function. Not that they were allowed to wander very far. They were to remain state pensioners to the end of their lives, but if they left the district where they were known they risked losing their pensions.

In the year 1315 when Alan de Nesse was prior of St Bees, Robert

Bruce invaded England and ravaged the northern counties. During this period Sir James Douglas did much mischief at Egremont, and spoiled the priory, and it was probably either in this invasion, or that of 1322 (in which the Scottish king 'spoiled the Abbey of Holm Cultram where the body of his father was buried, and proceeded through Copeland devastating and plundering'), that damage was inflicted on Calder Abbey that was never repaired.

His contemporary as lord of Egremont, Thomas de Multon, died about the time of this second invasion, leaving a widow, Eleanor, who had for her dower 'the Castle of Egremont, with a multitude of lands to the said Manor and Castle belonging'. John de Multon, the last of his name, died childless 23 November 1335, whereupon the Barony passed to his three sisters as co-heiresses, and the partition was made much in the same way as in the case of the Barony of Kendal.

The Caput Baroniae, 'the Castle with a due proportion of lands', fell, as in that case, to the eldest daughter, Joanne, wife of Robert, Baron Fitzwalter; a third passed to Elizabeth, wife of Walter de Bericham who subsequently married Robert de Harrington; the remaining portion went to Margaret, who married Thomas de Lucy, of the kindred line of Cockermouth.

In 1371, when Thomas de Brignal was prior of St Bees, Walter Fitzwalter, the grandson of Robert, was taken prisoner during the invasion of Gascony by the forces of Edward III. He had to mortgage the Castle to raise one thousand pounds for his redemption.

On 20 November 1449, about the time when Roger Kirkeby was prior, Thomas Percy, a younger son of Hotspur, was created Baron Egremont, of Egremont Castle. He died at the battle of Northampton, 10 July 1460, and the Barony is held to have expired. This creation took place during the minority of John Ratcliff, son of John Ratcliff and Elizabeth, heiress of the Fitzwalters. It is possible that the Castle may have been still unredeemed, and the money advanced by the Percies.

Between 1527 and 1529, when Robert Alanby was prior at St Bees, Henry Algernon Percy, sixth Earl of Northumberland, called 'the unthrifty', the unfortunate lover of Anne Boleyn, bought from Robert Fitzwalter (then Viscount Fitzwalter) the third part of the ancient barony, including the Castle, and he thus became possessed of two-thirds, the other portion being then vested in Henry Grey, second Marquis of Dorset, father of Lady Jane Grey, whence the share is called the 'Marquis's share'. During this time Whitehaven was regarded as the port of St Bees, but nothing was done to develop it as a harbour. It remained an open creek until the seventeenth century.

At the time of the dissolution of the monasteries the property of the priory of St Bees remained in the hands of the King. In 1553 Edward VI granted to Thomas Chaloner the manor, rectory and cell of St Bees, with all its rights in St Bees and Ennerdale, not granted away by the Crown before, to be held in fee farm, as of the manor of Sheriff Hutton in Yorkshire, in free and common socage, but not in capite, paying to the Crown the fee farm rent of £143 16s 2½d, which is practically the same as the clear income as set down in 1535.

Chaloner was a man of considerable importance and was employed on several missions abroad on behalf of the Crown. He married as his first wife, Joan Cotton, widow of Thomas Leigh, one of the most active suppressors of the monasteries.

From the Chaloners the manor of St Bees passed, in 1599, to Thomas Wybergh, who in the following year mortgaged it to George Lowther and thereby began the Lowther connection with the district.

Wyberg of St Bees.

Arms;– Or, three bars, Sable and in chief, two mullets of the second.

Chapter 4

The Lowthers

The Lowther family is one of the most ancient in the country. The first mention of it occurs in a deed to which William and Thomas de Lowther were witnesses in the reign of Henry II but it is claimed that they were located at Lowther before the Conquest. Certainly the name 'Lowther' is pre-Conquest, being derived from the Celtic *Gled-dior*, limpid stream.

In the reign of Henry III (1227-72) we find mention of Sir Thomas de Lowther and Sir Gervase de Lowther, but it was not until the following reign that the family achieved prominence. Sir Hugh de Lowther was Attorney-General to Edward I, and afterwards Justice Itinerant and Escheator on the north side of Trent. He was also a Knight of the Shire in 1299 and 1302, and at the commencement of the reign of Edward II (1307-27) was made a Justice of the King's Bench. From that time, and through the reign of Edward III (1327-77) the Lowthers filled various offices of trust and honour in the land. They served as Knights of the Shire for both Cumberland and Westmorland, and in Cumberland as Sheriff. They intermarried with such families as the Cliffords, the Curwens and the Wyberghs. Three of the Lowthers fought at the Battle of Agincourt. In the reign of Elizabeth, Sir Richard Lowther was twice sheriff of Cumberland. He was Lord Warden of the West Marches and was custodian of Carlisle Castle in 1568 when Mary Queen of Scots was lodged there. He incurred Queen Elizabeth's displeasure by permitting the Duke of Norfolk to visit her.

His grandson, Sir John, had three sons, John who succeeded him, Christopher, who was created a baronet in 1642, and William, from whom are descended the Lowthers of Swillington. To Christopher he gave the estate of St Bees and Whitehaven.

It is interesting to note how thie estate came into the hands of the Lowther family. The Wybergh connection with the district began with the marriage in 1586 of Thomas Wybergh to Anna Dacre, widow of William Dacre, and niece of Archbishop Grindal. At the time of his marriage, Wybergh, who was lord of Clifton, in Westmorland, purchased the Manor of St Bees from Sir Thomas Chaloner. He appears to have mortgaged it in 1600 to George Lowther, the eighth son of Sir Christopher Lowther, of Lowther. Gerard, the second son, took an interest in it. Gerard and George died without issue, and their interest passed to their brother, Sir John.

Wybergh disputed the title and it was not until far into the seventeenth century that an arrangement was arrived at.

Christopher took over the Whitehaven estate about 1630. To provide an outlet for the coal that was being mined on his estate he initiated or encouraged trade with Dublin. As Whitehaven was simply an open creek he built a pier in 1634 as a shelter for the shipping using the port. This structure is now incorporated in the Old Quay.

In 1638 he married Frances, one of the co-heiresses of the Lancasters of Sockbridge and Hartsopp Halls in Westmorland. He was Sheriff of Cumberland in 1640.

He had two children, Christopher, who was baptised in February 1640, and died in May 1641, and John, baptised 20 November 1642, who succeeded him.

Sir John Lowther, of Whitehaven (1642-1705), was one of the outstanding characters associated with the development of Whitehaven. Of his infancy and early youth we know nothing. It was presumably spent alternately at the family mansion on the Strand and at Lowther. In 1657 he went to Oxford where he stayed little more than a year. On 6 March 1659, he married at Lowther, Jane Leigh, a ward of his uncle Sir John Lowther, of Lowther. In April 1660, he and his wife went to London. One of the fruits of that visit was the confirmation of Whitehaven's right to hold a market and fair. In September 1660, he set up house at Sockbridge and there their first child, Elizabeth, was born in 1661. Two years later he took up residence in London where Katherine, their second daughter, was born in 1664. In January 1664, Sir John made a short visit to Cumberland and was elected M.P. In 1665 the plague caused Sir John to bring his family back to Sockbridge and there, on 17 May 1666, his first son, Christopher, was born. He attended the Parliamentary session at Oxford in October 1665, returning to Sockbridge in December.

This was an anxious year for Sir John in another respect. A claim to the foreshore between high and low water marks was advanced by the Earl of Carlingford, Sir Edward Green and William Dyke, Esq. Sir John secured a grant from the Crown that protected his rights but it is probable that the Earl of Carlingford and his friends had to be bought off.

In 1675 Sir John bought the mansion at Whitehaven known as the Flatt, from Sir George Fletcher of Hutton. He improved and extended it. In 1688 he was appointed one of the six commissioners of Admiralty, a post he held until 1693.

From the time that he came into authority until his death Sir John devoted himself to the development of the town of Whitehaven. An estate map that can be dated round about 1695 shows the he planned that the new portion of the town between the Pow Beck and the Flatt should grow up in an orderly fashion.

During his lifetime Whitehaven grew from a village of forty or fifty houses with a population in the neighbourhood of 250 to a town with over 2,000 inhabitants. At the time of his death in 1705 it had an exten-

Whitehaven c. 1693.

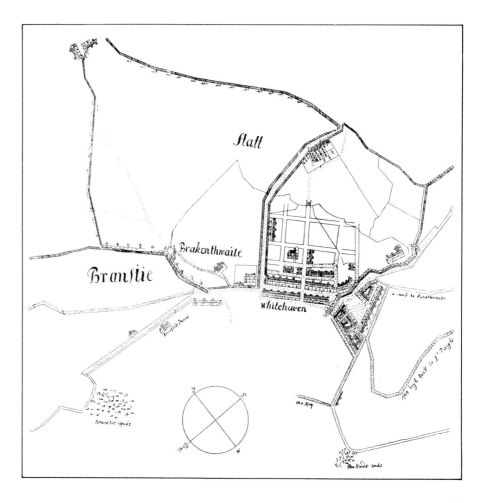

Scotch Street

Scotch Street

Ropewalk

Duke Street

The Church

New Street

Tangier Row

Lawries Street

King Street

East Strand

Chapel Street

Spring Lane

Fair Lane

Castle Lane

Bone Lane

Queen Lane

Fish Street

Gaol Street

James Street

Low Way to Street & Col

Market place

West Strand

Ember yard

East Way to Bridge

High Water Mark

High Water Mark

~ Scale of 300 Yards. ~

Low Water Mark

22

sive coal trade with Ireland and a considerable tobacco trade with Virginia and Maryland. It also had the beginnings of a shipbuilding industry, and a merchant fleet of some seventy-seven vessels. In 1702 Bristol had 165 ships and in 1709 Liverpool had eighty-four.

Sir John died in 1705 and was buried at St Bees. The estate passed to his second son, James, because he had quarrelled violently with his elder son Christopher on account of his dissolute life and his marriage, of which Sir John disapproved.

Mr James Lowther, later Sir James, spent the greater part of his time in London, but kept closely in touch with events in Whitehaven through agents, the Speddings.

In 1708 he secured the passage of a private act of Parliament which gave Whitehaven a body of Town and Harbour Trustees who were to be responsible for the development of the town and harbour until 1894 when Whitehaven received its charter of incorporation as a borough.

During his long life-time, Whitehaven grew rapidly along the lines laid down by Sir John. Matthias Read's famous 'Birds-Eye View' of 1738, the original of which is preserved at Holker Hall, shows the grid-iron pattern of the development plan filling in with substantial mansions set in spacious gardens. The census of 1762, taken seven years after Sir James's death, shows the population as quadruple what it had been at the end of the seventeenth century.

Sir James Lowther, Bt. (1673-1755), by Jonathan Richardson.

Mr James Lowther, as he was at the time, was M.P. for Carlisle from 1692 or 1693 to 1702. He was returned for Cumberland in 1708 and retained his seat until his death in 1755, with the exception of the period from 1722-27, when he either made way for or was defeated by Sir Christopher Musgrave. During this interval he sat for Appleby, being returned on the death of Sir Richard Sandford in 1723.

Sir James was Vice-Admiral of Cumberland, and an alderman of Carlisle. He was also appointed by William III, Clerk of the Delivery of the Ordinance.

Sir James died, unmarried, at his house in Queen Square, Ormond Street, London, on 6 January 1755, aged eighty-one years, with the reputation of being the richest commoner in England. With much enterprise and speculation combined with more than an ordinary love for economy and frugality which earned for him the nickname 'Farthing Jemmy' he accumulated and left behind him in hard cash and stocks a fortune of £600,000. He bequeathed his estates in Cumberland, with the coal mines, worth £15,000 per annum, to Sir William Lowther, of Holker; his estates in Westmorland and Middlesex, with his stocks, mortgages, etc, to Sir James Lowther, afterwards Earl of Lonsdale; to Robert Lowther, Sir James's brother, £20,000; and to sundry charities an aggregate sum of £2,400.

In 1745 James Lowther (1736-1802), second son of Robert Lowther, of Maulds Meaburn, succeeded his father; in 1750, on the death of Henry, third Viscount Lonsdale, he became heir to the Lowther estates; in 1753, on the death of Sir William Lowther, to the Marske estates; and in 1755 on the death of Sir William Lowther, of Holker to the Whitehaven estates.

Lowther had a passionate interest in politics and was quite ruthless in his efforts to dominate events at local and national level. This led to him being referred to as 'the bad earl', and Dr Alexander Carlyle said that he was 'more detested than any man alive, as a shameful political sharper, a domestic bashaw, and an intolerable tyrant over his tenants and dependents'.

Matthias Read's *Bird's Eye View of Whitehaven, 1738.*

To the Honble Sr JAMES LOWTHER BAR.^T F.R.S. & Knight of the Shire for the County of CUMBERLAND this East Prospect of the Town and Harbour of WHITEHAVEN is humbly Inscribed——

In the art of electioneering he had few equals. By combining a lavish expenditure of money with the unscupulous exercise of his enormous influence he was generally able to command nine seats in the House of Commons. The representatives of these seats became known as 'Jemmy's ninepins'. These seats were the two each for Westmorland and Cockermouth, one seat each for Cumberland, Appleby and Carlisle, and the two seats for Haslemere, Surrey, a nomination borough which he had purchased from a London attorney.

Lowther started out as a Whig but following his marriage to Lady Mary Stuart, eldest daughter of John, third Earl of Bute, he swung over to the Tory side. His great rival in the north was William Henry Cavendish Bentinck, third Duke of Portland.

During Lord North's administration, however (1770-82), Lowther acted with the Whigs. In 1775 and again in 1776 he unsuccessfully moved a resolution condemning the use of foreign troops within the dominions of the Crown without the previous consent of Parliament. In 1781 he moved, without success, two resolutions for putting an end to the American war. He was acutely aware of how the activities of French and American privateers were affecting the prosperity of Whitehaven. At the time of the outbreak of the American War of Independence Whitehaven had a fleet of some 200 ships and during the course of the war half of these were either captured by privateers or sunk. This was presumably why in 1783 he offered to build and equip at his own expense a seventy-four gun ship, but the conclusion of peace in that year made the execution of the offer unnecessary.

But his interest in the financial welfare of Whitehaven did not stop him acting with complete dictatorship when the occasion arose.

Two episodes are often quoted in this context. The first is his closing of the coal pits when sued for compensation for damage done to certain property due to mining subsidence which is noted in the chapter on mining. The other is the imprisonment of certain actors which is detailed in the chapter on literary associations.

On the other hand it must be remembered that in 1769 he rebuilt the Flatt in its present form and gave to the town its most gracious architectural feature. He took a keen interest in the affairs of the harbour, but did not always see eye to eye with the Trustees. He was a complex character, and although far from likeable, was the most interesting of all those who bore the title of 'Earl of Lonsdale'.

Upon his death in 1802 without issue all his titles became extinct except the Viscounty and Barony of 1797 which descended upon his next male heir, Sir William Lowther of Swillington. Sir William was over forty when he succeeded to the Viscounty by special patent. He was, however, created the Earl of Lonsdale on 7 April 1807. He is remembered as a munificent patron of the arts. He rebuilt Lowther Hall which had been destroyed by fire in Henry Viscount Lowther's time, according to plans drawn up by Sir Robert Smirke. The new building became known as Lowther Castle.

Joseph Farrington, R.A., was his guest at Whitehaven Castle and left as a souvenir two sketches of the town as it was in 1815.

In 1808 he built the Whitehaven Subscription Library which was let to the management at a nominal rent. He died in 1844 at the age of eighty-six. Of him it has been said that 'In the long line of Lowthers he stands out pre-eminent as a man willing and anxious to use his high station and immense means for the benefit of the generation in which he lived.'

He was succeeded by his eldest son, William (1776-1872), who had a reasonably distinguished political career. He had entered Parliament in 1808 as M.P. for Cockermouth and served continually till 1841, in all thirty-three years. He was Post Master General when he was summoned to the House of Lords in his father's barony. Although a good business man, he shunned the public eye but his ability and great wealth gave him considerable influence in the Tory party. He was the distant original of Lord Eskdale in Disraeli's *Tancred*, 'A man with every ability, except the

William the Good, First Earl of Lonsdale by the Second Creation.

William the Bad, Second Earl of Lonsdale.

Henry Lowther, Third Earl of Lonsdale.

St George Henry Lowther, Fourth Earl of Lonsdale.

Hugh Lowther, Fifth Earl of Lonsdale, in the garden at Lowther Castle.

ability to make his powers useful to mankind', a statement which is far from true. The Earl was a good landlord, keenly interested in agriculture and had spent very considerable sums on drainage. He had been in his earlier days, a patron of John McAdam, the roadmaker, and maintained an interest in roadmaking up to the end. He also played an important part in railway development in West Cumberland. He was at the time of his death Chairman of the Metropolitan Roads Commission. He died in 1872 and being unmarried was succeeded by his nephew, Henry Lowther (1818-76).

Henry Lowther, the third Earl, sat as Member of Parliament for West Cumberland from 1847 until 1872 when he succeeded his uncle.

He was succeeded by his son St George Henry (1855-82). He was only twenty-seven at the time of his death, which came as the climax to several years of ill health. His obituary in the local press says that 'though shy and retiring, with an apparent aversion to much society, his disposition was generous and kindly' and goes on to point out that, had circumstances permitted it, 'a closer personal acquaintance with a town and port in which he had so great an interest would have very much increased the estimation in which he was held'.

His only child was a daughter, so that the title passed to his brother, Hugh Cecil (1857-1944), who became a legendary figure in the world of sport and one of the finest horsemen of his day. He served as Whitehaven's first mayor and presented the corporation with its mace and mayoral chain. His long life spanned a period of great economic and political change and World War I saw the passing of a lavish and colourful era. Before his death the vastly changed economic situations witnessed the severance of the financial interest of the Lowther family in the coal mines, brought about by the nationalisation of coal royalties and later of the mines themselves.

After the death of Hugh Lowther's brother who succeeded him for thirteen years, the present holder of the title, James, seventh Earl of Lonsdale, was forced to sell the Whitehaven properties to pay the double death duties on his uncle's and grandfather's estates. The present Earl has brought his property at Lowther into a high standard of proficiency and modernisation. His interest in West Cumberland continues through his wide connections not only in industry but through the British Legion, County Playing Fields Association, and various youth organisations of which he is President, and as a member of the Northern Region Economic Planning Council.

Chapter 5

Whitehaven in the seventeenth and eighteenth centuries

The Whitehaven to which Sir Christopher Lowther came in 1630 was a village lying mainly on the west bank of the Pow Beck. Its main axis was Quay Street-Swingpump Lane, the latter leading to an area known as Townhead, and later as Old Town. From Townhead a road followed the path now known as Rosemary Lane to Arrowthwaite. Another straggle of houses built along the line of what is now Chapel Street lead to a tiny chapel which was situated where Chapel Street now joins Lowther Street.

This layout is quite clear on the print of Whitehaven in 1642 which shows the chapel with its little belfry. At this time the village had a population of about 250 persons. There is no indication of any strong growth during the period of the Commonwealth. The manor was managed by the guardian of Sir John Lowther who had succeeded to the estate when he was only two years of age. As has been remarked Sir John became one of the most outstanding of all the Lowthers associated with Whitehaven. His first action after the Restoration was to secure confirmation of Whitehaven's right to hold a weekly market and annual fair. The proclamation of the fair is still made each year on 12 August at 10 am by the agent of the Earl of Lonsdale.

His father had built a small pier to give shelter to the coal vessels dealing with Ireland. Sir John extended the coal trade and improved the harbour facilities. He was elected as a member of Parliament in 1664, and quite obviously spent a good deal of time in London, but he was well served by his agents in Whitehaven, first the Gilpins and later the Speddings. The village grew into a small town. By 1693 when the old chapel was pulled down and a larger one built on the site of the present St Nicholas Church, the population had increased to 2,222 and by 1713 was to rise to around 4,000.

He appears to have been reasonably tolerant in his religious outlook. The Gales who became one of the leading local families, were non-conformists, as were the Lutwidges. Owing to the fact that they were excluded from offices of state and of command in the armed forces by the Test Act, non-conformists found an outlet for their talents in business.

In 1672 the house of Isabella Dixon was licensed as a Presbyterian meeting house in Whitehaven. Twenty-three years later Elisha Gale, Henry Palmer, William Atkinson, William Feryes and John Shepherd had collected money for a chapel to be used by Protestant dissenters. Some of these names we shall come to again later.

The town grew because of the increased demand for coal, and as the main market was in Ireland it had to be carried by sea. This meant a demand for more ships which had to bought at other ports. In 1676 the town had a fleet of thirty-two ships; in 1682, forty; in 1685, forty-six; in 1689, fifty-five; and in 1706 the total had reached seventy-seven.

Sir John brought ship carpenters into the town and started a new industry that was to be an important factor in local economy for the next two centuries.

In 1685 the town, which till then was under the administration of the head port of Carlisle, became a separate customs port with responsibilities for the coast between the Duddon and Ellenfoot (later known as Mary-port).

Some ten years before this one of the local sea captains had sailed for Virginia and brought back a cargo of tobacco which became another

Grant of Arms to the Family of
Gale 1712.

Argent on a Fess between three
saltires Humette Azure, an Anchor
between two Lions heads erased
or; and for their Crest, on a wreath
or and Azure an Unicorns head
couped Argent charged with two
Pallets Blew Armed and Crined or,
over all an Anchor Gold.

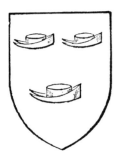

Lutwidge
Arms:— Azure, three morions,
or steel caps, or Crest:— A lion
rampant.

important factor in local affairs during the following century. The ships that sailed to the new world carried out emigrants and materials required by the settlers, and brought back tobacco. None of these ships sailing from Whitehaven was large. The biggest of them, the *Resolution*, had a keel length of sixty feet. Local records suggest that the round trip across the Atlantic was taking about a year.

It is difficult now to imagine that Whitehaven had a thriving trade in the importation of tobacco. Gone are the vast warehouses where hundreds hogsheads of tobacco were stored. Yet at the beginning of the eighteenth century Whitehaven was one of the dozen or so ports that were allowed to import tobacco. With the Union of 1707 Glasgow was accorded the privilege and then a trade war started which culminated in the House of Commons setting up a select committee to investigate the allegation that the Glasgow merchants were defrauding the Customs.

The early ventures of the Glasgow men were made in Whitehaven vessels, and in 1722 the officers of the port declared to the Commons committee that most of the Glasgow trade was carried in Whitehaven ships, the Glasgow merchants paying ten to twenty shillings per ton more than those at Whitehaven, yet the same Glasgow tobacco lords could sell tobacco in Cumberland at ½d to 1¾d cheaper than Whitehaven merchants.

In 1723 the Commons committee reported adversely on the Glasgow merchants, but despite that, Whitehaven's tobacco trade gradually passed into the hands of merchants in the rival city. The event which finally killed Whitehaven tobacco trade was the American War of Independence.

Whitehaven's pioneer in the tobacco trade was Richard Kelsick, master of the *Resolution*. By 1712 the amount of tobacco imported was 1,639,193 lbs and had increased to 4,419,218 lbs in 1740. The importance of the trade will be realised when these figures are placed against the figures for England and Wales as a whole — 28,000,000 lbs; and for London alone for the period 1689-1709 — 20,000,000 lbs.

The import trade was carried on by a few considerable merchants. The Gales followed the Kelsicks and it was tobacco business that brought George Gale to Virginia when he met and married Mildred, the widow of Lawrence Washington and nearly altered the course of American history. In 1712 the principal dealers in tobacco were Thomas Lutwidge, Robert Blacklock, Sheriff of Cumberland, 1710-11, and John Gale, jnr, and in 1740 Lutwidge, Peter How and Richard Kelsick, a son of the Richard Kelsick mentioned above.

The export trade was organised on different lines, persons who took no part in the import trade exporting small consignments to Ireland, Holland and elsewhere, or adopting the more popular course of taking shares in large consignments. One of the more important figures in the tobacco trade in the second half of the eighteenth century was Samuel Martin who built Somerset House.

Walter Lutwidge, the brother of Thomas Lutwidge, was also a merchant with wide ranging interests. A considerable amount of information about him has recently come to light, and will be found in Prof. E. Hughes *North Country Life in the Eighteenth Century. Vol. II Cumberland and Westmorland, 1700-1830.* In 1708 he was a ship master trading with Virginia. Thirty years later he owned some half dozen ships besides having shares in several others. When he temporarily handed over the direction of the business to his son Thomas in 1746, he described himself as 'A man of opulency' with a fortune of £30,000.

He was instrumental in the 1730s in establishing a glass bottle manufactory in the Ginns, which was acquired by Sir James Lowther in 1739. This business must have continued for a considerable period after that as the name is perpetuated in Glass House Yard, and in the Glass House School, later the Colliery Mission. Adjoining it was the copperas works.

The Ginns also became the focal point for the pottery industry which in the nineteenth century employed some two hundred people.

While coal mining and ship building were the two main industries of the eighteenth century, there were a number of subsidiary trades such as rope-spinning, sail-making, anchor-smithing, iron-working, figure-head carving and so on, that provided work for skilful hands. In addition a fair amount of linen-weaving was done locally.

But the sea was probably the greatest employer of labour. In 1682 Whitehaven's fleet of forty employed some 480 seamen, and in 1790, when the fleet totalled 214, the number employed was certainly not less than 1,600, and may well have been more. In 1751 Liverpool's fleet of 220 ships employed 3,319 men. The reason for the apparent discrepancy may lie in the number of Liverpool ships of the period fitted out as privateers. The latter carried very considerably more men than an ordinary merchantman. This number does not include Whitehaven men serving in the navy. The number so engaged is not clear, but there is no doubt that many West Cumbrians did serve in the Navy. The Thomas Lutwidge referred to above had three sons in the service, Thomas Henry who fought under Admiral Sir J. Jervis off Cape St Vincent in 1797; Samuel, a lieutenant, who died of wounds; and Skeffington, who rose to the rank of admiral, and lies buried in Irton church near Vice-Admiral Brian Hodgson.

The eighteenth century was the period of Whitehaven's emergence as a serious rival to Bristol and Liverpool. In 1725 Daniel Defoe had written of the town as 'grown up from a small place to be very considerable by the coal trade, which is increased so considerably of late, that it is now the most eminent port of England for shipping of coals except Newcastle and Sunderland, and even beyond the last, for they wholly supply the city of Dublin, and all the towns of Ireland on that coast'.

Not that Whitehaven achieved any great size in the eighteenth century although it grew fourfold. The population rose from 2,222 in 1693 to 4,000 in 1713 and 9,063 in 1762. The census for 1801 would seem to point to a decline to 8,742 but this is misleading because it does not take into account the shift of population to Mount Pleasant, New Houses and the Ginns, which were built outside the boundary of the township of Whitehaven expressly to accommodate work-people. It was not physical size that made Whitehaven important. It was considerably smaller than Liverpool, which had a population of 5,000 in 1700, rising to 18,000 in 1750 and 25,000 in 1760, and very much smaller than Bristol which had a population of 100,000.

Nevertheless, Whitehaven, even as late as 1816, was recognised as the largest town in the north of England ranking after Newcastle and York.

It was on Whitehaven's mercantile fleet that her prosperity depended. The following table which appeared in 'The Political Magazine and Parliamentary, Naval, Military and Literary Journal' for 1783, under the title *Accurate Estimates of the Trade and Resources of Britain at former periods compared with the Present* shows the tonnage of ships, English and foreign, cleared outwards from the five principal ports as representative of the whole.

	Tons English 1750	Tons Foreign 1750	Tons English 1751	Tons Foreign 1751	Tons English 1752	Tons Foreign 1752
London	146,187	33,673	140,508	25,051	145,999	25,502
Whitehaven	100,068	710	113,092		123,154	210
Liverpool	33,233	9,429	32,675	2,228	31,213	6,682
Newcastle	41,826	3,400	56,448	920	48,406	1,550
Bristol	24,411	3,225	25,720	2,511	25,057	3,673
	1770	*1770*	*1771*	*1771*	*1772*	*1772*
London	178,220	34,656	196,230	38,335	198,758	47,077
Whitehaven	187,448		203,368		192,436	
Liverpool	67,043	9,535	69,868	7,968	76,026	11,284
Newcastle	52,704	1,560	52,154	3,470	61,603	1,866
Bristol	30,063		31,482	7,333	31,529	4,185

Daniel Defoe.

It is probable that the Whitehaven figures in this table refer to the 'port' of Whitehaven which comprehended Whitehaven, Workington, Maryport, Harrington and Parton where the shipping in 1772 totalled 197, ninety-seven, seventy-six, twelve and five respectively, but even halving the port of Whitehaven figures still leaves the harbour as busier than Liverpool, Newcastle or Bristol. This was due to the pattern of Whitehaven's trade, the relatively quick traffic with Ireland helping to build up the tonnage figures. The weakness of Whitehaven's economic situation lay in the surrounding fells. They gave no support to large centres of population and cut Whitehaven off from the towns on the eastern side of the country. It was not until after 1750 that serious thought was given to road improvements, and even for a long time afterwards these were not very efficient.

It was the industrial revolution and the growth of the Lancashire cotton spinning industry that gave impetus to the expansion of Liverpool. Its fleet which numbered 393 in 1775 reached 796 in 1800. Liverpool had an expanding industrial hinterland to feed, Whitehaven had not. Whitehaven's fleet declined from 214 in 1790 to 188 in 1810, and 181 in 1822 but rose to 195 in 1828 and 217 in 1840.

The eighteenth century saw the growth of Whitehaven along the lines laid down by Sir John Lowther. The old part along the Quay Street axis had grown up fairly closely built. The new part on the east side of the Pow Beck grew on an organised plan. Sir John had ordained that the houses on the main streets should be three storeys high. In the beginning, as can be seen from Matthias Read's well known painting of 1738, the houses were well spaced out, set in gracious gardens. The main streets, King Street, Duke Street, Lowther Street, Scotch Street, Irish Street and George Street gradually filled in. Unfortunately, towards the end of the century the need for more and more houses for workers led to the gardens being built over and along side and behind the large houses grew up dark alleys of tiny houses that created slums that became the breeding ground for disease. This slum legacy lingered throughout the nineteenth century and presented the local authority with a major problem in the twentieth.

Nevertheless, we owe some of our best and most interesting architecture to the builders of the eighteenth century. Holy Trinity Church (demolished in 1947) was built in 1715. Like St James', built in 1753, it was not particularly striking externally, but internally it was extremely attractive.

Wrought-iron screen from Lowther crypt in Holy Trinity Church, now used as the Duke Street entrance to St Nicholas Church grounds.

Whitehaven Castle. Pen and ink
sketch by William Gaythorp
(1806-41).

In 1769, Sir James Lowther, later Earl of Lonsdale, rebuilt the Flatt in
its present form and changed its designation to Whitehaven Castle. It is
the distinctly eighteenth century air overshadowing Whitehaven that has
captured the hearts of so many visitors.

Not everyone has been rapturous about the town however. A nineteenth century visitor looked at the slums around the harbour area and
in 1858 wrote: 'There is only one street in England that we have seen to
beat Quay Street, Whitehaven, for squalor and filth; and that was Lace
Street, Liverpool, before the sanitary act came into operation. From
what we noticed there is some analogy between the two. The sprinkling
of Manx people, whose wide mouths, high cheeked bones, and broad
speech there is no mistaking, will not tend much to promote the cleanliness or purity of Quay Street. Houses, shops, jerry shops, courts, public
houses everything you come on speaks plainly of overcrowding. Sallow
looking women, covered with rags, thrust their heads and half their
bodies through the windows to look after you, and as they do this, they
appear to gasp for fresh air'.

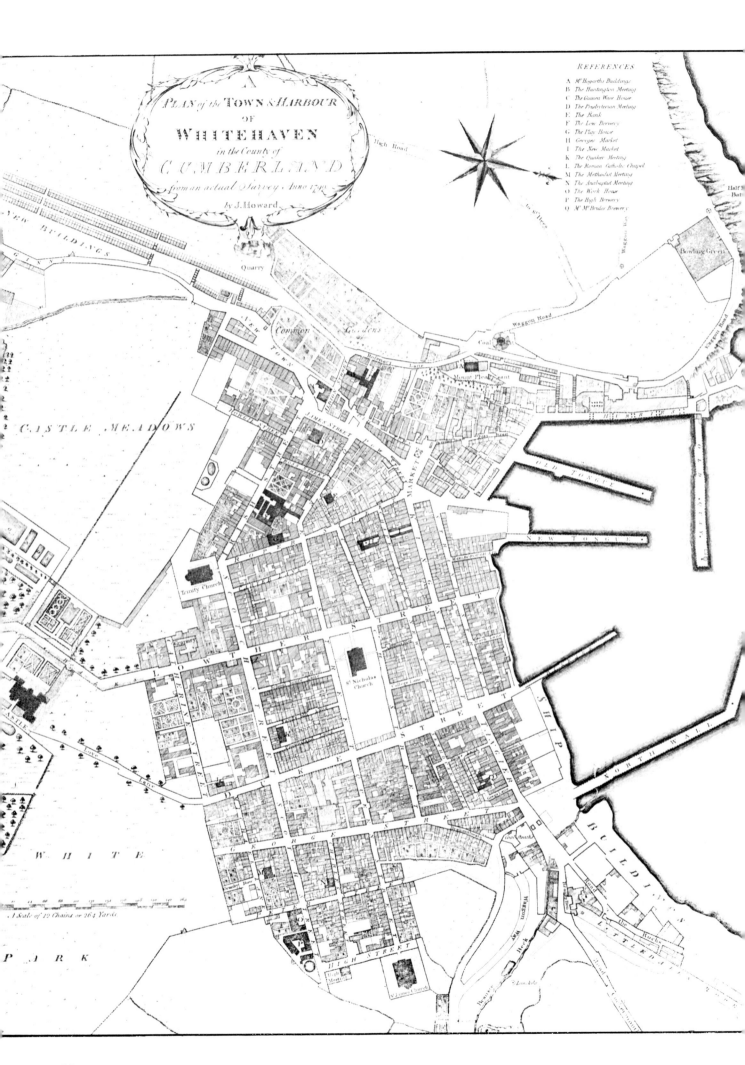

A
PLAN of the TOWN & HARBOUR
OF
WHITEHAVEN
in the County of
CUMBERLAND
from an actual Survey Anno 1790
by J. Howard

REFERENCES

A Mr Hogarths Buildings
B The Huntington Meeting
C The Guinea Ware House
D The Presbyterian Meeting
E The Bank
F The Low Brewery
G The Play House
H Georges Market
I The New Market
K The Quaker Meeting
L The Roman Catholic Chapel
M The Methodist Meeting
N The Anabaptist Meeting
O The Work House
P The High Brewery
Q Mr Mr Beules Brewery

A Scale of 12 Chains or 264 Yards.

Chapter 6

John Paul Jones and Whitehaven

John Paul Jones (1747-92).

◁ John Howard's street plan of Whitehaven, 1790.

One of the most romantic characters associated with the history of Whitehaven is John Paul Jones, who achieved fame, or notoriety – it depends upon one's viewpoint – during the American War of Independence, 1776-83. John Paul – he did not assume the appellation Jones until 1773 – was born at Kirkbean in Kirkcudbrightshire in 1747.

The event which was to have important repercussions later is described in the *Memoirs of the Rear-Admiral Paul Jones* (Oliver and Boyd, Edinburgh, 1830) which is based on the documents bequeathed to Janette Taylor's mother, a sister of Paul Jones. 'A sailor's life was his decided choice; and at the age of twelve he was sent across the Solway by his relations and bound apprentice to Mr Younger of Whitehaven. This gentleman, who was then a respectable merchant in the American trade, he found a kind and liberal master ...' His first voyage was made to America, the country of his after adoption. He sailed in the *Friendship* of Whitehaven; and, before he was thirteen landed on the shores of Rappahanock. While the *Friendship* remained in port, young Paul lived in the house of his brother William, and assiduously studied navigation and other branches of learning, either connected with his profession or of general utility.

'In the course of a short time, his good conduct, intelligence and knowledge of his profession, procured him the confidence and friendship of his master, who promised him his future protection and favour. From the subsequent embarrassment of his own affairs, Mr Younger was unable to fulfil this promise; but in giving the young seaman up his indentures, he did all he could then perform. Thus honourably released from his early engagements, Paul Jones, while still a mere boy, obtained the appointment of third mate of the *King George* of Whitehaven, a vessel engaged in the slave trade.'

Whitehaven does not appear to have been deeply involved in the slave trade, and this is one of the few references that can be traced to the port's connection with the traffic. In 1766 Paul was appointed chief mate of a Jamaican owned brigantine, *The Two Friends*, which was engaged in the slave trade between Africa and Jamaica, but in 1768 he appears to have become nauseated with this lucrative form of employment – he had managed to save a thousand guineas – and decided to return home. He bought a passage in the brigantine *John*, belonging to Messrs Currie, Beck and Co., of Kirkcudbright. While the vessel was still off Tobago both the captain and the mate died of yellow fever. Paul assumed command and sailed the vessel home. In recognition of his services the owners confirmed him in command of the vessel, but on his arrival off Tobago a second time there was trouble with Mungo Maxwell, the ship's carpenter, so that Paul had him severely flogged and on further provocation knocked him down with a belaying pin. Maxwell left the *John* and shortly afterwards died on another vessel bound for the Leeward Islands. The captain of this vessel later testified that Maxwell died of 'fever and lowness of spirits', but the unfavourable reports of Paul's brutal conduct on the *John* and the open talk of his murder of Maxwell poisoned the minds of the inhabitants of Whitehaven and his native village of Kirkbean. He later obtained command of the *Betsy* of London, in which he traded to the West Indies, but the mutiny of the crew over arrears of pay led to the death of the ringleader of the mutineers. His friends persuaded him to flee from Tobago to the mainland, and during the period that he was living incognito he assumed the name of Jones.

In the meantime relations between Britain and the Colonies were rapidly approaching a state of high tension and the ineptitude and tactlessness of the Government precipitated war. Jones applied for and received a commission in the infant Congressional Navy. He was appointed first lieutenant of the *Alfred* under Captain Saltonstall, and so distinguished himself that on 14 June 1777, he was put in command of the ship *Ranger*. On 1 November he sailed with despatches for Benjamin Franklin, the American ambassador in Paris, and arrived at Nantes on 2 December. After a dramatic dash to Paris on horseback he found that duplicates which had been forwarded on another vessel had arrived twenty-four hours earlier.

After a period of considerable intrigue, Jones was eventually permitted to sail from Brest on a privateering voyage round the British coast with a view to inflicting as much damage as possible on the enemy. Embittered by the events which had clouded his career as a merchant seaman he was prepared to wreck the entire merchant fleet at Whitehaven. On 18 April 1778, he attempted a descent on the town, but was foiled by contrary winds. A project against ten or twelve vessels at anchor in Loch Ryan similarly failed, but on the evening of the 22nd he was lying off Whitehaven. His call for volunteers for the hazardous enterprise which he had planned met with a poor response. The first and second lieutenants, Simpson and Hall, feigned illness, but Jones eventually set out with three officers and twenty-nine men, amongst whom was a young man of twenty-two, enrolled in the ship's books as David Smith.

Jones assumed command of one boat himself, and entrusted the other to the lieutenant of marines, Wallingsford, and a midshipman, Benjamin Hill. In each boat were two lanterns and a plentiful supply of tinder and flint, pine faggots and torches. Each sailor was armed with a pistol and cutlass. Before setting out Jones explained his design fully to his men and exhorted them to stand by him. The wind, however, had become so light that the *Ranger* could not approach the shore as closely as had been anticipated and the long pull against the tide proved unexpectedly arduous. 'When we reached the outer pier', Jones stated in his report, 'the day had begun to dawn; I would not, however, abandon my enterprise, but I despatched one boat under the direction of Mr Hill and Lieutenant Wallingsford, with the necessary combustibles, to set fire to the shipping on the north side of the harbour, while I went in with the other party to attempt the south side.'

This portion of the harbour was defended by a small fort and an open battery, known as the Lunette or Half Moon Battery. The actions of the party in the south harbour promised success. In the words of the leader, 'We took the fort by storm, lacking ladders, we had to climb it by mounting upon the shoulders of our largest and strongest men, and entered it in this fashion through the embrasures. I commanded this operation, and I was also the first who entered the fort. The morning was cold, and the sentinels had retired to the guard-room; they were not expecting such a hostile visit. No blood at all was shed in securing this post; we spiked thirty-six cannon of the fort and battery, and I advanced at length to the southern part of the harbour to burn all the ships there, when, to my great astonishment, I saw the boat to the northern part had returned without accomplishing anything. Those who had gone in it pretended to have been frightened by certain noises which they had heard, but I told them that these noises existed only in their imagination.'

As an additional apology for their failure to achieve their object they offered the excuse that their candles had burnt out ... At the same time Jones' own party stated that their candles had also become extinguished. This may have been a cover for trepidity and lack of zeal, as Lincoln Lorenz suggests, on the other hand it may have been a natural consequence due to the time consumed in rowing from the *Ranger*. In any case it did not deter Jones. 'The day too came on apace, yet I would by no means retreat while any hopes of success remained. Having again placed sentinels, a light was obtained at a house disjointed from the town (a watch house on the quay) and a fire kindled in the steerage of a large ship (the *Thompson*), which was surrounded by at least a hundred and fifty others, chiefly from two to four hundred tons burthen, and lying side by side, aground, unsurrounded by the water.

'There were besides, from seventy to a hundred large ships in the north arm of the harbour, aground, clear of the water, and divided from the rest only by a stone pier of a ship's height. I should have kindled fires in other places if the time had permitted. As it did not, our care was to prevent the one being kindled from being easily extinguished. After some search a barrel of tar was found, and poured into the flames, which now ascended from all the hatchways.'

Time was passing quickly, and the town was not only beginning to stir, it was becoming as active as an hive of enraged bees.

'As it was almost eight o'clock in the morning, and as the inhabitants came running by thousands, I was not able to delay longer my retreat, which I made in very good order. When all my people had re-embarked, I still remained for some minutes upon the outside mole to observe at my leisure the terror, panic and stupidity of the inhabitants, who in numbers of at least ten thousand remained motionless like statues or ran hither and thither like madmen to reach the hills on the other side of the town. The retirement had already carried my boats some distance from the shore when the English dared to draw nearer from their fort; finding the cannon spiked there, they brought some pieces taken from the vessels and fired upon my boats. I answered their salute with several swivel guns which I had placed in the stern of my barge.'

Whether Jones' retiral was as leisurely as he implies, he does not appear to have checked up on his party until afterwards. David Smith, or Freeman, as he called himself when he appeared before the magistrates, was missing. Lincoln Lorenz paints a lurid picture of him as a traitor, but the story that Freeman told the magistrates is nothing more than that which an enterprising prisoner might have told to save his neck. Had Freeman been the traitor he has been named, it is exceedingly doubtful whether there would have been time for the *Thompson* to have been set on fire. The raid achieved little in the way of material damage, but its moral effect was great. It spurred Whitehaven into considerable activity in improving its fortifications, and throughout the ports of the kingdom more than doubled the insurance rates. He became a sort of bogeyman, akin to the Black Douglas of an earlier period.

With his subsequent adventures we are not really concerned in this chapter as he never afterwards impinged on Whitehaven history. He was an intrepid man of action, but lacked the qualities that make for inspired leadership. At the instigation of Jefferson he accepted service as a Rear Admiral in the Russian Navy. His temperament was ill-suited to cope with the internecine feuds at the court of Catherine the Great and his career in Russia was wrecked by an accusation of 'rape' that has never been proved or disproved. He returned to Paris, and died there at the early age of forty-five. In 1913 his remains were removed to the crypt in the U.S. Naval Academy in Annapolis.

Chapter 7

The fortifications at Whitehaven

The earliest occasion on which we hear of fortifications at Whitehaven is on 8 April 1639, when Sir Christopher Lowther determined to resist any attempt by Parliamentary forces to land there and wrote to an acquaintance to say that he had bought 'two pieces of ordinance (2 sacres) of Captain Bartlett, and his brother' and wanted two more as he proposed to 'make a fortification for them on the peere'.

The next important occasion is in November 1745, when the town was put in a state of readiness to resist the Jacobites. James Ray in his *Complete History of the Rebellion* says: 'At this time Whitehaven had raised ten Companies of fifty men each, for the Defence of the Place, and raised Breastworks before the Avenues leading to the Town on which they planted Cannon; but on hearing that Carlisle, altho' a strong Garrison, had surrendered, Whitehaven being an open Town, it was thought advisable to dismount the Guns, and put them on board the Ships, that they might not fall into the enemy's hands'. The Minutes of the Town and Harbour Trustees for June 1746 show that £236 7s 3d was paid by the treasurer of the Trustees as a result of the preparations to resist the Jacobites; this included £17 2s 6d 'paid by order to the Gunner of the Fort for his salary for three quarters, and charges of oiling the great guns'.

In the minutes for August 1740, there is a note of 'Seven Guns of Four Pound Shot to be added to the Great Guns upon the Battery'; which I take refer to the Lunette, or Half Moon Battery, and in August 1762, there is reference to 'John Wooler, Esq., having pursuant to an order from the Board of Ordinance made a Survey of the Harbour of Whitehaven, Forts and Coasts adjacent in order to Erect further Forts, Platforms and other Works necessary for the reception of the Guns and Stores his Majesty has been graciously pleased to order to be sent here for the Defence of the Town and Harbour, from any attempts that may be thereupon by the Enemy in time of War, this Day delivered his Report to the Trustees, together with the Plans of the Buildings to be erected necessary for the Reception of the said Guns and Stores, and for the further Protection and Security of the Town and Harbour. Ordered that the said plans be laid before Sir James Lowther, Bart. and Gentlemen of the Town, for their Consideration, in order to be carried into execution with all convenient speed, and that the Estimates be made of the charge and Expense of Erecting the said Works.'

On 21 March 1763, the Trustees 'Ordered that the Guns in the Lunette Battery be dismounted, and properly laid on Beds, the Carriages put into the Storehouse and that two of the Six Pounders be removed from the Old Fort, to the Lunette Battery, and then mounted, that the Ten Eighteen Pounders be likewise dismounted and properly laid on Beds, and the Carriages put into the Storehouses. That the Forty two and Twenty four Pound Guns be placed on Beds under the Shed in the Harbour yard, and the carriages put into the Storehouse and that such of the Stores as can be put into the Storehouse placed there and all the Guns and Carriages that want painting be sufficiently painted'. We hear nothing more about the fortifications of Whitehaven until 23 April 1778, when John Paul Jones, quoted by Lincoln Lorenz from Le citoyen Andre's *Memoires de Paul Jones* which is said to have been dictated by Jones: 'We spiked thirty-six cannon of the Fort and battery'.

Old Fort at Whitehaven Harbour. The structure on the right is a nineteenth century lime kiln built from stonework from the fort. The fort itself was about the same time used as a smithy.

Mrs Reginald de Koven in *The Life and Letters of John Paul Jones* quotes Jones as saying that the townspeople of Whitehaven 'found at least thirty heavy cannon, the instruments of their vengeance, rendered useless'.

After the raid the townspeople subscribed £857 within the space of four days to put the defences of the town in order. According to Parson and White's *Directory* of 1829 'an additional supply of guns was received from Woolwich making the total number ninety-eight, of which eighteen were thirty-six pounders, and twelve thirty-two'. I am certain that this figure of ninety-eight is an error and that the number was considerably less than that. The number of strong points was increased to five. A battery was placed on the cliff top above the Half Moon Battery, another on the top of Bransty Brow and another, known as the Jack-a-Dandy Battery, on the site of the Old Gasworks, near William Pit.

If one analyses the statement about these fortifications as they were about 1810, as related in Mannix and Whellan's *Directory of Cumberland* (1847), there were :

42-pounders	mounted	3
	dismounted	3
	unserviceable	4
24-pounders	mounted	8
	unserviceable	8
18-pounders	mounted	7
	dismounted	10

Total 43

In May 1903, the late Mr Joseph Wear who had a profound knowledge of local history wrote to the *Whitehaven News* about these old fortifications and quoted from an article which had appeared in a local newspaper of some thirty years previously. From this account the disposition seems to have been:

Old Fort	8-9 guns
Half Moon Battery	9 guns
Sea Brows Battery	7-8 guns
Jack-a-Dandy Battery	6 guns
Bransty Battery	5 guns

Total 35-37 guns

This account is not very specific. All that one can deduce from it is that the Half Moon Battery consisted of nine large guns and there were eight or nine guns at the Fort. The Seabrows Battery had seven or eight guns of varying calibre; the Bransty Battery consisted of two 42-pounders and three long 18s, while the Jack-a-Dandy Battery was composed of six guns of 36- and 42-pounder calibre. The guns of this latter battery were removed about 1819.

In November 1817, the Minutes of the Town and Harbour Trustees notes that extensive damage had been done by the sea to the Half Moon Battery. This was repaired at the expense of the Trustees.

Correspondence with Mr Dalrymple, store-keeper, Carlisle, shows that there were at Whitehaven in 1818 ten 42-pounders, eight 32-pounders, eight 24-pounders, and ten 18-pounders.

In the following year the Ordnance Officer proposed to withdraw all the guns from Whitehaven, but at the request of the trustees the guns at the Fort and Half Moon Battery were retained. Two brass field-pieces were sent to Carlisle and the heavy pieces to Plymouth. This correspondence shows that there were at this time at the Fort 'Eight Guns mounted on Iron Carriages'.

A more exact picture is obtained from a document in the Public

Record Office, dated 21 February 1820, listing the heavy ordnance at Whitehaven. The sites and guns are as follows:

Redness point, on the Height		
Dismounted and skidded	3	42-pounders
Bransty, near high water		
Dismounted and skidded	2	18-pounders
	4	42-pounders
Bowling Green		
Dismounted and skidded	3	42-pounders
Thwaitefield, on the Heights		
Dismounted and skidded	3	18-pounders
Half Moon Battery under the cliffs at high water	8	32-pounders
Fort on the New Quay		
Dismounted and skidded	5	18-pounders
Mounted on iron carriages	8	24-pounders
Commands the entrance to the harbour		

Total Cannons 36

It would appear that the guns were last fired in 1824 on the occasion of the laying of the foundation stone of the West Pier. For a number of years two old artillery pensioners looked after the guns and the Fort but it seems to have been abandoned about 1830 and the largest of the guns of the Sea Brows Battery were taken away. All of them cannot have been removed because Mannix and Whellan indicate that in 1847 one battery remained, although in rather a useless state. Referring to the Jack-a-Dandy Battery the following note appears in the index to the minutes of the Town and Harbour Trustees:

'Memoranda: The site of this Fort or Platform was situated a little beyond the last Ship Building Yard in a line with William Pit Raised Waggon Way and then placed nearly on the level of High Water Mark; the Guns supplied were 42-pounders, these and all other Guns that were placed on the Heights and in and about this Town for its protection, were recalled by order of the noble Duke of Wellington and the Government, and being a party to the negotiation and transmission of all these Guns I am induced to make this declaration — John Peile — then a Trustee — the date of recall was during the high and prevailing state of Chartism and Radicalism in the Nation — A few guns and Iron Carriages were allowed to be retained in the Harbour Fort where they now remain by consent of the Government Authorities. The noble Duke replaced a pair 6-pound field pieces to the care of the late Earl of Lonsdale in the place of a pair taken away by General Grindall and now remain in the possession of the present Earl. Sep. 1850 — John Peile.'

Nicholson and Peile's *Directory of Whitehaven* (1864) has a short note about the old fortifications, and concludes: 'The only battery now, however, belonging to the town is the one recently constructed for the use of artillery Volunteers, on the hill above Wellington Pit'.

This in turn suffered from subsidence. In April 1872, there was a great landslip at the Sea Brows which brought thousands of tons of rock and soil crashing down upon the site of the Half Moon Battery. The newspaper account of the incident shows that the battery consisted of two guns and that neither came down with the debris. About this period, four old guns were removed from the site of the Half Moon Battery and taken to Chester.

Guns were on the Sea Brows site within the memory of many persons now living but seem to have been removed during the course of the First World War.

A cannon retrieved from the shingle behind Tom Hurd's Rock by the Sea Cadets in 1963 may be one belonging to the Half Moon Battery.

Chapter 8

Coal mining
at Whitehaven

The advent of the Normans at the end of the eleventh century and the establishment of the Priory of St Bees saw the inauguration of an era of record keeping which enables us to form a fair idea of what the Whitehaven of the period between the Conquest and the Reformation looked like. It formed part of a scattered rural community which raised horses, cattle, sheep and pigs, grew and ground its own corn, and maintained one or two minor industries. There were salt-pans at various points along the coast, and it is obvious from a charter of Nicholas de Langton, prior of St Bees from 1256-82, that there were coal mines and quarries at Arrowthwaite which were being worked after a fashion. There is evidence of some of the stone being exported as far as Windsor.

The parish of St Bees by the mid-fourteenth century was owned by the priory of St Bees, and the monks made no great effort to exploit the mineral resources of the territory under their control.

After the dissolution of the minor religious houses in 1538, the lands belonging to St Bees priory passed to Sir Thomas Leigh and from him to Sir John Chaloner (1553) and his son; and eventually into the hands of the Lowther family.

In 1560, however, Sir Thomas Chaloner, Lord of the Manor of St Bees, granted certain bases of land within that manor to various persons for the purpose of digging coal, at the same time reserving to himself the right to take coals from them.

In 1586 he granted the Governors of St Bees Grammar School liberty 'to take forty loads of coal at his coal pits in the parish of St Bees for the use of the School'.

Dr Nef has suggested that the substitution of the lay landlord for the ecclesiastical landlord helped the rise of the coal industry. The layman, urged on by the profit motive, was more likely to develop his mineral resources to the utmost, to invest heavily in his miners, and lay holdings could be purchased, unlike ecclesiastical holdings which were rarely for sale. The monks had done very little about the coal mines and Leigh and the Chaloners had not done a great deal but the Lowthers were more ambitious and energetic.

In the Workington area coal mining was carried on at the end of the sixteenth century, and by 1750 the Curwens were working pits there. Nearby, the Lowthers were then working coal at Distington, Clifton and Seaton, and Messrs Cookson obtained fuel for their furnace at Little Clifton from their pits at Little Clifton and Greysouthen.

It was at Workington that the first recorded shipments of coal were made. Coal was also being worked before 1750 in the vicinity of Maryport — by Humphrey Senhouse at Ellenborough, by John Christian on his Ewanrigg estate and at Dearham by Sir James Lowther.

But it was at Whitehaven that the major contribution to coal mining was made. Sir Christopher Lowther (1611-44) became lord of the manor of St Bees in 1630 and saw the possibilities of the coalfield and in 1634 built a pier which formed the first stage of what was to grow into a large commodious harbour. He died in 1644 before the Civil War reached its crisis, and the estate passed to his infant son, John, who was only two years old. He was placed in the charge of a guardian. By 1660, when he was old enough to take charge of his own affairs, King Charles II had been restored to the throne.

Although Whitehaven had grown somewhat during the early part of the seventeenth century it was still by 1642, only a village of about fifty houses and possibly some 250 inhabitants, and I doubt whether it had grown very much in the intervening eighteen years. But Sir John was a young man with ideas. One of his first public acts was to secure in 1660 the confirmation of a market charter for Whitehaven and the right to hold an annual fair at Lammas, originally granted in 1654.

The Whitehaven coalfield is divided into two distinct and separate portions, one embracing the vast tract lying between St Bees valley and the sea and under the sea, and the other lying to the north-east of the same valley. Until comparatively recent years the former was called Howgill Colliery and the latter Whingill Colliery. Each side had its separate staffs of management.

It might be as well to point out that there are eight principal seams in the Whitehaven area, as follows:

Seam	Thickness of coal ft	ins	Depth at Wellington Pit
1 Metal (Upper)	3	6	48 fathoms
2 Preston Isle Yard (Burnt)	2	6	53 fathoms
3 Bannock	6	0	74 fathoms
4 Main (Prior)	9	0	96 fathoms
5 Yard	3	0	109 fathoms
6 Little Main	2	0	127 fathoms
7 Six Quarters	6	0	139 fathoms
8 Four Feet	2	3	187 fathoms

The dip of all these seams is seaward with a fall of approximately 1 in 12. The Main seam crops out near the line of the low road to St Bees, and has been worked at a very early period along the main line of outcrop as far as Partis Pit, near Stanley Pond. The Bannock seam crops out at a correspondingly higher level and another seam twenty fathoms above it still higher on the eastern face of the hill; whilst on the coastline the Main seam is found at depths varying from about eighty fathoms at Saltom to 240 fathoms deep at a borehole put down near the sea at St Bees in 1877.

It was probably on the outcrop of the Bannock seam on the hillside close to the town that about 1620 coal was first worked for sale and exportation. The Howgill colliery up to 1660 must have been small and primitive.

As coal was first worked in this county on the rise, or along the level from 'day-holes' made from the outcrops or where the seams were exposed, no machinery was needed. The men dug the coal and women and girls carried it out in baskets on their backs. The workings drained themselves. The places still known as 'bear-mouths' at Whitehaven were the entrances to the roads (made from the outcrops of the seams) along which the coal was thus carried from the pits.

The next development in mining practice in West Cumberland took place about 1650 when, to win new tracts of coal, pits were sunk and drifts cut horizontally through the strata from the lower grounds to drain the workings. That arrangement was called the 'pit and adit system'. At the pit the coal was originally raised by jack-rolls and later by horse gins.

In addition to inheriting the lands of the dissolved priory of St Bees, Sir John Lowther obtained from Charles II a grant of the land between high and low water marks from Bransty to Moresby. He also leased the Fearon mines in Distington and the Duke of Somerset's Bransty estate, which lay to the north of Whitehaven harbour.

The acquisition of land adjoining his own property not only reduced competition but also enabled him to move his coal freely above ground, thus avoiding the payment of extortionate wayleave rents.

Sir John's first engineering feat of any importance was effected in 1663 when he drove a level from Pow Beck at a point a little to the west of the town, near the copperas works in the Ginns, in a westerly direction under the farmhouse at Monkwray and into the Bannock seam. This level drained a sufficient area to serve the needs of the trade until near the close of the seventeenth century. This drain is still known as the Bannock Band surface water level and is used to drain the outcrop water into Pow Beck.

Sir John claimed to be the first to introduce engines for the purpose of drawing water from low levels. The district in Whitehaven known as the Ginns derives its name from the wind and horse-driven water-gins that he established about this time to carry the water to the Beck.

It was probably about 1675 that corves were introduced into West Cumberland pits for the conveyance of coal. The corf was a circular basket made of hazel rods, provided with an iron bow for attachment to the hook at the end of the winding-rope. Originally two-and-a-half cwt capacity, they gradually increased in size as large pits were sunk and when horse-gins were superseded by steam winding engines.

The first mention of these corves comes in two wages books for 1675 relating to the Greenbank and Three Quarters Band Collieries. According to these documents, there were five haggers employed at the Greenbank Colliery at a fixed rate of 8½d per day. Four bearers conveyed the coal to the bearmouth at a fixed rate of 7½d per day each. There the coals were turned into a bank, whence they were either carted or taken by pack-horses to the harbour at a cost of 1s 0d per ton.

At the Six Quarters Band Colliery four haggers were paid a fixed rate of 8½d per day, three trailers 7½d each per day, whilst two winders and one banksman shared 3s 2d per day between them.

The Knockmurton Pit, near the southern boundary of the cemetery, was sunk between 1665 and 1670. It was not the workings from this pit which in the 1960s affected Meadow View House and caused its evacuation, but some other workings of outcrop coal in the vicinity. Up to 1679 several pits had been sunk in the Howgill Colliery. In that year the Woodagreen Pit was sunk near the Ginns.

Up to this time the coals appear to have been conveyed from the Whitehaven pits to the harbour in sacks, carried on the backs of horses, and there emptied into the ships. If one looks at the sketch of the south-east prospect of Whitehaven in 1642, one can see such a convoy of pack horses in the foreground. In 1682, Mr Gale advocated the construction of a 'coalway' to the Woodagreen Pit to enable 'carts and wains' to be drawn with great facility and to obviate the use of sacks in loading the vessels in the harbour. This intended road was described as a 'causeway' bounded on each side with wooden baulks on which the cart-wheels would run.

Such a cartway was constructed during the following year and proved to be a great improvement on the old mode of transport which was still used for the more distant pits. This cartway was the forerunner of other more ambitious projects.

Prior to 1738, John Spedding constructed a wagon-way from Ravenhill Pit to the south harbour. This wagon-way is quite clearly visible on Matthias Read's well-known 'Bird's Eye View of Whitehaven', engraved by Richard Parr in 1738. It also shows the better known wagon-way from Parker Pit to the harbour. This latter is often claimed as the first wagon-way in the country, but the Ravenhill wagon-way was earlier.

The wagons, carrying forty-four cwt of coal, were mounted on cast iron wheels and ran on wooden rails.

In 1680 a Mr Christian was one of the principal workers of coal in the Whitehaven district. He held leases of coal in Hensingham, at Corkickle and other royalties in Moresby and Distington. In 1682 a violent explosion occurred at his colliery at Priestgill, Hensingham, by which one man was killed and six injured.

Two of the principal landowning families in Moresby were the

Fletchers of Moresby Hall and the Lamplughs of Lamplugh, who, for generations, mined coal there and shipped it at Parton. The coal from Moresby entered into keen competition with Whitehaven coal in Dublin.

Sir John Lowther thwarted his rivals in two ways. He had obtained from Charles II in 1666, a grant of such land of the dissolved monastery of St Bees, but which still continued in the possession of the Crown, and in 1678 he procured a further grant of the land between high and low water marks. It was on the latter that it was proposed to build a new pier at Parton, and he was in a position to refuse consent of the pier. In addition, he had Whitehaven appointed a member-port under the head-port of Carlisle (Exchequer Commission, 24 October 1681), the terms being so devised that further development at Parton was impossible. As a result, all vessels engaged in the export trade had to load and unload at Whitehaven and the merchants to pay fees to the Lowthers for the use of the pier there. Nevertheless, an Act was passed in 1705 for enlarging the pier and harbour at Parton, despite Sir John's opposition, and coal was shipped from Parton until 1795 when the pier was destroyed by a storm and the harbour closed.

In 1692 Sir John was working the Prior Band at Howgill and Greenbank, and Lattera Colliery, Moresby. He was also actively engaged in negotiations for the purchase of neighbouring coal properties.

The output of his collieries for 1695 were: Howgill, 15,196 tons; Greenbank, 2,321 tons; Lattera, 1,387 tons; total, 18,904 tons.

In 1697 Mr William Gilpin (Sir John's agent) suggested the establishment of the Copperas Works which were eventually erected in the Ginns. There, green vitriol (ferrous sulphate) was made from the iron pyrites, or 'marchasites' as they were called by Mr Gilpin, which were picked out of the coal.

About this time the Main seam of coal, far superior in quality and thickness, had been discovered at a depth of about twenty-one fathoms. It extended under that part of the town now occupied by the lower portions of Lowther Street, Duke Street and George Street. In order to win it the new Ginns Pit was sunk in 1700, and Stone Pit was also sunk nearby to the Prior Band. They were eventually connected to the 'end Gills' of the various pits to the south in the same seam, thereby forming one continuous watercourse as far as Fish Pit.

Sir John Lowther died in 1705 after a life of unceasing endeavour to develop the trade of Whitehaven. The measure of his success can be gauged by the fact that in 1693, when St Nicholas Church was re-built, the population of the town was estimated at 2,222. He had enlarged the pier built by his father. In 1685, Whitehaven had a fleet of forty-six vessels.

He acquired the mansion known as The Flatt and improved and enlarged it. He was elected a Member of Parliament in 1664 and held office until 1701. He spent most of his time in London; and was a Commissioner of the Admiralty, 1688-93. He had two sons, Christopher and James. Christopher contracted a marriage that displeased his father and appears to have led a dissolute life. He was disinherited in 1700 and his younger brother succeeded to the estates and eventually to the title in 1725.

James Lowther showed the same energy as his father and helped by the brothers John and Carlisle Spedding, made great progress at the Whitehaven Colliery. Like his father, James Lowther spent most of his time in London, but his correspondence shows that he took a keen interest in the development of Whitehaven and the collieries. John Spedding's token book, which records the shipments of coal from Whitehaven for the year April 1707 to 31 March 1708, shows that during those twelve months 35,304 tons of coal had been shipped from Whitehaven.

Defoe, in 1725, described Whitehaven as 'grown up from a small place to be very considerable by the coal trade, which increased so considerably of late, that it is now the most eminent port of England for shipping off

Bransty Arch in Tangier Street was used in transporting coal from the Whingill Colliery site to the harbour. It was demolished in 1927.

coals, except Newcastle and Sunderland, and even beyond the last, for they wholly supply the city of Dublin, and all the towns of Ireland on that coast'.

Many new pits were sunk — Saltom, Thwaite, King, Duke, Kells, Ravenhill, Fish, Arrowthwaite, Parker, Newtown, Country, Moor and Hind pits on the Howgill (western) side of the town; and Carr, Pearson, Pedlar, Taylor, Fox, Daniel, Jackson, Hunter, Watson, Harras, Green and other pits on the Whingill (eastern) side of the town.

At this time the steam engine was coming into use as a means of clearing water from mines. The first steam pumping engine or 'fire engine' in Cumberland was erected by Mr James Lowther at Stone Pit, Ginns, under licence from the Committee of Proprietors, of which Thomas Newcomen, the inventor, was one. The agreement is dated 10 November 1715, and under it, Mr Lowther paid £182 per annum for the hire of it. This engine had a copper boiler about ten feet in diameter with a lead top, a brass cylinder twenty-eight inches in diameter, wooden pumps eight inches in diameter, with a brass working-barrel. This engine proved so superior to the horse-pump that the fate of the latter was sealed once and for ever. Other pumping engines were installed in the Whitehaven pits and the example was followed by the Curwens at Workington.

It was Mr James Lowther who opened out the Whingill colliery. The first pits were sunk near to the outcrop of the Main Band on the top of Harras Moor, at a height of about 450 feet above the sea. In the year 1716 the output from them was about 200 tons a week. At this time Mr Lowther or his agents conceived the idea of draining the coal under Harras Moor by means of a level watercourse, which was commenced from Bransty Beck at the bottom of Wheelbarrow Brow, on the east side of Whitehaven. This level in course of time, was driven past the Harras, Jackson, Fox and Hunter pits, through the fault which separates the Bateman pit workings from the remainder of the Whingill colliery, and terminates in the Main Band level end, close to the Bateman pit, a distance of about one-and-a-half miles.

This was the fourth great winning of the Whitehaven collieries and drained all the Whingill colliery in the Bannock and Main Bands, except the workings in the George, Lady and James pits, which are below its level. The water from the George and Lady pits was pumped at the George pit up to a level 750 feet long, by which it was discharged into Bransty Beck, about 600 feet south of Lonsdale Place. The James pit Main Band was drained to the Saltom pit in the Howgill side through the single stone drift, which was driven in 1796 underneath the town, through the Norway dyke and which, until a connection was made many years afterwards, seawards, was the only communication underground between the Howgill and Whingill collieries.

In 1685 William Gilpin succeeded Thomas Tickell as chief steward of the Lowther estate at Whitehaven. Gilpin was a lawyer and the mining interests were supervised by John Gale who was followed by John Spedding. When Spedding became chief steward management of the mines passed to his younger brother, Carlisle Spedding, a man of great ability.

It is on record that Sir James Lowther sent Carlisle Spedding to Newcastle to learn all the improvements in coal-mining to be seen there, in order to apply them at Whitehaven. Spedding got himself engaged as a hewer at various collieries in that neighbourhood under a fictitious name. After being there some time, he had the misfortune to be severely burnt in an explosion. The extraordinary care and attention, bestowed by the best doctors whose services could be procured, upon an apparently humble collier led to the discovery of his identity and of his mission and ultimately to his return to Whitehaven to put into practice what he had seen and learned.

He not only borrowed ideas from Newcastle but also men, for many miners from that area were employed at Whitehaven. One Newcastle

Spedding steel mill.

mining engineer wrote to him: 'There is nine or ten more run away from our place and I hear some of them is with you', but Spedding in his reply omitted to comment on the absconding Newcastle pitmen.

Spedding was of an inventive turn of mind and in 1730 he produced the steel-mill, which was the first attempt to produce a safe means of working in an atmosphere containing fire-damp. It was merely a steel disc fixed to a small cog wheel which was geared into a larger wheel. When the handle attached to the larger wheel was turned the small cog attained a high speed and when a piece of flint was held against the edge of the disc it shot off a stream of sparks. The use of the steel-mill spread throughout the north of England and it was used up till the invention of the Davy lamp in 1819.

He was also the inventor of a system of ventilation known as 'coursing the air', which consisted of threading the air-column up certain workings and down others until it ventilated the whole waste.

The success attendant upon the introduction of the steam engine for pumping was undoubtedly the factor that led Spedding to propose to Sir James Lowther the bold project of sinking a pit close to the seashore, as far to the dip as possible, for the purpose of winning and working not only the land coal which lay between the coastline and the workings to the rise, made from the Greenbank, Corporal, Wilson, Radcliffe Bank, Causey Head, Burnt, Swinburn, Grayson, Bell, Fox, Double, Miller, Skelton Bank, Howgill Heads, Pickeron Bank, Senhouse, Gill Close, Gibson, Murray, Knockmurton, Mawson, Pow, Andrew, Forbes, Granger, Darby, Gameriggs and Baxter pits, but also to work the coal under the sea.

The site selected for this new undertaking was Saltom, close to high water mark, and work commenced on the shaft in 1729. It was sunk oval in form, ten feet by eight feet, a shape that commended itself to Carlisle Spedding and his son James who succeeded him in office. All the pits sunk during their administration were of this form.

This winning was the most remarkable colliery enterprise of its day, and a curious incident during the sinking process led Sir James Lowther to communicate to the Royal Society in the year 1733 a paper entitled 'An account of the damp air in a coal pit within twenty yards of the sea'.

When the pit was down 252 feet from the surface, a strong blower of gas was pricked, and was piped to the pit top, where it burned for many years afterwards. Mr Spedding offered to supply the Trustees of the Town and Harbour with whatever gas they required to light the town, if they would be at the expense of conducting it through the streets, but the offer was not taken up.

It is a fact, however, that Spedding conducted gas in pipes from an adjacent pit to the laboratory of Dr William Brownrigg, an eminent scientist then living in Whitehaven, and Brownrigg used it to heat furnaces.

Saltom was completed to the Main Band, a depth of 456 feet, in 1731. At the pit-top, a fire-engine, with a twelve foot boiler, a cylinder forty inches in diameter and a pump seven inches in diameter, was erected. The pumps were in four lifts, and the engine was a Newcomen atmospheric, similar to that at the Ginns. In the course of a few years it was found to be inadequate and a second engine, a duplicate of the first, was erected and these continued working until about the year 1782, when the engines 'being nearly worn out', were pulled down, and a new engine of gigantic proportions for that day was erected.

This great mechanical wonder was an atmospheric engine with a cylinder seventy inches in diameter and six feet stroke. It had an air-pump three feet in diameter and three feet stroke. The beam was oak, twenty-four feet three inches long, twenty-one inches deep and nineteen inches broad. There were four lifts of pumps, the two top sets being eleven inches and the two bottoms sets eleven-and-five-eighths inches in diameter. There were three malleable-iron boilers, each thirteen feet six inches in diameter, nine feet four inches high, with hemispherical

Saltom Pit.

tops. This engine continued to work until the year 1866, when it was broken up, and the water pumped at the Wellington pit. In 1832 the great Saltom pumping engine was supplemented by a high-pressure engine with a cylinder two feet eleven inches in diameter and seven feet stroke, working ten-and-a-half inch pumps.

Saltom pit ceased to draw coals in 1848 after the long period of 107 years.

At this point it might be convenient to look at an incident that created a great deal of bad feeling. It is recorded in Ashton and Sykes *The coal industry of the eighteenth century* (Man. U.P., 1929), p.192, in the following terms: 'Sometimes, however, a powerful industrialist was able to exert undue influence over the owner of the property. In 1742, Sir James Lowther (afterwards the "Bad Earl" of Lonsdale), induced the Governors of St Bees School to grant him a lease for 867 years, of all their coal at the absurdly low rental of £3 10s 0d a year.

'The mines proved highly productive, and in 1819 the Charity Commissioners instituted an inquiry which elicited the fact that, at the time the lease was granted, both Sir James and his steward, John Spedding, were themselves Governors of the school. The Attorney-General took proceedings and, after a protracted suit, the successor of the delinquent was obliged, in 1827, to pay £13,280 in additional royalties, and to accept a fresh lease, the terms of which were settled by disinterested viewers'.

It should be pointed out that in this instance, Ashton and Sykes are at fault — the person concerned was Sir James Lowther of Whitehaven, not his nephew, the notorious 'bad Earl'. Whatever crimes against society the Earl committed this was not one of them.

The expenses of the law suit had to be defrayed out of the £13,280 award.

In fairness to Sir James Lowther and his agent, one must look at the background of the St Bees lease before accusing them of sharp practice. In 1604 King James I granted by letter patent to the governors of St Bees Grammar School certain lands in St Bees and Sandwith that had been acquired by the Crown.

In the leases of 1608-09 the tenants covenant that they will permit the governors and their successors to sink pits and dig for coal in the demised premises; but there is no record of any advantage having been taken of this until 1650, when the governors demised 'all that pit of Coalgrove or Bearmouth, already sunk within the closes called Stephen Ridding, in the parish of St Bees, holden of the school under the rent of 4s, with liberty to dig for coal therein, for the term of four years at the yearly rent of £3'.

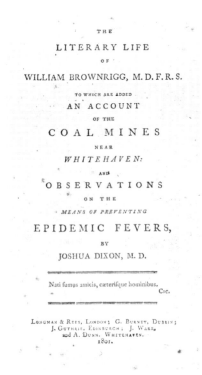

Title page of *The Literary Life of William Brownrigg, M.D., F.R.S.*

Dr Joshua Dixon (1743-1825).

In 1664, the governors granted to another set of lessees a lease of the same coal-pit for a term of seven years at the same rent. In 1679 these tenants quitted this 'coalery', the coal having given out.

No profit seems to have been made out of the coal under the school lands from 1680 until 1742 when the lease under consideration was drawn up. There seems to have been good historic grounds for the amount offered, what was wrong was the inordinate length of the lease.

One of Carlisle Spedding's great friends was Dr William Brownrigg (1711-1800) who was elected a Fellow of the Royal Society in 1741. Dr Brownrigg was one of the outstanding scientific figures of the eighteenth century and his achievements were recorded by his friend and fellow practioner Dr Joshua Dixon, one of the best-loved men who ever practised medicine. In his *Literary Life of William Brownrigg, M.D., F.R.S.* (1810) Dixon writes: 'In some explanatory notes to "A descriptive poem addressed to two ladies at their return from viewing the mines near Whitehaven," published in 1755 by John Dalton, D.D., is contained a short account of those mines, which proceeded from the pen of Dr Brownrigg. These notes are not intended to form a history of the collieries or a philosophical treatise upon their peculiar exhalations but merely to illustrate and confirm the poet's description of the operations and appearances in the mines. An accurate relation is given of the various expedients, which attentive observation and melancholy experience have, at different periods suggested, for the purpose of preventing the explosions of the fire-damp, and fatal effects of the choak-damp. The scenes exhibited in those subterraneous regions, which fill the mind with awe, surprise and terror, and delineated with equal elegance and perspicuity'.

A later version of Brownrigg's notes are published in Dixon's *Literary Life*.

On the death of Sir James Lowther in 1755, his successor increased Carlisle Spedding's wage to £150 per annum, an increase he was not to enjoy for very long because he was killed in a pit explosion in that same year. His son, James (1720-88), became the next engineer at the Whitehaven collieries and he sank more new pits — Wolfe, Davy, Lady, George, North, Bateman, Howe and Scott pits on the Whingill side, and Croft and Wilson on the Howgill side. Of these the most important was Croft pit, sunk in 1774 to a depth of 910 feet, which was worked continuously until 1903.

Gabriel Jars inspected Saltom pit in 1765 and was much impressed by the workings which extended one-and-a-half miles from the day-hole, some of them being three-quarters of a mile under the sea.

R. W. Moore says that there is every reason to believe that the coal worked under the Solway at Saltom was the first ever worked beneath the sea in any part of the world. The sea-coal at Saltom, and afterwards at the William and Wellington pits, was worked free of royalty until the year 1860, when the Crown put forward a claim to the minerals lying below low-water mark.

From 1860 until 1880, the submarine coal was worked under a Crown lease. In 1880, Henry, Earl of Lonsdale, purchased the minerals under the sea down to the bottom of the coal-measures, and for the distance of ten miles seawards.

According to Fletcher, the following pits were exhausted before 1755: Taylor, Hunter, Carr, Fox, Daniel, Green, Watson, Pedlar and Harras, while Wolfe, Scott and Moss pits were stopped. Mr William Watson has pointed out that many of these pits only lasted from ten to twenty years and usually carried the same name as the manager or sinker.

But Moore says that in 1765 the pits in production on the Howgill side were Duke, Kells, King, Fox, Wilson, Hinde, Saltom, Fish and Thwaite pits, and implies that the pits mentioned by Fletcher were in operation until about 1780.

The pits in operation at Whingill were: Jackson, Pearson, Fox, Hunter, Pedlar and Scott. It will be noticed that the name Fox appears in both collieries.

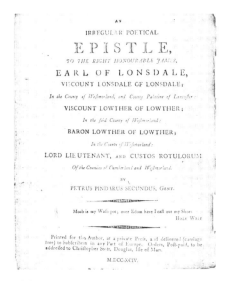

Title page of *An Irregular Poetical Epistle*.

The number of horses employed at this time in the colliery was very large. For instance, at the Howgill side, there were underground sixty-nine tram-horses, and above ground eighty gin-horses and twenty-four bank horses, a total of 173. Of this number, fifty-six were provided by the neighbouring farmers. If Whingill required horses in the same proportion they would probably need 140, so that the aggregate would be about 313.

Between the years 1755 and 1780 the average annual output was about 150,000 tons, and the average price on board ship was 3*s* 4*d*. Between 1780 and 1800 the average output was 160,000 tons and the selling price was about four shillings per ton.

Mr James Spedding retired in 1781 and died on 22 August 1788, at the age of sixty-eight. He was buried at Trinity Church, Whitehaven.

He was succeeded by Mr John Bateman who remained for ten years and was followed by a Mr Thomas Wyley.

The reason for his departure appears to lie in one of the more famous incidents in local mining history. The old workings of the Main Band under a portion of the town were worked at very shallow depths. In 1791 the workings had reached in the neighbourhood of Duke Street where on 31 January a holing was made in an old waste, and liberating a large quantity of water, drowned two men, one woman and five horses in the workings. The ground subsided in the garden behind Somerset House which, with some houses in Scotch Street, George Street and Church Street, were cracked and otherwise damaged.

The inhabitants of this locality, thoroughly alarmed, deserted their dwellings and camped with their furniture in the streets until they were assured by competent viewers that the danger was over.

One of the victims was Mr Henry Littledale of Somerset House, a mercer, who brought a successful suit against the Earl of Lonsdale at the Carlisle Assizes. In a fit of temper the Earl closed his collieries at Whitehaven, regardless of the colliers and others dependent, directly or indirectly, upon the continuance of coal mining.

Not until he received a petition signed by 2,560 people begging him to continue working the mines and promising to indemnify him against all such actions in the future, was work resumed.

The savagery of the Earl's treatment of those dependent upon him, drew down on his head the bitter denunciation of John Wolcot, the satirist, who wrote under the name of 'Peter Pindar', but Wolcot's attack was nothing to the bitterness with which Lonsdale was scourged by a local writer who hid behind the pen-name of Petrus Pindarus, Secundus. In *An Irregular Poetical Epistle* he lashes Lonsdale with an invective that is quite unequalled in a century that was used to strong language.

Coal mining
at Whitehaven – Part II

It seems incomprehensible that the steam engine should have been in use for pumping purposes for upwards of seventy years before it was applied to drawing coals, but such is the fact, and probably arose from the idea that seems to have possessed our early engineers — an idea wholly unfounded — that the crank was not a practical medium for converting rectilinear into circular motion, and at a later period that the steam engine could not be made sufficiently delicate in its movements to render it available for winding coals; it is remarkable that its first application to this purpose was by making it pump water on a waterwheel to the axis of which the rope rolls were fixed. The wheel was provided with two sets of buckets on its circumference, set in opposite directions so that by turning the stream of water from one set to the other the revolution of the wheel could be reversed. A machine of this sort was erected at George Pit in the year 1787, and cumbersome and difficult to manage as it must have been, it was said to be a great improvement on horse power. A model of this apparatus was in existence in 1878.

The first direct application of the steam engine at Whitehaven for winding was at Davy Pit where an atmospheric engine was erected in 1791 and another at Lady Pit in 1795. About the same time an engine of a novel construction, made at Seaton Iron Works, Workington by Messrs Heslop and Millward, was erected at Kells Pit and drew coals for many years from a depth of 114 fathoms. This form of engine was patented by Mr Heslop in 1790 and came into extensive use at the various West Cumberland collieries.

In the late eighteenth century a foundry was established at Lowca by Adam Heslop and his two brothers, Crosby and Thomas. Adam Heslop left West Cumberland early in life to work at the Madeley Wood Colliery in Shropshire and in 1790 patented a steam engine. On returning to Cumberland he set up the Lowca Ironworks, taking into partnership William Stead, Mr Johnson, Mr Millward and a lady named Ritson, the firm being styled Messrs Heslop, Johnson, Millward and Company, the total capital involved being less than £3,000.

The firm's lease from Mr J. C. Curwen included the right to work the thin bands of ironstone on the beach at Harrington. Their intention was to produce iron as well as to manufacture Heslop engines, but after laying the foundations of one or two blast furnaces, they abandoned them. This was the last attempt to establish blast furnaces in West Cumberland until the Whitehaven Haemetite Company built their works at Cleator Moor in 1841.

The foundry, however, continued and for over a century made a notable contribution to the industrial life of the area.

It should be noted, however, that the first direct application of the steam engine for winding coal in Cumberland was made not at the Davy Pit, Whitehaven in 1791, as has hitherto been believed, but as the Curwen records show, at Workington in 1789. According to an agreement, dated 1 July 1788, between John Christian and Messrs Boulton and Watt, the latter undertook to provide at Workington 'a Steam Engine of the said James Watt's invention — The Cylinder of the said Engine to be fourteen inches in diameter and four feet long in the stroke and the piston thereof to be acted upon by the force of steam both in its ascent and descent with a rotative motion of the said James Watt's invention applied thereto for the purpose of drawing coals and water from the said Colliery'.

This was a six hp engine, its materials costing £251 13s 7d. In addition Christian had to pay an annual premium of £30 for the use of the engine, since the firm charged £5 per horse-power. This engine was 'calculated to wind Coals at the rate of four-and-a-half feet per second', and its success persuaded Christian to order a sixteen hp engine which was built in 1789 at a total cost of £1,300 8s 3½d. Other engines followed and by 1790 eight or nine of them were in use at Workington.

Mr Isaac Fletcher, M.P., in his *Archaeology of the Cumberland Coal Trade* writes: 'As the Heslop engine played a very important part in the development of our coal fields, and was (I believe) not in use elsewhere, I may be allowed to give a very brief description of it. I have already described the old atmospheric engine and alluded to the invention by Watt of the separate condenser, for which he obtained an extended patent right. Mr Heslop's object was evidently to maintain a hot steam cylinder without infringing Watt's patent, and he effectively carried out his object by adopting two cylinders, one at each end of the beam. One of the cylinders called the hot cylinder worked exactly in the same manner as in the ordinary atmospheric engine, but instead of condensing the steam in the cylinder or using a separate condenser and air pump as in Watt's engine, it was passed into the other cylinder, which was immersed in cold water and there condensed. The cold cylinder was fitted with a piston connected with the beam in the same manner as the one in the hot cylinder, and the early engines were without an air pump. Mr Heslop made two or three very large pumping engines on this principle, and numerous winding engines, both great and small, all of which did their work efficiently, and economically as regards the consumption of coal, far more so indeed than the modern high pressure engine which unfortunately has now come into such general use.'

The Heslop engine at Kells was removed to Low Wreah Pit in 1823 and was in operation until 1878. It is now in the Science Museum, South Kensington, London.

One of the last men to have charge of it was Robert Bland; his son, John, followed in the same job; and his grandson, 'Joe' Bland had in 1939 completed forty-one years at the engine in William Pit. Many other members of the Bland family have been engine men and none were better known in that capacity in West Cumberland mines.

After William Pit was sunk in 1804, an atmospheric pumping engine was installed. It has been described in the following words: 'The cylinder is eighty inches diameter, and the stroke eight feet. The beam is of cast-iron, with parallel motion at each end, and the diameter of the air-pump three feet. She works a twelve inches pump, lifting 109 fathoms, and at her usual speed of eight strokes lifts 320 gallons per minute, with a consumption of nine tons of coal in the twenty-four hours. She is still working (1878) and is in excellent order. The original winding engine was a "Heslop" engine of large dimensions. The hot and cold cylinders were, respectively, forty-four and twenty-eight inches diameter with a five-and-a-half feet stroke. This fine engine was pulled down and broken up in 1850, and a high pressure erected in her place.'

Since the days of Heslop engines many improvements have been made in winding and pumping machinery; firstly with closing in the cylinder tops, adopting parallel motion, and making the steam act at both sides of the piston, which led to the vertical and beam engines of the Boulton and Watt principle. These in turn have been replaced by the horizontal high-pressure engines now in general use in all pits. The winding engine in use at William Pit was considered one of the best engines of its class. It was erected in 1871, had two horizontal cylinders each thirty-two inches in diameter with a six foot stroke; and the winding drum was eighteen feet 4 inches in diameter. It was fitted with steam brake and ran with sixty pounds steam pressure.

Haig pit was sunk during the years 1914-16 and Mr William Watson

Old Pumping Engine at Work · From Cumberland · Till 18?

This illustration of the Heslop
pumping engine removed from
Low Wreah Pit made the front page
of the weekly newspaper
The Graphic, 3 January 1880, when
it went on public display for the
first time at the Science Museum
in London.

has this note about the winding engine. 'The last word in winding engines
is, of course, at Haig Pit. There the twin shafts are provided with double
engines of enormous capacity. We have seen this machinery recently
(1939) and have been courteously supplied with the following details:
The east, or Number Four shaft, designed for riding men principally, is
engined as follows: Each cylinder thirty inches diameter, stroke five feet,
and winding drum fourteen feet diameter. That engine was erected when
the pit was sunk in 1914-16. The engine at Number Five shaft is indeed a
monster, and was erected in 1920. Cylinders are forty inches diameter,
stroke seven feet, and drum twenty-one feet diameter. Each cylinder
weighs thirteen tons, the trunks, i.e. the connecting rod guides, weigh
eleven tons each, and the drum shaft weights twenty-five tons. This
enormous machine was built by Beaver and Dawley of Bradford, a firm
now defunct, and required a train of seventeen wagons to deliver it.'

To return however, to the management of the Whitehaven pits. At
Whitehaven, mining had declined following John Bateman's departure in
1791, but his return to the employment of the Lowthers in 1802, at a
salary of £500, was followed by steady improvements. Whitehaven
exports of coal which had dwindled to 90,628 tons in 1802 rose to
153,728 tons in 1803. New pits were sunk, the most important being
William Pit on the shore near Bransty, begun in 1804 and completed in
1812. Coal was first shipped from this pit on 10 March 1806 and the pit
worked continuously until 1955.

William Pit in the early nineteenth century was regarded as the best
equipped colliery in the kingdom — a pumping engine erected in 1810
could lift 320 gallons of water per minute. The original winding engine,
a Heslop engine made at Seaton Iron Works, was in operation until 1850
when it was replaced by a high pressure engine.

The surface buildings of Wellington Pit were designed by Sidney Smirke, brother of Sir Robert Smirke. The detail of the chimney is traditionally alleged to be based on a candlestick in Whitehaven Castle — hence its popular name.

In 1811 John Bateman retired and was succeeded by John Peile who had long experience of the Whitehaven pits. Mr Bateman died in 1816, at the age of sixty-seven, and was buried in Holy Trinity Churchyard, Whitehaven.

Under John Peile's direction the Whitehaven collieries made great progress. In 1813 he constructed the Howgill surface incline down to the Howgill staith. In 1818, he sank Croft pit from the main band down to the six-quarters seam, and drove therefrom a level drift until it cut the main band seaward. In 1819 he did a similar thing at Saltom pit. He sank a new shaft at Duke pit from the surface to the six-quarters, and also at James pit from the main band to the six-quarters.

In 1832 he began the Parton drifts and Countess pit. The Parton drift was intended, like the Whingill levels, to drain a vast amount of inland coal; but, although it was driven for a distance of one and a half miles, it failed to win the extent of coal that was done by this means under Harras Moor. Nevertheless, it has been described as the seventh great development in the history of mining at Whitehaven.

Countess pit worked until 1863, when it was abandoned, and when the Parton drifts were stopped. Wreah pit was also sunk during Mr Peile's tenure of office.

The importance of the Whitehaven Collieries may be judged by the fact that, in 1816, 900 persons were employed there.

Peile's greatest mining achievement was the sinking of Wellington Pit, which was begun in 1840. In 1843, one of the shafts was down to the main band and the other to the bannock band; both reached the six-quarters coal in 1845 and thence level stone-drifts were driven seaward and intersected the main band at a distance of 2,700 feet. He proposed to sink the pit to a further depth of 960 feet, a total depth of 1,800 feet from the surface. The last 600 feet would have been in the Carboniferous Limestone. From the bottom of the pit, in the limestone, he proposed to drive a pair of level drifts westward until they intersected the six-quarters coal and main band, and finally the bannock band at a distance of 13,500 feet from the shaft. The first 6,000 feet of these drifts would have been in limestone.

In 1843 Mr George Stephenson, the celebrated engineer, and Mr Frank Forster made a report on the Whitehaven collieries. They approved of Peile's proposals in the main but objected to the last part because at such a depth 'it would be expensive and inconvenient to raise the quantity required, setting aside the dangers arising from the breakage of ropes', and 'notwithstanding the compact nature of the limestone in this district', it might be 'so affected by faults as to leave cavities and fissures yielding such a quantity of water as to render the colliery unworkable, such cavities and fissures being very common in the Mountain Limestone'.

The Wellington pit winning stopped at the six-quarters seam and no further exploration of the strata below that seam has been made.

Mr Peile introduced screens at the Whitehaven collieries in 1839. He also began the manufacture of coke and patent fuel but there was no demand at that time for these products and, during the term of office of his successor, these branches of industry ceased.

During Mr Peile's tenure of office the output of the Whitehaven collieries reached about 250,000 tons a year.

He retired in 1847 and died on 17 January 1855, after a few days' illness, at the age of 79. He was interred in St James' Churchyard.

The *Cumberland Pacquet* paid a graceful tribute to him as an engineer and as a man. He took a wide interest in public affairs. He was forty years a member of the Board of Trustees of the Town and Harbour and during the three years prior to his retirement, was chairman of that body.

As R. W. Moore remarked: 'Excepting perhaps Mr Carlisle Spedding, he was without doubt the ablest viewer and citizen that Whitehaven has produced'.

He was succeeded as principal colliery agent by Mr Peter Bourne, with

Mr William Anderson, South Shields, as consulting viewer. In 1847 the following pits were in operation: at Howgill colliery, Saltom, Croft, Wilson and Wellington, and at Whingill colliery, William, North and Wreah pits. Their total output was 93,744 wagons or 224,985 tons.

An important development of the collieries took place during the period that Mr Bourne was agent. In the year 1849, the workings in the Croft pit main band had reached the down throw fault, known as the St Bees dyke, that had already stopped the workings in that seam in Wilson pit to the south.

In 1862 the main band was proved in the St Bees Grammar School royalty, at a depth of nearly 318 feet. This fault has since been crossed seawards by the main dip haulage road, in Croft pit and Bannock and Main bands have been won therefrom.

The other important event that occurred during Mr Bourne's time was an extensive outbreak of fire in the six-quarters seam at Wellington pit on 24 August 1863. At that time there were two underground hauling engines, with boilers, placed near to the level drifts, leading from the six-quarters seam to the main band. The smoke from the boiler fires was carried by means of a chimney drift to Duke pit. This underground flue passed through the six-quarters coal near Wellington Pit and it was there that the fire was discovered. It was thought by some that the fire originated in the chimney drift from the ignition of some soot by a spark and that the fire thus created had penetrated through some crack in the arching to the coal. Others thought that the fire was the work of an incendiary.

On the advice of Mr T. E. Forster, the consulting viewer for the colliery, it was decided to exclude all air from the fire by hermetically sealing Duke pit and by flooding the entrance to the workings in the six-quarters seam at Wellington shaft foot.

This latter operation was effected by putting in four dams, two in the drifts leading through to Saltom pit and two in the drifts leading from the six-quarter seam at Wellington pit to the main band seaward, and by pouring in the sea-water down one of the Wellington pits by means of a drift, fitted with sluices, that was driven from shore between high and low water marks. In addition, steam was blown through a pipe in the light stage at one of the Duke pits. It was not until 1866 that the fire was extinguished; and it was not until 1872 that the water was got out of the dip districts so as to enable work to be resumed there.

On the resignation of Mr Bourne in 1867, the consulting viewers, Messrs T. E. Forster, G. B. Forster and T. G. Hurst of Newcastle-on-Tyne, took over the direct management of the Whitehaven pits, having first appointed Mr Henry Mulcaster as resident viewer and after his death, Mr Matthew Harper.

Henry pit (alongside William pit) was sunk 1870-72 to a depth of 930 feet, whence drifts were set away and won over faults, the six-quarters seam, a considerable area of which, both under land and sea, was worked up to 1891 when the workings were abandoned.

In 1874, Mr R. F. Martin became viewer. During his three years in office, he modernised the plant, abolished the use of baskets and introduced compressed air haulage on the main roads in William pit. He erected a Guibal fan at William pit and also at Kells pit, and abolished the last of the underground furnaces. Both above and below ground he made many improvements.

In 1866, the total output derived from William, Croft, Wellington and Wreah pits was 255,505 tons, and the greatest output of these collieries, while controlled by the Earls of Lonsdale, was obtained in 1886 when 417,039 tons were produced from William, Henry, Croft and Wellington pits.

The direct Lowther control of the Whitehaven collieries came to an end in 1888. It has been suggested that one factor that may have contributed to the decision to lease the collieries to a company may have been a series of fraudulent dealings by employees that resulted in the prosecu-

Typical pit headgear circa 1882.

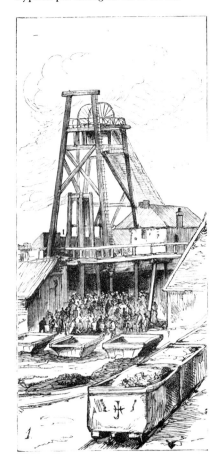

tion and imprisonment of several. On 11 August 1888, the collieries and their ancillaries were leased to the Whitehaven Colliery Company. The shareholders were Sir James Bain, his sons Col J. R. Bain and Mr J. D. Bain, and Mr J. S. Simpson.

The property leased to this company consisted of Henry, William, Wellington, Croft, James, Duke, Saltom and Kells pits, with their equipment, seventy-two coke ovens and 578 cottages. For the pits, including a sub-lease of St Bees School coal, the certain annual rent was £10,000 with further annual payments of £3,000 for the fixed plant and coke ovens and £1,014 for 139 cottages. After five years a further rent, equal to their rateable value, was payable in respect of the remaining 439 cottages. Royalty rent was 8d per ton when sold below 9s 0d and above 9s 0d, one-tenth of the excess was to be added to the royalty rent. This firm was very successful for the next twenty-five years. Through a subsidiary company it owned a large fleet of steamers that carried coal to Ireland where the coal was sold from the company's coal depots situated in various Irish towns.

In 1893 the six-quarters and main band seams were being worked and all coal of the Whitehaven mines, except for a small district in Croft pit, was under the sea. Between 1900 and 1902 Ladysmith pit was sunk to a depth of 1,090 feet, near Croft pit which ceased to draw coal in 1905, after a working life of 129 years. By 1903 only the main band was being worked and at that time the undersea workings were the most extensive in the world – in William pit they extended nearly four miles from high water mark, the cover at that point being 600 feet.

In 1900 the output of the Whitehaven collieries were as follows:

William Pit	246,850 tons
Wellington Pit	112,094 tons
Croft Pit	176,549 tons
Total	536,493 tons

The numbers employed were as follows:

William Pit	1,055 men
Wellington Pit	500 men
Croft Pit	626 men
Total	2,181 men

The company continued until 1913 when, owing to death, the number of partners diminished and steps were taken to form a new company. A limited liability company, formed chiefly by local businessmen, next leased the collieries.

This company made further developments. Haig pit was sunk 1914-16 and in the same period a battery of up-to-date coke ovens was erected near Ladysmith pit to replace the old 'bee-hive' ovens near William pit. Electricity was installed at all the pits from a central generating station near Ladysmith. They also built over 300 houses for employees. In 1927 the company produced the record output of 881,239 tons from William, Wellington, Haig and Ladysmith pits. The number of employees was at that time about 3,800.

But it had not been a period of uninterrupted progress. An admirable review of the first three decades of the twentieth century was made by Alderman John McAllister in a speech to the Whitehaven Rotary Club, printed in the *Whitehaven Review*. Alderman McAllister spoke of the events which had coloured the life of the mining community since he first started work on 12 June 1902. There were many bitter memories of strikes and accidents which would take a long time to eradicate and which left a difficult legacy even for a nationalised industry.

The first event which occurred after he started work was the with-

Contemporary engraving of a typical Victorian pit after a fatal accident, relatives flocking to the pit mouth anxious for news.

drawal of horses from Croft pit in 1903 and the institution of the man-handling of tubs. This led to a seventeen weeks' strike which was followed by a sixteen weeks' strike in 1904 when horses were withdrawn from Wellington and William pits.

Five men were killed by an explosion in Number Six Drift, William Pit on 26 November 1907, the victims being James Rowe, Joseph Kennedy, William Vincent Fitzsimons, William Hanlon and Alfred Burns.

On 11 May 1910, there occurred the greatest calamity ever experienced by the town — an explosion of gas and subsequent fires in Wellington pit which caused the death of 136 men and boys. In 1912 there was a five weeks' national coal strike — the only national strike which the miners won — when a minimum wage award was achieved. *See appendix VII.*

In 1920 there was a short national strike and again in 1921 there was a seventeen weeks' national strike which resulted in the Sankey award.

On 11 July 1922, there was an explosion at William pit which resulted in the deaths of two men, and in September of the same year there was another major disaster, an explosion at Haig pit which claimed the lives of thirty-nine men.

Wellington Pit, c. 1910.

Board with message:
All's well in this airway at 4 o'clock thirty-five men and boys. J. Moore.
Board recovered from Wellington Pit after the 1910 disaster.

The famous 'Bully' Smith strike which lasted seventeen weeks occurred in 1923 and three years later there was the national strike when the miners were out for eight months. He was proud to recall that at that time Mr Hugh Gibson and other traders advanced credit to the strikers to

Rescue team ready to go down Wellington Pit following the explosion on 11 May 1910.

Soup kitchen — probably at Colliery
Mission — during a miners' strike.

H. W. Walker with H.R.H. the
Prince of Wales at Haig Pit, 30 June
1927, just prior to the official
opening of the Recreation Ground
and Aged Miners' Homes.

the amount of £40,000, and that within a remarkably short time after the resumption of work the debt was cleared.

Haig pit was the scene of another disaster in 1927 when, on 13 December, four men lost their lives in an explosion and the pit was sealed for several weeks.

On Sunday morning, 12 February 1928, a party of workmen, accompanied by representatives of the Colliery Company, Government inspectors and miners, descended to inspect beyond the portion which had been sealed. A series of explosions resulted in the deaths of thirteen members of the party.

A further major catastrophe occurred at Haig pit on the 29 January 1931, when twenty-seven lives were lost.

Ladysmith pit closed in 1931, Wellington pit in the following year, and on 10 August 1933, the Whitehaven Colliery Company Ltd went into voluntary liquidation and was succeeded on 11 August by the Priestman (Whitehaven) Collieries Ltd. This company was financed chiefly by Messrs Piele and Priestman from Durham and the Lowther Estates were also shareholders. Great credit must be given to this company for the vastly improved ventilation of Haig pit and also for the introduction of more up-to-date screening plant and other machinery. In fact this company probably expended more money on improvements than the output of coal warranted at the time.

The company ceased on 12 October 1935 and the pits closed for eighteen months. During that period unsuccessful attempts were made to form a company and as the months passed away many thought that the pits would never work again.

It was only when assistance was made available from a fund set up by Lord Nuffield to help struggling industries that the Cumberland Coal Company (Whitehaven) Ltd was formed. The company was an offshoot of the Coltness Iron Company Ltd of Glasgow, well-known as colliery owners on both sides of the border. Work was resumed in March 1937.

The dangers attending work in the pits is forcibly brought out by R. Arnot Page in *The Miners: a history of the Miners' Federation of Great Britain*, where he says: 'Mining has always been one of the more dangerous trades. Roman poetry and the earliest English poetry (as in *The Seafarer*) have told of the perils of the sea. But have they amounted to so much more in loss of life and bodies maimed than the perils of the mine. For many years more accidents were reported in mines than in all the factories and workshops of the United Kingdom. The families of the miners live in all times under the shadow of calamity, great or small. The total number killed annually in the mines in the period from 1880 to 1910 was for most years between 1,000 and 1,500. On the average four miners were killed every day in the British coal-fields.

'The non-fatal accidents also run to a high figure. For every man killed, a hundred and more were injured. The number of persons injured by non-fatal accidents at mines, reported under the Notices of Accidents Act, 1906, was:

143,258 in 1908	168,360 in 1911
154,740 in 1909	152,302 in 1912
160,638 in 1910	178,962 in 1913.'

The fatility figures rose to 1,818 in 1910. Of these 501 had died in explosions, 658 through falls of ground and 286 through haulage accidents. There were two major disasters that year, an explosion of firedamp at Wellington Pit, Whitehaven, whereby 136 miners were killed and an explosion of coal dust at Hulton, in Lancashire, in which 344 miners died.

Between 1910 and 1940 eighty-five miners had been killed in explosions in the Whitehaven pits and then on 3 June 1941, an explosion occurred at William Pit which resulted in the death of ten men and injury to eleven more. Once again the price of coal was underwritten in sorrow and bereavement. But this was not the last sacrifice that William

Haig Pit, new coal washing unit and land sale loading point.

Wagons being loaded at South Harbour.

Pit was to claim before it closed in 1955. On the evening of 15 August 1947, an explosion occurred in the main haulage road some two-and-a-half miles from the shaft when 117 men were working below. It was soon ascertained that only ten men were safe and that 107 were trapped behind heavy falls. Three only of the entombed men escaped alive — John Birkett, Daniel Hinde and James Weighman.

The question of the nationalisation of the coal mines had been under discussion for many years. It became a reality with the passing of the Coal Industry Nationalisation Act on 12 July 1946 and the constitution of the National Coal Board three days later. Vesting day was 1 January 1947. Nationalisation did a great deal to improve working conditions in the mines, and at a public dinner on 11 November 1964, Mr J. Lomax, area manager of the National Coal Board, said that at Haig Colliery £1,125,000 had been spent on development and mechanisation and that

William Pit
Sinking commenced 1804.
First coal shipped 1806.
Closed 1955.
Photograph taken 1967.

during 1965 it was intended, at a cost of £150,000, to increase operations in the Metal Band seam to ensure the working of the colliery for a further forty years.

Modernisation of surface installations by 1972 was expected to cost a further £500,000.

Unfortunately, the mines in the Cumberland area were not profitable and resulted in closures with a consequent diminution of the labour force. William Pit was closed in 1955, Walkmill in 1961 and Harrington No.11 in 1963. In November 1965, Lord Robens, Chairman of the National Coal Board, announced the closure nationally of 150 collieries. As a result Risehow Colliery closed in April 1966, St Helen's Colliery, Siddick in September 1966 and the West Cumberland coalfield which had employed 5,764 workers in 1947 was reduced to 2,918 by 1966-67.

At a press conference on Tuesday, 24 November 1966 at Workington, Lord Robens pointed out that there were sufficient reserves of coal to keep Haig and Harrington No.10 collieries working for the next twenty years — but to ensure their continuance there must be a lowering of the rate of absenteeism and the high incidence of injury.

He gave Solway Colliery, Workington, little hope, anticipating that it would close in about a year. In actual fact coal winding ceased at Harrington in July 1968 and despite every effort coal winding ceased at Solway in May 1973.

The labour force continued to diminish. By 1976-77 the number of men employed at Haig, the sole remaining colliery, was 1,158.

As part of the National Coal Board's *Plan for Coal*, published in 1974, which envisaged a £600 million capital investment, extensive improvements to the surface facilities at Haig took place during 1975 and 1976 at a cost of £2 million. The old Ladysmith washery was abandoned and replaced by a new one which was opened in October 1976. A new coal silo, or dockside store, was brought into operation in December 1976 to facilitate the loading of coal on wagons.

As Haig is an undersea colliery with its working faces receding further and further from the shaft thereby increasing transport costs and diminishing working time, National Coal Board engineers have been making a survey of the Keekle-Moresby Parks area and the St Bees valley in order to assess the viability of opencast mining. A decision on this has yet to be announced.

Heslop's engine formerly at Low Wreah Pit and now in the Science Museum.

Crown Copyright. Science Museum, London.

Chapter 9

Whitehaven in the nineteenth century

Brockbank's fish shop, 7 King Street, c. 1840. Painted by Robinson Wilson (c. 1828-64).

Students who learn of the high rating of Whitehaven as a port in the eighteenth century are inclined to ask why it declined in the nineteenth, and especially why it lost ground to Liverpool. Actually although the shipbuilding industry ceased to be a factor in local economy in the late nineteenth century the trade of the harbour, as the following table shows, was higher in the mid-nineteenth century than it was prior to the American War of Independence when it was relatively at its zenith.

| | Ships | Tonnage | Exports | |
			Iron Ore	Coals
1853	3,706	317,732	115,731	222,987
1854	3,687	332,267	145,526	215,544
1855	3,693	285,476	129,490	201,853
1856	3,886	322,506	160,691	219,500
1857	3,911	375,820	193,850	199,218
1858	3,770	313,821	196,140	181,274
1859	4,125	316,723	213,843	185,472
1860	4,206	335,932	223,795	199,606
1861	4,206	364,304	250,347	183,841
1862	4,787	412,073	307,079	196,294

The interesting point to note from this table is that the average displacement of the vessels using the port is less than 100 tons.

As has already been pointed out the style and size of vessels built during the eighteenth century were fairly static, brigs and brigantines of 100 to 200 tons, and ships or barques of 200 to 300 tons and although the shipbuilding yards began turning out larger and larger ships as the nineteenth century advanced, Whitehaven, because it was a tidal harbour, was used mainly by small vessels. Furthermore, because of the fact that there were only a few small towns in its hinterland, exports were in the main limited to coal and iron ore whereas Liverpool had behind it the galaxy of towns that had grown up in Lancashire as a result of the Industrial Revolution and became the focal point for a great import and export trade. The Cumbrian fells not only failed to support any large centres of population, they also effectively barred Whitehaven from becoming a port through which Irish and American produce could be imported for onward transit to the more populous northern counties of Durham and Yorkshire.

The population of the town rose from 8,742 in 1801 to 19,370 at the end of the century, although part of this increase came from the inclusion in the town of the Ginns, New Houses and the Mount Pleasant which formerly were in Preston Quarter; but the population was increasing, just as it has increased throughout the twentieth century despite the economic depression of the nineteen thirties.

Mr J. E. Williams in a thesis on the rise and decline of the port of Whitehaven writes: 'Whitehaven was still of considerable importance during the first quarter of the nineteenth century. Since the wars the mercantile marine of the British Isles had been almost stationary in numbers with an aggregate tonnage which fluctuated between 2,400,000 and 2,200,000. Of that aggregate a full quarter (573,000 tons) was owned

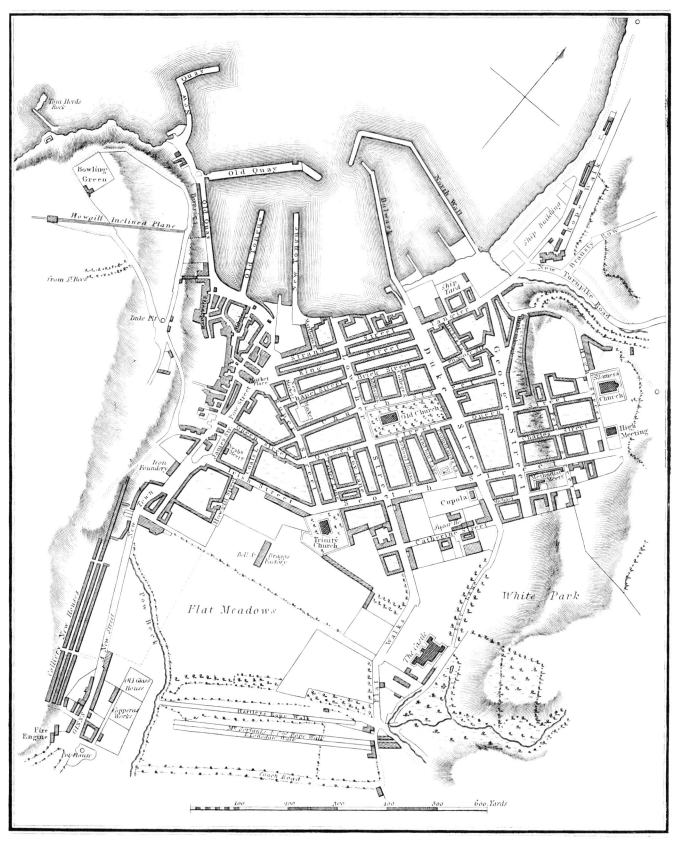

Street plan, 1815.

62

and registered in London in 1828. Second to London came Newcastle with 202,000; third, Liverpool with 162,000; fourth, Sunderland with 108,000; and fifth Whitehaven with 73,000. No other port in the country, except Hull (72,000), had as much as 50,000 tons of shipping, although Glasgow, Port Glasgow and Greenock taken together had 84,000.'

These figures are governed by the same caveat as those for 1750-52 and 1770-72; they refer to the port of Whitehaven which still in 1828 included the coast from Millom to Maryport. The actual shipping and tonnage for Whitehaven itself is given below:

Year	Vessels	Aggregate tonnage
1772	197	
1790	212	26,129
1810	188	29,312
1822	181	26,220
1828	197	30,960
1840	217	36,800

Coal was still the primary industry upon which Whitehaven's prosperity depended, but shipbuilding remained an important factor until the end of the century; and pottery making which at the time of the coronation of Queen Victoria employed some 200 persons gradually declined, the last pottery closing in 1915.

Sailmaking which was an important subsidiary of shipbuilding suffered when steam replaced sail but it lingered on until the 1930s.

Chapter 10 Shipbuilding

At the present moment little is known about the beginnings of ship-building except that somewhere about 1690, when the coal trade with Ireland was expanding rapidly, Sir John Lowther brought ship carpenters into the town to begin a new industry.

The extraordinary influx into Whitehaven that doubled the population between 1693 and 1715 turned agricultural labourers into miners and helped these new key workers to turn village carpenters into shipbuilders. The names of the early master shipbuilders are unknown, and even those operating at the beginning of the eighteenth century remain to be identified. The first names are names and little else: Thomas Sibson (1686-1775), Benjamin Hadwen (1704-96), Joseph White (1714-66) and Roger Martindale who died on 3 August 1784. The most outstanding member of this early group was William Palmer (1702-78).

The earliest vessel that can be definitely attributed to him was the

Whitehaven Harbour, 1856.

Cookson, seventy-nine tons, built in 1757, but it is obvious from his obituary notice in the *Cumberland Pacquet* that he had begun operations at a much earlier date than that. The *Cookson* had a fairly long life and was wrecked at Port St Mary, in Scotland, on 6 March 1832. Equally long-lived was the *Mary and Betty*, 156 tons, launched in 1762. She was lost in Dundalk Bay on 14 December 1837; but Palmer's *Kitty*, 138 tons, launched in 1765, had the most remarkable life of all lasting 118 years. She was lost on a run from Dieppe to Runcorn in December 1883.

As the *Cumberland Pacquet* was not established until 1774 and as the registration of shipping was not compulsory until 1786, it is exceedingly difficult to secure information about vessels built prior to these dates. Even after 1786 it is sometimes difficult to trace the names of builders as the habit of including their names in the register was not introduced until the nineteenth century. However, an analysis of the entries in the early registers at Whitehaven Customs House and of the files of Lloyd's Register shows that at least 187 vessels were built at Whitehaven between the years 1743 and 1786. The total is likely to be much higher than that but will require prolonged research to establish it.

Within this period the busiest years were 1764 and 1765 when eleven and fourteen vessels, with an aggregate of 1,503 and 1,921 tons respectively, were launched; and 1785 and 1786 when the launches were ten and eleven respectively and the tonnages 1,735 and 1,865.

The activity at this latter period is understandable; Whitehaven merchants alone had lost about one hundred vessels during the American War of Independence. Two of Palmer's contemporaries concerning whom all too little is known, are the brothers John Wood (1717-89) and William Wood (1725-1804), who had come to Whitehaven from Rockcliffe. According to a local census of 1762 they were both living in Coates Lane at that time and were engaged in shipbuilding, but there may have been some misunderstanding with regard to John as he seems to have started business at Workington prior to 1756. The association of the Wood family with shipbuilding at Workington covers a period of over sixty years. In 1765 William Wood obtained a grant of ground at Maryport where he set up a shipbuilding yard and the Woods dominated the shipbuilding scene at Maryport for nearly a century. During that time they launched 157 vessels with an aggregate tonnage of 27,627.

Best known of Whitehaven's eighteenth century shipbuilders is Daniel Brocklebank (1742-1801), the founder of the oldest shipping line in the country. He was the younger son of the Rev Daniel Brocklebank, curate-in-charge of the Parish Church of Torpenhow. In 1770, when he had

▽ Watercolour by William Jackson, Liverpool, of the barque *Boyne*. Launched at Whitehaven by William Bowes and Son, 1794.

▷ Watercolour of the ship *Hartley*, 243 tons, William Thompson, commander. Launched by James Shepherd, 1795. Captured on voyage to West Indies, 1796. By courtesy of the Misses M. I. and W. A. Wandless.

BOYNE of Whitehaven Joseph Hodgson Master. 1794.

HARTLEY of W:HAVEN William Thompson Commander.

Watercolour of the ship
Lady Gordon, 283 tons, Capt. John
Bell, 1828. Launched by Whiteside
and Scott, 7 January 1817. By
courtesy of Mr W. R. Roan.

reached the age of twenty-eight, he left his native country and established
a shipbuilding yard at Sheepscutt, Maine, where he constructed five
vessels. At the time the fifth was nearing completion the trouble between
the colonists and the mother country became acute and it was patent
that a choice had to be made. Daniel Brocklebank decided to establish
himself in Whitehaven, and on 8 May 1775 left Sheepscutt, arriving at
Whitehaven thirty-two days later.

For a time he was engaged in trade but, although in all he made
twenty-five voyages across the Atlantic, he did not allow his seafaring
activities to interfere with his shipbuilding ambitions and in 1782 he
established a yard at Whitehaven where he built twenty-seven vessels
before his death in 1801. The yard was carried on by his sons Thomas
and John who gave their name to the business and under which title it is
still maintained. In 1819 a connection was commenced with Liverpool
and in the course of time the management of the business gradually
drifted to the larger port.

The yard was maintained at Whitehaven until 1865 when two factors
contributed to its closure. In 1863 the firm decided to go in for iron
ships instead of wooden ones and the contract for building the *Alexander*
and *Baroda* had been given to Harland and Wolff of Belfast. Brocklebanks continued to obtain almost all their vessels from that firm until
1889 when they went into steam. On the other hand the lease of the
Whitehaven yard had expired without hope of renewal. Further reference
to this will be made when dealing with the fate of another local firm,
Lumley Kennedy and Company. During these sixty-five years, 131
vessels with an aggregate of 36,746 tons had been launched.

To return to the eighteenth century, a firm concerning whose activities
all too little is known, is that of James Spedding and Company. It built
eight vessels between 1775 and 1763; the *Sovereign, Phoenix, Eliza,
Pollux, Carson, Castor, Carlisle* and *Cyrus*. The *Pollux, Castor* and *Cyrus*
were built for Daniel Brocklebank, but the *Pollux* was renamed *Precedent*
after she was launched and under that name sailed from Whitehaven

under the command of Capt Brocklebank on 14 December 1780. From other sources we know that the *Castor, Carlisle* and *Cyrus* were built by Henry Stockdale, so the question naturally arises whether Spedding and Company was simply another name for Stockdale's yard, or whether James Spedding, agent for the Earl of Lonsdale, had an interest in Stockdale's business. If that is the case, Stockdale's entry into the shipbuilding industry must be dated several years prior to the time so far accepted. According to the register at Holy Trinity Church, Whitehaven, Henry Stockdale was baptised there 30 September 1749. Between the years 1782 and 1789 Stockdale built twenty-two vessels, the largest of which was the ship *Castor*, launched in 1782 for Daniel Brocklebank. In 1776 another shipyard was opened at Whitehaven. The owner was William Bowes who was born about 1752. His family consisted of a son, William, born about 1783 and at least two daughters. William Bowes, senior, died at Whitehaven in May 1817 aged sixty-five. His son who had been a member of the Town and Harbour Trustees from August 1820 to July 1826, died 12 July 1831 'after an indisposition of many years' duration'. At least sixty-seven vessels were built at the Bowes's yard during the period of its existence and one authority makes the total seventy-seven. The largest of these was the *Prince Regent*, 434 tons, twenty-man, master, launched on 8 May 1811.

In 1778 Henry Jackson commenced business as a shipbuilder, but for some reason which is not clear decided in 1783 to move to Chester, advertised the sale of his yard and probably would have gone if his legs had not been broken in an accident. He died in Quay Street on 30 November 1789. Jackson built fifteen vessels which varied between ninety tons and 287 tons.

The next person to make an incursion into the shipbuilding industry was James Shepherd who took over or laid out a yard in 1785 and who, during his eighteen years' activity, built thirty-six vessels, the aggregate displacement of which cannot be ascertained as particulars regarding the individual vessels are not available.

Shepherd himself is a shadowy figure, a pale ghost concerning whom little biographical data is at present available. He married Julia Casson at Holy Trinity Church on 19 May 1776.

He was associated at the beginning of his career with a William Coulthard, and in the *Cumberland Pacquet* they are named as the joint builders of the *Mary* in April 1785. Coulthard is credited with building three vessels under his own name between 1789 and 1792. Shepherd died at his home in King Street on 30 May 1803.

Like Shepherd, Samuel Nicholson was another local shipbuilder about whom we know singularly little, except that he had gained his experience as foreman to Henry Jackson. He married a Miss Ann Pearson of Marlborough Street in 1783. He commenced business in 1792 when he launched the *Hope*, 220 tons, and from then on seems to have worked steadily and energetically, scarcely a year passing but one or more vessels slid from the stocks in his yard. The most prosperous year was 1804 when he launched four brigs and a hopper, the *Ant, Divina, Dale, John* and *Whitehaven*, an aggregate of 554 tons. In all he constructed twenty-nine vessels between 1792 and 1814. The 4,980 tons of shipping he built included smacks, sloops, schooners, scows, brigantines, barques and ships.

According to *Jollie's Directory*, 1811, his home was in Bardywell Lane.

Nicholson's yard appears to have been taken over by a firm which is mentioned first as Harrison and Younghusband and later as Harrison and Company who built seven vessels there between 1817 and 1821. The William Younghusband of this partnership was a substantial shipowner. He died at 'Floraville', Corkickle, which was at that time a residential suburb on the outskirts of Whitehaven, on 23 June 1845 aged seventy years.

Thomas Kirk's business was the last of those established in the eighteenth century. He was born about 1749 and from his association with the Secession Church in High Street, may well have been of Scottish birth or extraction. He was forty years old when he launched his first vessel, the *Nancy*, 100 tons, in 1793. In the twenty years he was in business he constructed nineteen vessels. His latter years were spent in retirement at St Bees. Prior to moving there he resided in a house in Queen Street at the junction of Queen Street and Carter Lane.

He had three daughters. The eldest married a Mr Gibson at Liverpool in 1819. The second, Mary, married Mr John Christopherson at Liverpool in 1807, while the third, Jane, died at Barbados in 1810 at the early age of twenty-four years.

The eighteenth century closed with five yards in operation, Brocklebank's, Shepherd's, Bowes's, Nicholson's and Kirk's, and the launching of thirteen vessels with a total displacement of about 2,900 tons. During that century Whitehaven's population had more than quadrupled. Although considerably smaller than either Liverpool or Bristol it had for a time threatened to outstrip them both but the tobacco trade was ruined by the American War of Independence and the Industrial Revolution gave its rivals the industrial hinterland Whitehaven could never hope to possess.

Its position at this time will be more clearly gauged against the following background. During the four years 1799 to 1802, 3,429 vessels totalling 414,002 tons had been built and registered in Great Britain. Of these London had furnished 179 vessels, 45,777 tons; Liverpool ninety vessels, 16,752 tons; and Whitehaven thirty-eight vessels, approximately 7,500 tons.

In the first years of the new century a new combine appeared, the active partners in which were William Wilson and Musgrave Walker, although William Stitt, a prominent ship owner had a strong financial interest in it. Wilson was a mere stripling of twenty but he possessed a great ability as a draughtsman. He designed the *Clarendon*, a ship of 505 tons, launched in 1807 and the *Earl of Lonsdale*, of 502 tons, built in 1810. These were the largest vessels built at Whitehaven in their day and were not exceeded in size until Brocklebanks constructed the *Princess Charlotte*, 514 tons, in 1815.

Throughout the eighteenth century the design of Whitehaven ships had remained fairly static. The majority of the vessels in the American, Baltic and Mediterranean trades were brigantines of 100 to 200 tons and ships of barques of 200 to 300 tons. Spedding and Company's *Sovereign*, 363 tons, launched in 1776, was an unusually large vessel for her time. Even a quarter of a century later the local press was acclaiming William Bowes's twenty-gun ship *Neptune*, 363 tons, as 'the most valuable ship ever built in Cumberland'.

With the advent of the nineteenth century conditions changed, particularly with the development of the East India Trade and there was more and more demand for larger vessels. By the middle of the century yard vied with yard and port with port in turning out vessels of ever increasing size. Wilson fell victim to a cholera epidemic that was raging in Dublin in August 1834 'and was interred, in the evening of the same day of his death, in the burial ground attached to St Mark's Church, in the city'. His younger son, Joseph Dickinson, died at his father's house in Lowther Street in 1829 at the age of nineteen. His only daughter, Mary Ann, married Captain John Moore in 1835.

Musgrave Walker (1770-1826) was the seventh child of John Walker and Eleanor Piper.

In 1799 he was the owner and master of the 237 ton ship *Urania* built by Thomas Kirk in that year. He was captured by the French in 1805 when he was sailing in the West Indies. He was held as a prisoner of war for four years, escaped in an open boat and was picked up by H.M. Brig *Banterer* returning to Whitehaven in November 1810. In 1813 he took over the ship chandlery business carried on at the low end of Duke Street under the name of Messrs Bragg, Bowes and Wilson. Three years later he was appointed Lloyd's agent at the Port of Whitehaven. In the following year he was one of the chapel wardens at St Nicholas.

He died at his home in Catherine Street, 24 November 1826, in his fifty-seventh year. His wife, Ann Greenhow, by whom he had eight children, survived him until 1846. Their youngest son, Captain Thomas Walker of the *Superior*, died at the age of twenty-four on 28 November 1838. He was washed overboard on a voyage to Rio de Janeiro. Their eldest son, John, died in London in 1824 aged twenty-three and their next son, Joseph Greenhow, in 1845 aged forty. Forty-eight vessels were constructed at this yard between 1802 and 1836. Of these, two exceeded 500 tons, two 400 tons and five 300 tons. James Shepherd ceased building in 1803 and Thomas Kirk three years later leaving four yards in operation, but the vacant yards were not idle long. In 1806 John Scott took one over and in 1808 Thomas Cowen the other.

Born about 1775 Cowen started in business in 1808 and although he built half a dozen largish vessels, such as the *Wellington*, 224 tons and *Julius Caesar*, 296 tons, it was as a boat builder that he was regarded by his contemporaries rather than as a shipbuilder. Between 1808 and 1816 he built twenty-three vessels most of which were comparatively small. In 1813 he seems to have experienced financial difficulties for in July of that year he assigned all his property to Abraham Sibson, Edward Clementson and James Bulman. He died in 1840.

Not very much can be said about the personalities controlling the firm of Whiteside and Scott which commenced in 1806. John Scott, born about 1775, was the son of Joseph Scott of Hensingham who died 15 April 1828 aged eighty-three years. He had two children, John who died in February 1838 at the age of twenty-five and Elizabeth who married Richard East, clerk in the Colliery Office, in September 1836. Scott died 12 July 1842 and his obituary states that he 'was an excellent draughtsman and was always regarded as a very superior builder'. His home was at Sea View, Bransty. His wife predeceased him in May 1835. The forty vessels built by Whiteside and Scott run the usual range of sloops, schooners, brigantines, barques and ships.

The following interesting note about the *Elizabeth Buckham*, built by Whiteside and Scott in 1837, appeared in the *Cumberland Pacquet* for 23 April 1844: '*Elizabeth Buckham*, Bewley, from South Australia off Folkestone on the 4th instant, and at London on the 17th, all well after a splendid passage of 118 days to the Downes and considered the quickest

Visitors' day on the *Eleanor Dixon*.

trip ever made to this country from the above colony'. The *Elizabeth Buckham* was only a 269 ton brigantine. If the trip seems long to modern eyes, it must be remembered that the big clippers of the 1870s and 1880s took over 70 days for the trip to or from Australia. She was wrecked off the Mersey on 26 November 1866.

Captain William Middleton and his sons built the schooner *Lowther Castle*, launched 5 January 1833.

Robert Eilbeck built two schooners, *Sarah*, fifty-nine tons and *Elizabeth*, seventy-one tons, in 1839 and 1840.

Lumley Kennedy and Company is not only interesting *per se* but also on account of its relationship to T. and J. Brocklebank. Lumley Kennedy, the practical partner in the firm, was the son of a former shipwright in the town and was himself, for nearly twenty years, manager for Brocklebanks. He left them in 1835 to become the managing partner in a firm, the other partners of which were Dr Robinson, Bolton Hall; Mr R. Jefferson, Springfield; Mr H. Jefferson; Captain Pew, R.N., Whitehaven (subsequently of London); Captain I. Mounsey, Whitehaven; Mr Thomas Beck, Whitehaven; and Mr John Peile, Somerset House, Whitehaven. The company was formed for twenty-one years but carried on for several years more. Two factors influenced its dissolution: the change from wood to iron shipbuilding and difficulties over the lease of the yard. In order to provide better facilities the company required a long lease of the foreshore used as a building site but, owing to possible rail and dock developments, the Earl of Lonsdale would not grant this.

Both Brocklebank's and Kennedy's yards closed almost simultaneously. In all Lumley Kennedy built sixty-five vessels of varying tonnages for customers in different parts of the country, all of which sustained the firm's reputation for sound workmanship and good sailing qualities. The largest was the *John O'Gaunt*, 871 tons, launched 2 May 1855. The list includes five vessels of over 600 tons, one over 500 tons, twelve over 400 tons and nine over 300 tons. Lumley Kennedy himself was a quiet, retiring man who took little interest in the political life of the period.

He married Mary Riley at St Nicholas Church in 1816 but was himself a nonconformist. They had several children. His second son, Captain Lumley Kennedy, was master of the steamer *Calder* of Whitehaven.

When the yard closed he moved from Whitehaven to Beckermet where he died in 1882 at the ripe old age of ninety-one. His yard was taken over by Joseph Shepherd and Company. Shepherd had previously been in Kennedy's employment. The new company operated from 1865 to 1879 and built seventeen vessels, the largest of which was the *Beckermet*, 229 tons.

Brocklebank's yard was taken over for a short time by William Huddart who built two schooners and a trawler. The last named, the *Maria*, launched in 1870, was an elegant and sturdy piece of work. She survived until 20 August 1926 when she was wrecked at Harrington.

Three brothers, Richard (1800-59), Hugh (1805-73) and William Williamson (1815-47), were all apprenticed to shipbuilding and in course of time branched out on their own. Richard started a yard at Harrington at which he was joined by his brother William. Hugh migrated to Douglas, Isle of Man, where he started in business on his own building nine brigs and schooners between 1837 and 1841. The shipbuilding on the Isle of Man experienced a disastrous depression in 1842 and Williamson was forced to close his yard. He eventually returned to Whitehaven where he built fourteen vessels between 1851 and 1870.

The Harrington yard established by Richard Williamson was continued by his son Thomas and removed to Workington in 1870. Thomas retired leaving his two sons Richard and Robert Hardy Williamson to carry on the Workington Shipyard. The latter was so named in memory of his grandfather, Robert Hardy, a Whitehaven shipbuilder who launched eighteen vessels between 1825 and 1852.

Towards the end of 1869 the Whitehaven Shipbuilding Co Ltd took over the yard previously occupied by T. and J. Brocklebank. The chair-

Riggers fitting out the ship
Thirlmere, 1,711 tons. Launched by
the Whitehaven Shipbuilding
Company in May 1874.

man of the company was G. C. Bentinck, M.P. for Whitehaven, and the
shareholders were a fair cross-section of local shipping and business
interests. The result of their enterprise was the launching of the *Patterdale*,
1,200 tons, on 3 June 1871. The huge crowds which watched the launch
turned it into something of a gala occasion. The reason was not far to
seek. Following the closing of the Brocklebank and Kennedy yards the
shipbuilding industry experienced a very severe depression. The new
company was employing upwards of 450 men and boys whose wages
amounted to £1,200 per month and to carry out the contracts on hand
within the specified time it was estimated that at least twice as many
employees would be required.

Owing to various misfortunes and circumstances outside the control of
the company it was forced into voluntary liquidation in 1879 and once
more the yard closed after forty-two vessels had been launched, the
aggregate tonnage of which was 40,519.

Among them were many which are remembered as amongst the finest
examples of the clipper ship era, the *Wasdale, Greta, Thirlmere, Rydal-
mere, Cassiope, Candida, Silverhow, Grasmere* and *Blengfell*. The closing
of the shipyard hit the town heavily and as many of the shareholders
were convinced that under new management it could be run successfully,
a persistent effort was made to restart the yard. Eventually the necessary
capital was obtained but the unsettled state of the iron market made
buyers hold off in hope of a further fall in prices. However, by the time
that its first vessel, the schooner *Isabel* was launched for Mr W. Burnyeat,
on 3 November 1880, contracts to the value of £100,000 were in hand.
In all, thirty-four vessels were built by this company including such well-
known ones as the *Gilcrux, Dunboyne, Galgate, Lord Shaftesbury,
Windermere, Alice A. Leigh* and the *Englehorn*, but towards the end of
its life the firm experienced serious financial difficulty. On the contract
prices of the last five vessels £24,000 was lost. Faulty launches added to
its troubles. In 1889 both the *Alice A. Leigh* and the *Englehorn* stuck on

Whitehaven Lass, launched by Hugh
Williamson, Whitehaven, 1860.
Wrecked Parton beach, 1883.

Watercolour sketch by J. McMillan of
the *Alice A. Leigh*, 4-masted barque,
2,929 tons, launched September
1889 — the largest sailing ship built
at Whitehaven.

the ways as they were being launched and a further £3,004 had to be spent before they eventually entered the water.

Attempts to form a new company were unsuccessful and other firms were unwilling to take over the shipyard. As a result the yard and equipment were sold in 1891 for £3,000 and for the next ten years it was carried on as a repairing yard.

Share certificate of the Whitehaven Shipbuilding Company issued 6 May 1881.

No. 23

The Whitehaven Shipbuilding Company, Limited

Registered 9th Day of April 1880.

Capital £80,000 in 4000 Shares of £20 each.

This is to Certify that Mr John Brockbank of King St. Whitehaven is the registered Proprietor of Fifteen Shares Numbered _____ to _____ inclusive in The Whitehaven Shipbuilding Company, Limited subject to the terms and conditions contained in the Articles of Association of the said Company and that up to this day there has been paid up in respect of each of such Shares the sum of **Ten** Pounds

Given under the Common Seal of the said Company the Sixth day of May 1881

Augustus Helder
Wilson Dees
} Directors.

Ja. Hamilton Secretary.

Reprint commissioned by The Friends of Whitehaven Museum.

73

Chapter 11

The building of the harbour

Whitehaven harbour is the pivot around which the destiny of the town has hinged for several centuries and although its pristine glory is departed, it is still a vital factor in our economy.

Although the era of romance is over and we can no longer sit on a bollard and watch a full-rigged ship come sailing in from a distant port on the other side of the globe, there is still much to interest us about the harbour because every quay has its own story to tell of the days when Whitehaven was making a bid to become the most important port on the west coast of England.

From 1708 the problem of the expansion of the harbour to meet the needs of a growing merchant fleet was the constant preoccupation of the Town and Harbour Trustees. The first part to be built was that portion of the Old Quay erected by Sir Christopher Lowther in 1634 which was improved and lengthened in 1665 and again in 1687. Then between 1709 and 1711 the Trustees built the breakwater out from the end of Duke Street that was known first as 'Mr Lowther's Bulwark' and later simply as 'The Bulwark'. In 1804 the Bulwark was moved bodily about twenty yards to its present position and in 1872 was incorporated as part of the Queen's Dock. The Trustees also built a wharf or mole along the shore between Marlborough Street and Lowther Street.

Whitehaven Harbour, c. 1840.

House of Thomas Hartley, merchant, on Marlborough Street. Mentioned in Harbour Act, 1761.

Mr Thomas Hartleys house in Marlborough Street Whitehaven The end windows look down the New or Lime Tongue named in the act of 1761 as a boundary Point.

In 1726 twenty yards of wharf was built on the seaward side of the Old Quay and in 1730 the lighthouse on the end of the Quay was repaired. Two years later the Trustees decided to repair and strengthen the Bulwark and work was commenced in September 1733. They also decided to build a second bulwark or tongue. This is the structure known variously at different times as the Merchants' Quay, the Old Tongue, the Sugar Tongue and Fish Quay. Originally it was to be sited where the Lime Tongue now stands but the position was altered in the planning stage. It was completed in 1735. In 1734 a breakwater was built between Tom Hurd's rock and the shore.

In 1739 it was agreed to build a mole 'behind the present Pier (i.e. the Old Quay) for the reception of a few of the largest ships when fully laden'. In 1742 John Reynolds submitted a plan for extending this quay (now known as the Old New Quay) by 100 feet at an estimated cost of £1,250. As the work was proceeding it was agreed to buttress the quay and to build a nine foot high parapet.

In 1750 it was resolved to build a new tongue out from the end of Marlborough Street. In contrast with the Merchants' Quay or the Old Tongue it became known as the New Tongue and later as the Lime Tongue. In 1767 the Trustees agree to add thirty yards to the Old New Quay, to shorten the Sugar Tongue by twenty yards, to lengthen the Old Quay by sixty yards and to move the lighthouse to the end.

The North Wall was started as a result of discussions held in 1766, more work was done on it following another resolution in 1780 and in 1785 it was agreed to add a return to the North Wall. This is the straight part of the Devil's Elbow, the additional portion being added in 1804.

In 1823 John Whidbey and Sir John Rennie were consulted about extending the limits of the harbour. This resulted in the plan for the West Pier which they suggested run N.N.W. from the western corner of the New Quay for 145 yards, then canting N.E. for 110 yards and again canting E.N.E. for a similar distance. A North Pier was visualised by them but it was not until 1833 that Rennie provided a detailed plan for this.

Work on the West Pier started towards the end of 1823 and continued until the end of 1830 when it had reached a point 340 yards from the New Quay. As the work progressed it was found that sand was accumulating within the West Pier, a point which Rennie had anticipated when he proposed the North Pier. In 1832 Rennie was again consulted about the sand deposits and recommended the building of a pier extending seaward 1,100 feet, then taking a little cant to the westward and terminating with a round head. This work was begun in 1833, but a year later the plan was slightly modified and the building suspended while Mr Caird Logan, of Glasgow, was consulted about the completion of the West Pier. In 1836 he submitted his design for the circular head which was accepted by the Trustees. The work was started early in 1837 but Mr Logan died and the design was completed by Mr Ebenezer Stiven, his resident engineer, in 1838.

The ogee head has been described as 'the finest piece of work in the whole pier, and decidedly the most difficult in construction'.

As the North Pier remained to be finished the Trustees asked Mr Stiven to provide a design. He recommended that the jetty be taken down and that the pier be canted to the south-west and finished with a circular head. The Trustees approved the plan which was put in hand and finished in 1841.

In 1854, 1860 and 1866, the Trustees studied plans for the provision of a wet dock but rejected them. In 1869 they asked Mr Stiven to produce a plan which he did. The estimated cost of his scheme was £52,000 and the Trustees submitted the plan to Mr Brunlees who reported in its favour, although he proposed certain alterations and additions that added £5,000 to the cost. The report was accepted, the Trustees secured the passage of the Dock and Harbour Act in 1871 and the work commenced early in 1872. The dock was opened 22 November 1876. The dock, named the Queen's Dock in honour of Queen Victoria, is on the site designed by Mr Stiven.

The dock was opened with hopeful anticipations of an expansion of the shipping trade and traffic but, unfortunately, things did not go smoothly for long. There was a serious set-back which turned all calculations upside-down, causing considerable trouble and financial loss. The condition of the dock entrance became unsatisfactory — there was a shrinkage and cracking, said to be due to shifting foundations — and ultimately the dock gates failed to act. In 1880 the dock was closed to enable the necessary repairs to the pier heads. At this time there was

North Pier lighthouse.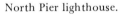

Oil painting by Charles J. de Lacy, of the paddle steamer *Refuge* in Whitehaven Harbour, 1901. By courtesy of the Whitehaven Harbour Commissioners.

much discussion as to the proposed conversion of the North Harbour into a wet dock, but the opposition to such a scheme prevailed.

The dock engineer, Sir James Brunlees, was asked to report on the accommodation for shipping with a view to deepening and improving the harbour. In his report to the Trustees in April 1880, he pointed out the inadequacies of the Queen's Dock and suggested the construction of a new dock and tidal harbour on the foreshore, north of the existing dock at a cost of £180,000. The prospect of further heavy outlay did not appeal to the Trustees and the subject was allowed to drop.

In 1879 the Trustees had suffered a severe financial loss of £10,000 due to the sinking of their steam tug *Whitehaven* in Ramsey Sound. The vessel was not insured.

The failure of the dock gates led to a dispute between the Trustees and the contractors with regard to a final settlement of accounts which ended in proceedings against the Trustees, a claim for £12,810 being made. The arbitration which followed resulted in an award against the Trustees.

The dock was reopened in 1882. When once in proper working order it proved of great service, but it would have been of greater advantage had it been made in the first place for the accommodation of larger vessels.

The dock gates were again renewed in 1939. Writing on the evolution of Whitehaven the late J. R. Thompson said: 'Whitehaven people, until the advent of railways and steamships, lived an industrious prosperous life. There was, as I have said, the extensive foreign trade, a brisk coal trade, shipbuilding, rope-making and other industries. The harbour was always busy, except on the occasion of a long spell of easterly winds when vessels could not get up the Channel or across from Dublin, and down to the early sixties the shipping trade was really a considerable affair.

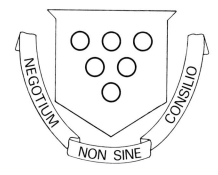

Coat of Arms of the Whitehaven Harbour Commissioners.

'The development of iron ore, followed by large exports to South Wales helped for some years to swell the shipping trade, but the extension of the railway system, the cessation of our West Indies trade, the advent of steamers and the collapse of wooden shipbuilding was a combination which struck at our very foundations — in fact, as a port and shipbuilding centre worked for us a gradual revolution.'

The following table shows the comparative use of the harbour in the mid-nineteenth century with that at the present time.

	Vessels	Tonnage		Vessels	Tonnage
1853	3,706	317,732	1968	371	196,405
1854	3,687	332,267	1969	338	201,161
1855	3,693	285,476	1970	446	269,769
1856	3,886	322,506	1971	423	274,232
1857	3,911	375,820	1972	363	249,576
1858	3,770	313,821	1973	427	281,443
1859	4,125	316,723	1974	316	271,522
1860	4,206	335,932	1975	259	230,412
1861	4,206	364,304	1976	282	263,543
1862	4,787	412,073	1977	264	251,954

Timber boat in the harbour.

In the first half of the present century the harbour was dependent primarily on the coal trade so that its prosperity was conditioned by events inside and outside the town. The most serious of these were the Wellington Pit explosion of 10 May 1910 which stopped the mining of coal from that pit until 15 August 1911, the Whitehaven Miners' Strike from 25 June to 1 October 1904, the National Strike of March-April 1912, the Dublin Dockers' Strike which began in September 1913 and lasted until January 1914, the long miners' struggle that followed the collapse of the National Strike in 1926, and the period of worst economic depression when all the Whitehaven pits were closed in 1935-37.

The advent of Marchon Products Ltd and the developments that have taken place there have given a new importance to the Harbour, as can be seen from the table of imports and exports in the appendix, although it still suffers from the fact that the size of ships that can be accommodated is limited.

In 1967 Marchon Products Ltd produced a plan for the improvement of Whitehaven Harbour so that it could accommodate vessels of 30,000 tons. The estimated cost of the scheme was between £2½ million and £3 million. An Action Committee consisting of representatives from various interested bodies was set up under the chairmanship of the Mayor of Whitehaven (Councillor A. G. Daugherty) with a view to implementing the scheme, but it was eventually dropped.

Marchon Enterprise entering Queen's Dock — a tricky manoeuvre as seen from this bird's eye view.

Chapter 12   Railways

A reminder of the days when we
had two local railways.
Publisher's Collection.

As was shown in the chapter on mining history there were tramways in Whitehaven early in the eighteenth century, but the wagons that ran along these ways did so by gravity. It was not until a century later that locomotives made their appearance.

In 1837 the promoters of the railway line from Maryport to Carlisle received Parliamentary powers to proceed with the work. The first section of the line from Maryport to Arkleby Pits was opened on 15 July 1840 and the line completed on 10 February 1845. In the meantime, William, Second Earl of Lonsdale, took an interest in the extension of the line from Maryport to Whitehaven and engaged George Stephenson, who had been engineer for a time for the Maryport-Carlisle line, to become the engineer for the new line which was to be built by a separate company known as the Whitehaven Junction Railway. The line was opened in three stages – Maryport to Workington, 19 January 1846; Workington to Harrington, 18 May 1846; and Harrington to Whitehaven, 19 March 1847.

Excursion to Windermere and
Lowther arranged by the Committee
of the Whitehaven Mechanics'
Institute, 24 May 1852.

CHEAP TRIP
TO THE
LAKE DISTRICT
ON HER MAJESTY'S BIRTH-DAY.

The Committee of the WHITEHAVEN MECHANICS' INSTITUTION beg to inform the Public, that they have arranged with the Whitehaven Junction Railway Company for a

CHEAP RAILWAY EXCURSION
TO
WINDERMERE LAKE,
AND LOWTHER,
TO TAKE PLACE
ON MONDAY, THE 24TH OF MAY, 1852.

FARES, There and Back, (a Distance of 200 Miles,)
FIRST CLASS,   SECOND CLASS,   THIRD CLASS,
's. 6d.   5s. 0d.   3s. 6d.

After the first 500 third Class Tickets are disposed of the Price will be advanced to 4s.; and Parties are urgently requested to procure Tickets before Noon, on Thursday, the 20th of May, in order that sufficient Carriage accommodation may be prepared.
The Trains will leave as follows :—

ST. BEES	at - 5 0 a.m.	WORKINGTON	at - 6 0 a.m.
WHITEHAVEN	- - 5 30	MARYPORT	- - - 6 20
HARRINGTON	- - 5 50	ASPATRIA	- - - 6 45
COCKERMOUTH	- 5 15	WIGTON	- - - 7 10
	CARLISLE, at 8 0 a.m.		

And arrive at Windermere at 10 30 a.m., & leave Windermere on their return at 7 p.m., & Penrith at 8 30 p.m.,
Thus affording ample time for visiting the romantic and magnificent Scenery of this charming locality.

" Among the English Lakes, Windermere confessedly stands unrivalled for the beautiful variety of scenery that greets him who sails along it."
" A visit to Windermere is a thing to be ever after remembered along with the very happiest of our reminiscences of natural scenery."
It hardly seems possible indeed that the beauties in Lake scenery could excel that from the bosom of Windermere."

Persons desirous of visiting LOWTHER CASTLE, BROUGHAM CASTLE, ULLSWATER, &c., may alight at the Penrith Station.

The EARL OF LONSDALE has kindly consented to allow the Grounds, &c., of LOWTHER CASTLE to be open to Visitors on the occasion.

THE WINDERMERE LAKE STEAM-BOATS WILL PLY AT LOW FARES.

An Excellent Band of Music will accompany the Train.

TICKETS MAY BE HAD AT THE FOLLOWING PLACES :—
Whitehaven, Mr. Joseph Brown, Lowther-street, and of the Committee.—*Harrington*, Mr. Thomas Williamson.—*Workington*, Mr. J. Pearce, Washington-street.—*Cockermouth*, Mr. John Hird, Grocer. *Maryport*, Mr. Adm. Bookseller, and of Mr. Sherwen, Mechanics' Institute.—*Aspatria*, Mr. D. Bouch. *Wigton*, Mr. Hoodless, Bookseller, and at the Mechanics' Institution.   And at the several Railway Stations on the Lines.

PRINTER, KING STREET, WHITEHAVEN.

Uniform button — Cleator and
Workington Junction Railway.

The close friendship between the Earl of Lonsdale and George
Stephenson led to the formation of the Whitehaven and Furness Junction
Railway, which was incorporated on 21 April 1847. Lord Lonsdale and
his fellow directors were undeterred by the trade slump and railway
panic that took place at that time and the construction of the line was
commenced in 1847. The original starting point was the Newtown
Station at Preston Street, now used as a goods depot. The engineer was
Mr Dees and the line was single throughout, apart from passing loops at
the stations.

The section from Whitehaven to Bootle was opened 1 July 1850 and
on 28 October 1850 it was extended to Broughton where it connected
with the existing Furness Railway. These two lines were united under
one management in 1866. The tunnel from Corkickle to Bransty Station
was started in 1850 and completed in 1852. Up to that time there was a
break between the Preston Street terminus of the Whitehaven and
Furness Junction Railway and the Bransty Station of the Whitehaven
Junction Railway. There was a link between the two systems in the form
of a mineral line which ran from the back of Preston Street through the
Market Place on to the West Strand of the harbour. From the West
Strand use was made of the lines along the harbour to reach Bransty
Station. The manoeuvring was awkward and limited in the main to goods
traffic in iron ore and pig iron.

The portion of the track which ran through the Market Place and
threw off a short spur to the flour mill in Catherine Street was taken
up some time after 1918, but it had not been used for a long time before
that.

In 1854 powers were obtained to establish the Whitehaven, Cleator
and Egremont Railway. It joined the Whitehaven and Furness Railway at
Mirehouse. There was a branch line which ran from Moor Row to Cleator
Moor and Frizington. The line was opened to goods traffic on 11 January
1855. The first passenger service started in the summer of 1857. In 1869
the line was extended from Egremont to Sellafield. In 1879 it was
acquired jointly by the Furness and London and North Western Railway
Companies. The Furness Company itself was absorbed into the London,
Midland and Scottish Railway in 1923, as was the Maryport and Carlisle
Railway in the railway reorganisation of that year. The Whitehaven Junction Railway had been acquired by the London and North Western in
1866.

Hutton Hall 0-6-0 S.T. taken in
September 1923 in Cleator and
Workington Colours.

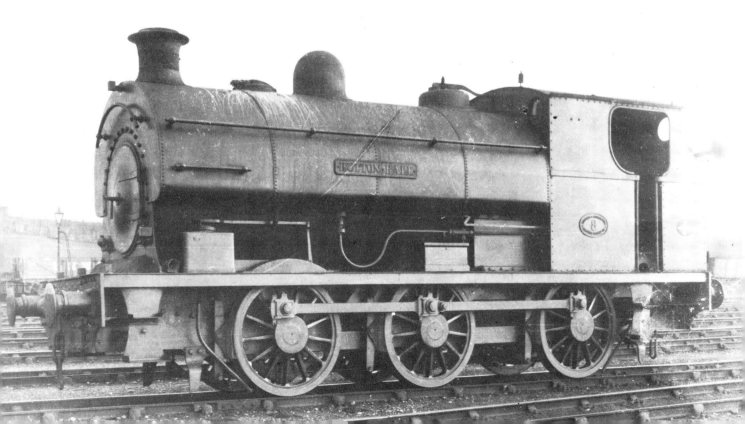

Chapter 13 Local government

During the early period of the development of Whitehaven under the Lowther family the parish vestry, which was responsible for poor relief, would probably meet at the mother church of St Bees. The most important factor in the lives of the people of the growing township would be the manorial court and although many of the powers and usages attached to the manorial court from medieval times had to a large extent disappeared, there is no doubt that the Lord of the Manor, or his deputy, played a major role in local affairs. Although no records survive, it is highly probable that in this small community up to the end of the seventeenth century, the merchant traders had some voice in harbour affairs.

Sir John Lowther realised that by the end of the seventeenth century Whitehaven needed a more representative governing body to deal with the needs of his growing town. He devoted his latter years to that end, but it was left to his son James (afterwards Sir James) to secure the passage of an Act of Parliament in 1708 that established the Whitehaven Town and Harbour Board of Trustees on a partially elective basis. This act described the harbour boundaries, regulated certain building operations adjacent to harbour property, imposed duties on imported goods and tonnage on exports. Under its authority the first members of the Board of Trustees were appointed and the method and times of subsequent elections are described.

The Board of Trustees numbered twenty-one, the Lord of the Manor, or his deputy, was always a member, and six others were to be nominated by him. Fourteen others are named in the Act, these were in the first instance appointed for seven years, afterwards they were to be elected by ballot every three years. Those eligible for election were: (a) inhabitants of the town who were merchants dealing in goods subjected to payments and duties; (b) master of any vessel belonging to the port; or (c) owner

Nos.80-83 Lowther Street. Drawn and engraved by W. Banks & Son.

82

or part-owner of not less than one-sixteenth share of a vessel belonging to the port.

The last provision is interesting. The value of a ship was divided into sixty-fourths. It was rather unusual for one person to own a vessel outright. Two or three persons, termed subscribing owners, might well own half the shares between them, the other shares would be divided among a considerable number of non-subscribing owners. People with money to invest in shipping preferred to spread it over a number of vessels. For example, when Robert Hardy, the shipbuilder, died in 1853 he had shares in twenty-five vessels which varied from two sixty-fourths to twenty-eight sixty-fourths.

In the Act those representing the manor were James Lowther, William Gilpin, Anthony Benn, John Gilpin, John Ribton, John Sheppard, John Golding and John Spedding, who deputised for the Lord of the Manor in his absence.

The other fourteen original members were William Feryes, Clement Nicholson, Thomas Lutwidge, Robert Blacklock, Elisha Gale, Thomas Coates, Richard Hodgson, Robert Bigland, Richard Filbeck, John Gale Jnr, John Gale Snr, Peter Senhouse, Ebenezer Gale and Christopher Dixon. The lord of the manor had a right of veto over almost every item of business dealt with.

The importance of the Gale family is underlined by the fact that four members were on the original Trustee Board and that William Feryes was a relation by marriage, but the other members also contributed to the development of Whitehaven.

The Act provided the means for improving the harbour. The accustomed Duties of Anchorage had become insufficient to defray the growing charges for maintaining the harbour. A new scale is set out in the Act. The Act provided for the building of a new mole or wharf and of a counter-mole that became known as Mr Lowther's Bulwark.

The Trustees were empowered to make orders for the management and care of the harbour and for the preventing and removing of annoyance from the town. They appointed a collector of harbour dues and a scavenger for the carrying away of 'dirt, ashes, or other annoyances from the town to such places as shall be appointed'.

Further Acts of Parliament followed periodically. The improved trade of the harbour meant that more goods had to be transported into and out of the town so that the Act of 1739 provided 'for the better surveying, ordering, widening, amending and keeping in repair of the roads', and a commission of fifty Trustees was appointed. This body, known as the Turnpike Trust, continued in existence until 1870. Toll-Houses for the collection of tolls for the maintenance of the roads were erected at Scragill, at Collier Flatt in the Ginns and at Long Bransty Gate.

The Act of 1761 allowed for the further enlargement of the harbour, the limits of which were to be those of the present day, without the additional protection of the North and West Piers. Shipbuilding was to be aided by the erection of wet and dry docks and the making of dockyards for repairing as well as buildings ships. The Act also allowed the Trustees to organise a water supply to the town and harbour.

Although street lighting was first discussed by the Trustees in 1763 it was not until 1781 that the proper system of street lighting by oil lamps was instituted. In 1764 the Pow Beck was covered over. Until then the Beck had been crossed by three bridges. The Act of 1792 sanctioned further extensions to the harbour and the Act of 1806 prepared the way for the paving of the streets and the establishment of a night-watch.

The Act of 1849 allowed the Trustees to proceed with a much needed scheme to take water from the river Ehen and Ennerdale Lake.

Any body which has to serve a variety of interests tends to form lobbies and power groups. The Trustees were no different from any other. There was a tendency for one group to coalesce around the lord of the manor and for another to support the interests of the merchants, ship owners and shipbuilders. This split into what in the nineteenth

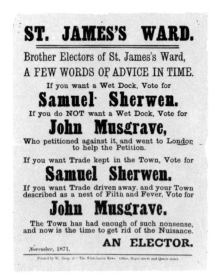

ST. JAMES'S WARD.

Brother Electors of St. James's Ward,

A FEW WORDS OF ADVICE IN TIME.

If you want a Wet Dock, Vote for

Samuel Sherwen.

If you do NOT want a Wet Dock, Vote for

John Musgrave,

Who petitioned against it, and went to London
to help the Petition.

If you want Trade kept in the Town, Vote for

Samuel Sherwen.

If you want Trade driven away, and your Town
described as a nest of Filth and Fever, Vote for

John Musgrave.

The Town has had enough of such nonsense,
and now is the time to get rid of the Nuisance.

November, 1871. AN ELECTOR.

Printed by W. Alsop, at " The Whitehaven News " Office, Roper-street and Queen-street.

John Musgrave (1822-1912), J.P.,
was a solicitor and the leading figure
in the movement to break the
Lowther control of Whitehaven. He
became a member of the Town and
Harbour Trustees but his election
was fiercely contended and equally
strongly supported. St James' Ward
contest, 1871.

GOOD TEMPLARS
Can you vote for a CANDIDATE who seeks supporters through the Public House?

VOTE FOR MUSGRAVE

AND PURITY OF ELECTION.

Good templars can you vote —
election broadsheet.

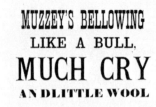

MUZZEY'S BELLOWING
LIKE A BULL,
MUCH CRY
AND LITTLE WOOL

Muzzey's Bellowing — election
broadsheet.

century came to be known as the Town and Castle Parties, resulted in
the Act of 1859 including arrangements for a comprehensive reorganisation of the annual election of the Trustees. The town was divided into
five wards, St James, St Nicholas, Trinity, Newtown and Harbour. Three
Trustees were to be elected for each ward. The Trustee with the least
votes at the time of his election was to retire at the end of one year, the
next lowest at the end of two years, in order to institute a system of
annual elections. The lord of the manor, or his deputy, remained a
Trustee but the number of his nominees was reduced from six to five.
This arrangement placed greater control in the hands of the elected
Trustees, but since some of the elected representatives supported the
Castle party, the two groups were fairly evenly balanced and meetings
were frequently rowdy. Elections between 1850 and 1880 were fought
with a much fiercer partisanship than we know today. Candidates for
election were supported or opposed vigorously in a variety of ways – in
humorous poems, complimentary and otherwise, in letters to the press
and in cartoons and election squibs placed on hoardings. If anyone could
be hoaxed into a ridiculous situation, so much the better.

In 1879 the boundaries of the town were extended to take part of
Bransty and part of Hensingham and the Ballot Act of 1872 was applied
to the election of Trustees. In 1883 came a very important change. From
1709 the town and harbour, although administered by one authority,
were dealt with as separate concerns and accounts for each kept apart.
The Board of Trustees was an elected body without powers of corporate
action. The Act of 1883 changed that and the Board became a corporate
body under the name of the Town and Harbour of Whitehaven, with per-
petual succession and a common seal, with the powers to purchase land
and property and to sue or to be sued in the corporate sense. The Act
also allowed the Board to merge town and harbour accounts.

In 1889 a meeting was held in the Oddfellows Hall 'to consider the
expediency of applying for a Charter of Incorporation for the town and
district'. Application was delayed but was finally approved in 1893 and
the Charter was in due course received from the Privy Council at a
meeting of the Trustees and twenty-one representative ratepayers at the
Town Hall on 20 July 1894. By this the long association between the
town and the harbour came to an end and each passed under separate
administration.

The principal changes effected by the charter were: (a) the extension
of the boundaries of the town to include a large part of Preston Quarter
and Bransty raising the area of the town from 679 to 1,620 acres; (b) the
creation of a new Bransty ward; (c) the lord of the manor no longer sent
nominees; (d) eighteen councillors were to be elected for three years by
the direct vote of householders and were to retire by rotation; (e) six
aldermen were to be elected by the councillors and retire by rotation;
and (f) the Council was to elect, for one year, a mayor who could be a
councillor, alderman or someone from outside the Council.

Mr John Collins, clerk of the Board of Trustees, and Mr James Gibson
Dees, chairman of the Board, were nominated in the charter to carry out
the duties of town clerk and mayor. They were responsible for conducting
the first municipal election which took place in all wards on 1 November
1894 and for convening the first meeting of the elected council on
9 November.

The eighteen elected councillors were: W. H. Kitchin, J. Pattinson,
J. R. Musgrave, T. Bowman, J. Cant, W. Hastwell, A. Wilson, T. Batty,
R. W. Moore, J. Davis, T. K. Metcalf, A. Kitchin, J. Dickinson, J. Kennedy,
J. Stoddart, H. Dixon, R. Cousins and J. I. Fisher. From these Messrs
Moore, W. H. Kitchin, Pattinson, Hastwell, Dees and Bowman were
elected aldermen; and the five vacancies thus created (Mr Dees as charter
mayor caused no vacancy) were filled at a bye-election on 27 November
when the following were elected: J. Barr, J. Bragg, J. Huddleston, J. L.
Paitson and H. M. James. The full council numbered twenty-four, the
majority of whom had had local government experience as members of

Hugh Cecil, Fifth Earl of Lonsdale.

Coat of arms of the borough of Whitehaven.

Mace and mayor's chain.

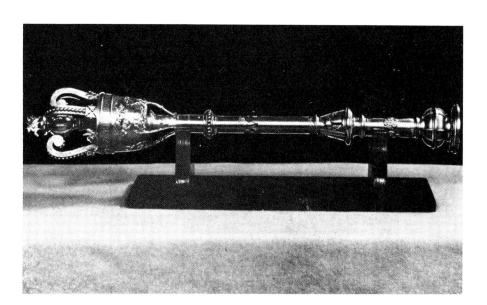

the late Trustee Board. The mayor of a municipal corporation is normally elected from among the aldermen or councillors, but it is not necessary that he should already be a member of the authority. At its first meeting the council decided unanimously to ask The Rt Hon Hugh Cecil, Fifth Earl of Lonsdale, to become the town's first elected mayor. His lordship was re-elected a second year and a two year term of office became the accepted pattern up to 1949 when the date for elections being altered from November to May, the opportunity was taken to dispense with re-election. There have been exceptions. Alderman J. R. Braithwaite continued in office for a third year in order to establish the Wellington Pit Disaster Fund and Alderman J. R. Musgrave held office twice, 1898-1900 and 1915-19. The town possesses a fine set of municipal insignia consisting of a mace, mayor's chain, mayoress's badge and fifteen badges for past mayors. The mace and mayor's chain were presented by the first mayor. The silver gilt mace is three feet long and bears the monogram and coronet of the Earl of Lonsdale. It is embossed with roses and adorned with the arms and mottoes of the borough and of the donor. The chain consists of eighteen shield links alternating with the letters composing the word WHITEHAVEN, twice repeated. The central link exhibits the arms and crest of the Earl of Lonsdale and from this depends a circular badge displaying the borough arms. Surrounding the badge are four small medallions with representations in enamel of local industries.

The mayoress's badge is an ornament of eighteen carat gold displaying the borough's coat of arms and adorned with precious stones. It was presented by Mr John Davis, then mayor in 1902, in honour of the coronation of King Edward VII.

The deputy mayor's badge was presented to the Town Council at a special meeting on Wednesday, 16 May 1956, by the Earl of Lonsdale. It is a pendant in heavy silver gilt and first quality enamel with a water-silk collarette.

The badges worn by ex-mayors on civic occasions were presented by Marchon Products Ltd in 1957. Each badge is of nine carat gold, chased and engraved. In the centre, the coat of arms of Whitehaven is engraved upon a quartic disc of convex section with matt surface; the disc is attached to the outer surround by eight strips, tapering towards the outer surround engraved with a herring-bone pattern. The outer surround is an almost square band of plain polished gold of concave section.

The coat of arms of the borough is that of the Lowther family differenced by a silver border. The six annulets or rings on the coat of arms came to the Lowthers through marriage with a member of the Veteriponte family and the six annulets are an heraldic pun on the contracted form of this name — Vipont. The borough motto, *Consilio absit discordia* —

'Let discord be absent from the Council', is sometimes forgotten when feelings run high, but on the whole business is transacted with a dignity that is conscious of two and a half centuries of tradition.

Mr William Watson has suggested that by 1894 party politics had died down and that the municipal contests were won largely by personal prestige, or lost by lack of it. This is not strictly accurate as the *Whitehaven News*, in reporting the election, carries a breakdown of their known political affiliations. Although Mr Thomas Batty, the miners' agent, was elected he was a Liberal in politics and not a Socialist. The first Socialist candidate was James Smallwood, a miner, who lost Newtown ward by forty-two votes. Mr James Burney, a postman, fought two unsuccessful elections before winning Newtown ward in 1903 and in 1904 Socialists contested all six wards and were successful only in Newtown ward where John Hanlon, the miners' agent, was elected. He served as a town councillor until 1918 with a short break between 1907 and 1908 and as a member of Cumberland County Council from 1910 until his death. He was also a member of the Whitehaven Board of Guardians and served on many other local committees. His death in 1918 at the early age of forty-six cut short a career that was full of promise.

Since the borough boundary was extended in 1894 there have been two further extensions. Under the first, in 1900, Lonsdale Place and the land in that vicinity was taken over from Moresby parish. Under the second, in 1934, the area of the borough was almost doubled by the inclusion of Hensingham, what remained of Preston Quarter, Sandwith and part of Moresby parish. As Newtown and Bransty wards had grown out of proportion to the other wards, an Order was obtained in 1937 to adjust the ward boundaries. The names Harbour Ward and Bransty Ward were retained but the other wards were renamed. The representatives of the former St Nicholas ward became the councillors for Harbour ward, St James representatives for Central, Trinity for Hensingham, Newtown for Kells, and the former Harbour ward councillors sat for the new Sandwith ward. At this time Councillor James Owen, a representative for Bransty, retired and his place was taken by Councillor F. A. Clayton who had sat as a representative for Harbour ward since 1934. The vacancy in Sandwith ward was filled by the unopposed election of Mr Joseph Blamire.

At this time there were two Labour aldermen, William Stephenson and Francis Harvey, and the election of Councillor Blamire had resulted in an equal distribution of council seats between Independents and Labour. Alderman F. Borland was due to demit office as mayor and to be succeeded by Councillor Walter Wear. Three aldermen were due for consideration for re-election: Aldermen Borland, Harvey and Stephenson. The Labour Party decided to make a bid for control of the Council. Councillor Wear was the next Labour councillor with a claim on an aldermanic seat. Unfortunately his elevation would have created a bye-election in a ward that Labour was not positive it could win. So Councillor Wear was asked to forego promotion and instead Mr John McAllister, who had been a councillor from 1921 to 1932, was elected in place of Alderman Borland.

By 1952 the building of the Mirehouse estate and the shift of population from slum property in the town centre had depleted Harbour and Central wards and unduly enlarged Hensingham so that in 1954 an Order was secured that united the two town wards under the name of Harbour ward and split Mirehouse off from Hensingham as a new ward. The Central ward councillors represented the new Harbour ward and the Harbour ward councillors sat for the new Mirehouse ward.

In 1967 a combination of Conservative and Ratepayers' Association representatives on the Council dismissed three Labour aldermen and broke the firm control of local affairs which the Labour Party had held for thirty years.

By 1970 the Labour Party had recovered most of its lost ground and, on the resignation of Alderman Alan Scriven, once more clinched its hold

Councillor John D. Davidson taking the oath of office as Mayor, before the Town Clerk, Mr W. H. J. Browne, May 1961.
Photograph courtesy of Mr Ivor Nicholas.

on the Council by repeating its 1934 manoeuvre. Mrs I. Cattenach was elected to the vacant seat.

The increase in the population of Hensingham ward due to the development of the Richmond and Fairfield housing estates and the diminution of the population of Harbour ward as a result of slum clearance caused the boundaries of these two wards to be redrawn in 1966 with a view to balancing the electorate in each ward.

The Town Council can honour those who have done distinguished service to the town or the country by electing them honorary freemen of the borough. It is an honour that is used sparingly. It was not until 19 March 1952 that the first presentations of the freedom of the borough were made to Alderman William Stephenson, J.P., C.C., and to Alderman Frank Harvey in recognition of their work on behalf of the community.

On 9 April 1953, the Rt Hon the Viscount Nuffield, G.B.E., O.B.E., F.R.S., F.R.C.S., and the Rt Hon the Lord Adams, O.B.E., J.P., M.A., C.A., became freemen of the borough. Lord Nuffield was so honoured because the Trust that he had established came to the assistance of the town at a very critical moment in its history, and Lord Adams because his drive and energy had resulted in the the development of new and existing industries in the district.

On 23 March 1961, the freedom of the borough was bestowed upon Mr Frank Schon and Mr Frederick Marzillier in recognition of the way in which the detergent industry they had established in Whitehaven had revitalised the community.

Another recipient of the honour was the Border Regiment which, on 24 May 1964, received the freedom of the borough and the right 'to march through the streets of the Borough on all ceremonial occasions with drums beating, bands playing, colours flying and bayonets fixed'. The title deed was presented by the Mayor (Councillor A. M. Garraway, J.P.) to Lt-Gen Sir Richard Anderson, K.C.B., C.B.E., D.S.O., Colonel of the King's Own Royal Border Regiment.

The note on the history of the regiment that was printed in the official programme is worth quoting: 'The Border Regiment can trace its history back to 1702 when the 34th Foot was raised. This Regiment, together with the 55th Foot which was raised in 1755, became respectively The

Cumberland Regiment and The Westmorland Regiment in 1782. In 1881 all Line Regiments were linked and given county titles. It was at this time the Cumberland and Westmorland Regiments were named respectively the 1st and 2nd Battalions The Border Regiment, the County Militia became the 3rd (Volunteer) Battalion and the 5th (Volunteer) Battalion was formed from the Cumberland Volunteers. Thus in 1881 we see the composition of The Border Regiment.

'The 5th Battalion The Border Regiment, in which so many West Cumbrians have served, has played a most distinguished and conspicuous part in the life of the Regiment. In 1899 the active service Companies of the Battalion reinforced the 1st Battalion in South Africa. In 1908 the word "Volunteer" was dropped from the titles of the 4th and 5th Battalions with the formation of the Territorial Force. The 5th Battalion T.F. was one of the first Territorial Battalions to land in France in 1914. The Battalion remained in France until the Armistice, when it then formed part of the Army of Occupation. The name of the Territorial Force was changed to Territorial Army in 1920.

'The 5th Battalion T.A. fought in France in May 1940 and was evacuated through Dunkirk. In 1941 the 5th Battalion The Border Regiment (T.A.) was converted to 110 Regiment R.A.C. In 1946, when the T.A. was re-formed, the 5th Battalion was remustered as a Heavy Anti-Aircraft Regiment R.A. This Regiment was disbanded in 1950. This resulted in the 4th Battalion being the only T.A. Battalion of the Regiment. However, the recruiting area of the 4th Battalion was enlarged to cover West Cumberland. This gave West Cumbrians, like their forefathers, the opportunity of service with the Regiment. At the present time the 4th Battalion has Companies based on Whitehaven, Workington and Cockermouth, the remainder of the Battalion being drawn from Carlisle and Kendal. In 1947 the Infantry of the line was re-organised with only one Regular and T.A. Battalion to each Regiment. Each Regiment was placed in a group. The Border Regiment became part of the group known as the Lancastrian Brigade.

'In October 1959, the 1st Battalion The Border Regiment was amalgamated with another Regiment in The Lancastrian Brigade, The 1st Battalion The King's Own Royal Regiment (Lancaster). This amalgamation formed The King's Own Royal Border Regiment of which The Border Regiment (T.A.) is part.'

Between 1970 and 1975, the Territorial Army went through a number of reorganisations. In 1975 the 4th (Volunteer) Battalion The King's Own Royal Border Regiment was formed, taking the place of the 4th Territorial Battalion The Border Regiment and the Territorial Battalion of The King's Own. The Drill Hall at Whitehaven was closed in 1970 and has since been demolished, the only Drill Hall in West Cumbria is now at Workington.

The Border Regiment has been awarded ten V.Cs. and The King's Own ten. Pte Abraham Acton, of Whitehaven, was one of The Border Regiment V.Cs. He won his V.C., together with Pte James Smith, of Workington, when serving with the 2nd Battalion, The Border Regiment, in France in 1914. The citation for the two V.Cs. of Acton and Smith read as follows: 'For conspicuous bravery on 21 December 1914, at Rouges Bancs in voluntarily going from their trench and rescuing a wounded man who had been lying exposed against the enemy's trench for seventy-five hours, to bring into cover another wounded man. They were under fire for sixty minutes whilst conveying wounded men to safety'. Pte Acton was mortally wounded in action on the 16 May 1915.

Since 1894 when the Borough of Whitehaven received its Charter of Incorporation there have been five ceremonies of the bestowal of the Honorary Freedom of the Borough and Mr John Wade, O.B.E., J.P., is only the seventh person to receive this honour.

The Mayor, Councillor James L. Johnston, wrote on 8 November 1972: 'We are very conscious of the part Mr Wade has played during his years with the West Cumberland Farmers Limited in the rapid expansion

Portrait of Pte Abraham Acton, V.C., by J. D. Kenworthy.

Memorial to Pte Abraham Acton, V.C., in Crosthwaite Memorial School.

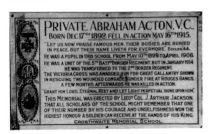

John Charles Wade, Esq., O.B.E., J.P.,
Lord Lieutenant of the County of
Cumberland, 8 November 1972.

The Presentation Scroll.

of this company. His zest and leadership whilst he acted first as secretary
and manager and then as managing director have been instrumental in
ensuring the prosperity of the company and such prosperity has also
reflected on the Borough indirectly.

    'In 1968 Mr Wade was appointed Her Majesty's Lieutenant for the
County of Cumberland (an office which he still holds) and Whitehaven
can be justly proud of the honour this has brought to the Borough. His
devotion to duty and his zeal for carrying out the many public functions
he is called upon to perform is a characteristic worthy of note. He has
also given his valuable time and the benefit of his years of experience to
many public bodies and local organisations without seeking any glory or
reward.'

    The passing of the Local Government Act, 1972, which came into
effect on 1 April 1974, saw the disappearance of Whitehaven as an
independent local government unit and its reappearance as six wards,
each with three councillors, in the new borough of Copeland which also
includes the former Ennerdale and Millom Rural Districts.

    The new Copeland Borough Council consists of 48 members. There
are no aldermen in the sense that local government has known that term

G. E. E. Lyon, last town clerk of Whitehaven.

for centuries; but the 1972 Act allows a local authority to recognise service to the community on the part of councillors who have retired from public office by their election as Honorary Aldermen. Copeland recognised the distinguished service given by four former Whitehaven aldermen, Joseph Blamire, William Edward Knipe, George Quinn McCartney and Henry McGill by electing them honorary aldermen. It also so honoured two former Ennerdale R.D.C. members, Councillors J. R. Gilbertson and C. Porter, and a former Millom R.D.C. Member, Councillor J. H. Knox.

A boundary review is under consideration which would divide Mirehouse and Hensingham wards and create eight wards with either two or three councillors as shown: Kells (2), Sandwith (2), Mirehouse, East (2), Mirehouse, West (2), Hensingham (3), Fairfield-Hillcrest (2), Bransty (3) and Harbour (3).

Chapter 14   Council achievement

Towns are living vital things that reflect the minds and ambitions, the spirit and aspirations of their inhabitants. Eighteenth century Whitehaven owed its growth to the plan set down by Sir John Lowther and the best of that development has been admired by discerning students of architecture. The Town and Harbour Trustees were concerned primarily with the harbour and the results of their deliberations down the years are obvious to all who look at the area enclosed by the 'lobster claws' that stretch out to the westward, a reminder of the days when graceful ships sailed to the West Indies and round the Horn to the Pacific.

Unfortunately, the hundreds of work people that flocked into the prosperous, growing town had to be housed, but the Trustees had no control over the building of the accommodation which they were to inhabit. Sir John's plan which by the mid-eighteenth century produced a gracious town with large houses and spacious gardens were unfortunately marred during the latter part of that century by the filling in of the gardens with rows of cottages that produced dark and ill-ventilated courts and closes. A lack of knowledge of sanitation, allied with a totally inadequate water supply, made these cottages the breeding ground of disease and infection and created a legacy of slums that became the major preoccupation of the Town Council during the twenieth century.

Two efforts were made to provide better working class accommodation. The first was by James Lowther, Earl of Lonsdale, who in 1788 planned to build 500 workmen's houses on the hillside between the Ginns and the town, but of these only some 250 were erected in three long rows that became known as the New Houses. The second was at Mount Pleasant where Mr James Hogarth had built a linen factory and houses for his workpeople. Lack of sewers and lack of water made them equally dangerous to health as houses in the town itself.

The Cupola, built by William Feryes, merchant, c. 1715. Purchased in 1850 by the Town and Harbour Trustees and rebuilt as the Town Hall.

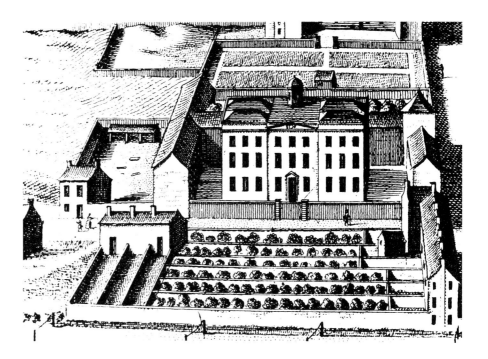

The *Cumberland Pacquet* for 11 July 1776 contains the news that: 'Small-pox appeared in Whitehaven last week and has since spread with most surprising rapidity'.

Diphtheria, typhus and other serious epidemics were common. In 1832 Whitehaven, along with other towns in England and Wales, suffered an outbreak of cholera and between 4 July and 30 September 1832 there were 273 deaths from this disease alone in the town.

Following the passing of the first Public Health Act in 1848 a local Board of Health was established and held its first meeting in the Savings Bank on 4 January 1848.

It was decided to divide the town into fourteen districts, with sub-committees appointed for each, to report on conditions under the following heads: (1) the lack of yards and conveniences for depositing ashes and nuisances; (2) the state of cleanliness in the houses; (3) density of population; (4) piggeries, stables and other nuisances in yards; (5) best sites for building public conveniences in the different districts; and, (6) to collect subscriptions for the expenses incurred.

The information was quickly collected and presented to the Town and Harbour Trustees on 26 January 1849. The investigation had been thorough and the situation revealed was appalling. The report says: 'In every district throughout the town it is the painful duty of your Committee to state that there is a very inadequate supply of water, and as this is so essential for the comfort, cleanliness and even health of the inhabitants, they cannot too strongly urge upon the Board that no effort be left untried to obtain such a supply, as may be adquate, to the fullest extent of its appreciation, to the wants of other people. In those districts in which this want has been alluded to in detail, we find that in Charles Street alone, which is part of No.2 District, there is a population of about 418 people without a single pump in the street. In No.6, the Strand Street District, for instance, there are no less than 216 families, comprising a population of about 700 people, without water on their premises and only two fountains at all conveniently situated for their supply which, it must be borne in mind, are also visited by an equally unprovided number of people in adjoining districts. In District No.8, comprising Albion Street, Swing Pumplane, etc, in which is contained 170 families, comprising a population of the poorer classes, amounting to upwards of 800 people, we found there are only fifteen pumps which belong to private individuals; consequently there is a very great want of water in this neighbourhood, sometimes felt to a serious extent by the numbers that may be seen waiting at the fountain near the Fish-market, at untimely hours, which fountain is the only one in the district.

'The Ginns District, No.12, comprising a population of 865 people or thereabouts, is equally unprovided with water, only four pumps were met with and these were private property. There is no fountain in the neighbourhood and the poor have a long way to fetch their water. In Mount Pleasant District, No.13, containing 108 houses with a population of upwards of 500 people, there are no pumps and the water has to be brought from a considerable distance, and at great inconvenience to the poor people, up a long range of steps from the fountain in Quay Street.

'In looking over the entire town, comprising a population, along with that part in Preston Quarter, of about 16,000 people, we find that there are only eleven public fountains; and, during the dry seasons, all classes of the inhabitants have frequently to remain waiting at them for a scanty supply of water to very untimely hours; indeed, in times of great scarcity, which do not infrequently occur, parties may be seen at the fountains waiting for their turn to obtain a supply all night long.'

This local demand for improved sanitary conditions was followed by an inquiry conducted in 1849 by Sir Robert Rawlinson, Superintending Inspector to the General Board of Health. Rawlinson's report is thorough, detailed and blunt. Mount Pleasant he describes as 'a congregation of most wretched dwellings, situated on the side of a hill, and they are principally approached by steps much worn, broken and in a ruinous

Title page of Rawlinson's 1849 Report.

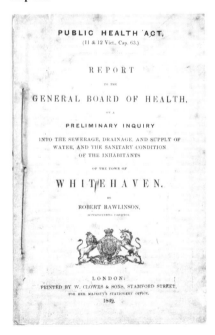

condition. Many of the tenements cannot be called rooms, they are so dreary, black and loathsome; some of them were formly used as nail-makers' shops and without any alterations or cleansing from that time ... There are about 1,825 inhabitants in Mount Pleasant without any form of privy accommodation or any regular supply of water. There are no public or private lamps throughout the year'.

Concerning New Houses, he writes: 'These cottages stand on the outskirts of the town, on sloping ground, and at an elevation considerably above the low part of the town; they were erected by a former Lord Lonsdale for the use of his miners and labourers. They are built on the side of a hill and form three rows or streets, the roofs being, in many instances, level with the roadway in front of the house behind, and the roofs of the highest run full against the hillside. There are no sewers or drains and consequently the roads and houses are damp. On the front row there are seventy-seven tenements and five ash-pits; on the middle row 111 tenements and nine ash-pits; on the back row seventy-eight tenements and seven ash-pits; total number of houses 266; total number of ash-pits twenty-one. There is not a single privy belonging to the whole property. The ashes are taken away every week by the Earl of Lonsdale's carts for agricultural purposes. The water supply is very inadequate. It is not uncommon to see twenty women waiting at the stand pipe for water. In the summer months this frequently fails and the inhabitants are then obliged to fetch their water for domestic use more than a mile; or they resort to any nearer place if it can be obtained, even when of inferior quality. Many of the tenants on the front row complain of the ash-pits belonging to the middle row as, these being on a level with the roof of their houses behind, the refuse sinks down into their back kitchens and causes a very bad smell through the whole house; the wind also blows the dust and dirt about. Pig-sties and stagnant water in contact with the houses are common. These houses are very seldom clear of fever.'

Rawlinson acknowledges that the fault does not always lie with the tenant: 'Amidst these scenes of utter destitution, misery and extreme degradation in Whitehaven there are, however, instances of a desire for cleanliness, even in some of the worst places; and it is most painful to contemplate the hopeless position of such persons, who are generally English and have known better times and happier days, confined to narrow courts or crowded rooms and surrounded with dirt and neglect, striving to keep their own particular place clean and neat.'

In the past various water schemes had been suggested, discussed and forgotten. The Act of 1761 had empowered the Trustees to take water from the springs in Stanley Wood. Two years later it was suggested that an estimate be obtained for bringing water from the Wood in wooden pipes of five-inch bore (but no action seems to have been taken on the matter).

The discussions on public health in the late 1840s made the Town and Harbour Trustees realise that something definite would have to be done and in February 1848 Mr Thomas Hawksley, Civil Engineer, of London, was engaged to draw up a scheme for a water supply. Acting on the advice of Mr Hawksley the Trustees obtained power under the Whitehaven Water Works Act, 1849, to take a supply of water not exceeding 1,000,000 gallons per day from the River Ehen at Bankhouse, a point one and a half miles below where it leaves Ennerdale Lake. The engineer's estimate for carrying out the work exclusive of Parliamentary and other expenses was £15,825. The work was completed in 1852.

Later Acts allowed for improvements to the service, but it was the Whitehaven Corporation Waterworks Order, 1947, which provided for the complete overhaul of the system. The estimated cost of the original scheme begun in 1949 was £321,000 but it was extended to cope with industrial developments in the Sandwith area of the borough and the final cost was about £603,000 towards which the Ministry of Health contributed £300,000.

The Order enabled the Corporation to abstract up to 98,000,000 gallons in any week, but in addition 4,000,000 gallons of compensation water per day had to be discharged. Thus some 14,000,000 gallons a day was available for supply purposes. A scheme is now in hand for the abstraction of the authorised quantity. Of this quantity 1,125,000 gallons a day was reserved for the Ennerdale Rural District.

The consulting engineers for the scheme were Messrs Rofe and Rafferty of London. In any consideration of the water supply at Whitehaven, a special tribute is due to Mr Arthur Wilson, M.I.Mun.E., A.R.I.B.A., who was appointed borough surveyor in 1925 and retired in 1957. In addition to the Ennerdale scheme he was associated with most of the development which has taken place in Whitehaven since the end of World War I — the town's extensive housing schemes, the Ginns-Kells Road, Kells Infants' School and the rebuilding of the public baths. He initiated the town's direct labour building department which has built a large proportion of the houses owned by the Corporation.

When the scheme was officially opened by the Minister of Housing and Local Government, the Rt Hon Harold MacMillan, M.P., tribute was paid to the work done by past chairmen and vice-chairmen of the Water Committee, Councillors H. S. Taylor, J. R. Kerr and J. W. Dick, and to Councillor F. Baxter who was chairman of the Committee from 1950 until 1 October 1961 when the assets and powers of the Whitehaven Corporation and the Ennerdale and Millom Rural Districts as water authorities passed to the South Cumberland Water Board.

The Board consisted of four representatives from the Whitehaven Borough Council, four from the Ennerdale Rural District Council, two from the Millom Rural District Council and one from the Cumberland County Council, eleven in all. There was a similar number of deputy members. The Board was the water authority until 1974 when its powers passed to the North West Water Authority under the 1973 Water Act.

In his report in 1849 Sir Robert Rawlinson had pointed out that a sewage disposal scheme was as vital as the water scheme which the Trustees had in mind: 'A full and copious water supply is necessary, but to produce that benefit intended there must also be as perfect a system of underground sewers and drains. The two systems cannot be divided but to the deterioration of both'. Although his report was adopted and copies of it published, no action was taken about the sewage scheme. Epidemics continued and a serious outbreak of enteric fever in 1862 in which there were 1,000 cases and nearly fifty deaths resulted in a petition to the Trustees in August 1963 requesting the adoption of the Local Government Acts, 1858 and 1861.

As a result of the petition a Local Government Board inspector held an enquiry into the existing sanitary conditions and upheld Rawlinson's recommendations. In January 1864 Mr Thomas Hawksley, who had designed the town's water scheme, was invited to design the sewage scheme. The work was carried out by Messrs Newell and Docuros whose tender amounted to £21,741. The effective disposal of town refuse is another factor in public health. At first the onus of keeping the town clean was placed on the inhabitants but in 1743 a scavenger was appointed with well defined duties. In 1848 the cleansing staff consisted of a surveyor of roads and streets, four scavengers and four horses and carts, and two night soil carts belonging to the Trustees and one belonging to a private individual. For a long time rubbish was taken out to sea in hoppers and dumped, but this practice was interrupted for a period between 1918 and 1925 when it was deposited on the north shore. Since 1946 Overend Quarry has been used as a rubbish tip.

In 1968 the cleansing department consisted of a force of thirty-seven men under a foreman who was responsible to the borough surveyor. They had a fleet of specially constructed vehicles which replaced the horses and carts of a bygone era.

The Act of 1761 allowed the Trustees to erect a number of glass lamps even if it meant removing sign-posts in streets and lanes. In March 1763 consideration was given to asking for tenders but it was not until 1780 that a tender was accepted for lighting the streets. By 1794 there were 300 oil lamps in the town, and oil lamps continued in use for a period of fifty years. In April 1830 the Trustees accepted the offer of a newly formed Whitehaven Gas Light Co Ltd to light the Town and Harbour for one year for £367 4s 7d. As Rawlinson notes: 'The best streets and harbour are tolerably well lighted, but the back streets, courts and confined yards are indifferently lighted. This is much to be regretted as light is needed more in these places than in other parts of the town'. In 1852 a rival company, the Whitehaven Gas Light Consumers Co, was formed and as the gas works were at opposite ends of the town, it was arranged by the Trustees that to prevent overlapping, each company should share the street lighting between them. Public lighting by gas ceased in 1893. The question of introducing electricity into the town was first discussed in 1883 but it was not until 1891 that the Trustees obtained their Electric Lighting Order and became one of the pioneers of the electricity supply industry.

In July 1892, a committee was appointed to consider a report by Dr John Hopkinson, F.R.S., on a suggested electricity supply system. This was adopted in October and application made to borrow the money needed to implement the scheme.

The first loan was for £14,000 and others for £7,000 and £5,000 followed. A generating plant was installed in the sewerage engine house on the West Strand and mains laid to most parts of the town. On 1 September 1893, 450 incandescent street lamps introduced the new lighting system to the town; and by the end of 1894 the number of private customers totalled eighty-one.

As with other pioneer undertakings there were snags and misadventures. Some of these were due to the small size of the cables, so that in 1898 these were relaid and the voltage increased from 110 to 210. Additional plant was installed and more mains laid so that as the new century came in the service improved and the demand increased.

In 1931 an Extension Order was obtained for the supply of electricity to Hensingham. The electricity generated locally was direct current. In September 1933 the outer areas of the town were changed over to alternating current at 230 volts taken from the Central Electricity Board, the first step in the abandonment of direct current in favour of power from the national grid. The change-over was finally effected in 1962.

The first office of the Electrical Engineer was located in a room in the Customs House; as business increased it was moved to Lowther Street. In turn, these premises became inadequate and in 1937 two shops, numbers 18 and 19 Lowther Street, were acquired by the Corporation, demolished and rebuilt as showrooms, offices and workshops. These were formally opened on 25 Febraury 1939 and by 1948 the number of consumers had increased to over 7,000.

Catalogue of the Curiosities at the Museum at Bishop's Court.

Old Library book label.

Initially the scheme had been run at a loss but by the time of World War I equilibrium was reached and after the War it showed a considerable profit that went to the relief of the rates. This advantageous condition continued until after the end of World War II when steps were taken to nationalise all electricity undertakings and on 1 April 1948, local owner-ship ceased and the entire undertaking passed into the hands of the British Electricity Authority.

The Town Council has not confined its activities to health and housing. As early as 1814 baths were erected on the Strand by the Town and Harbour Trustees where hot and cold fresh and salt-water baths could be obtained. The earl of Lonsdale, in 1858, erected in Newtown, baths and wash-houses for the benefit of his work-people. In 1883-84 the Public Baths Co Ltd erected premises on Duke Street to a design by Mr T. L. Banks at a cost of £5,665. These were taken over by the Town at the beginning of the present century and altered in 1937 at a cost of £11,600, part of this expenditure being met by a grant of £5,000 from the Special Areas Commissioner. Over the years much has been done to encourage the art of swimming.

The Whitehaven Museum came into existence in 1922 as a result of the demise of the Whitehaven Scientific Association, a body established on 19 November 1867 as the Whitehaven Natural History Society. It first met in a room in Queen Street, but on 10 November 1874, moved into the Old Assembly Rooms in Howgill Street which it had purchased. Here it flourished and had a very active life until the turn of the century, but it was dealt a heavy blow by the 1914-18 War from which it never recovered. In 1921 its premises in Howgill Street were handed over to the Whitehaven Town Council. The materials in the Society's museum were transferred to the former Whitehaven Subscription Library which was another war victim. The Subscription Library had been founded in 1797 and originally occupied a room in Duke Street. In 1808 the Earl of Lonsdale built the library on the corner of Lowther Street and Catherine Street. It ceased to function as a library in 1921 when the property was purchased by the Town Council and converted into a Museum. In 1957 the building was closed because of dry rot in the floor and the exhibits were stored in the Public Library. The building was demolished in 1961.

In 1974 Copeland Borough Council decided to convert the former Whitehaven Market Hall into a Museum, Art Gallery and Tourist Infor-mation Centre, the upper floor being developed as a local history museum.

The original market hall had been opened on 1 January 1819. The plans for it had been drawn up by Sir Robert Smirke. It was replaced by the present structure, designed by Mr T. L. Banks and opened 2 June 1881.

Other museums had existed in the town in earlier times. The White-haven Mechanics' Institute was founded in 1825. It was discontinued after a few years but reformed in 1844 when it met in some rooms in Duke Street. Here in 1847 it is reported to have had a 'small museum, consisting of some curious fossils, with various coins, relics, etc'.

There was also a museum at No.27 King Street (Mr George Bell's grocer shop, now Boot's chemist shop) 'tolerably well supplied with geological specimens and other curiosities'.

Locally, the public library service has its roots in the Mechanics' Institute movement. After an uncertain start the Institute bought 139 Queen Street and developed it as meeting rooms and library. By 1887 it was in financial difficulties and asked the Town and Harbour Trustees to take over its property. This was done after the adoption of the Public Libraries Acts in that year and the premises were opened as a public library on 15 May 1888. The book stock was 4,078 volumes and Mr John Simpson was appointed as librarian. He held that post until his death in 1933. The Library moved into a new building on Catherine Street that was opened on 5 November 1906. Mr Andrew Carnegie donated £5,000 towards the cost of the building.

Mr Daniel Hay was appointed as Mr Simpson's successor and remained as borough librarian until 1974 when the service was taken over by the Cumbria County Council as part of the changes brought about by the Local Government Act, 1972. During his absence, 1941-46, Miss G. A. Hanlon was acting librarian.

In January 1933, a small collection of books was loaned to the old Kells Miners' Welfare. That building was burned down in February 1938. The larger building that replaced it in 1940 contained provision for a library and a service was maintained there until October 1963 when the Welfare ceased to be used. Temporary accommodation was found in the Kells Infants' School until a new branch library, costing £3,500, was built. It was officially opened by the Mayor (Councillor Wm Fell) who had already opened a similar building at Richmond Hill Road, Hensingham on 18 October 1965.

A branch library service was initiated on Mirehouse in September 1953 when a room in the Valley Junior School was used. In 1961, a converted bugalow was made available and served until a purpose built branch was opened on 19 June 1972.

The central library was converted to open access in 1934, had a large stockroom added in 1963 and had a major extension built over the former museum site. This cost over £60,000 and was officially opened by the Mayor (Councillor Mrs F. M. Reed) on 29 January 1970.

At the time of the handover to the County Council the Library had a stock of some 90,000 books.

When Whitehaven Castle was purchased in 1926 for alteration into Whitehaven Hospital, the adjacent 13 acres of park was leased by the Corporation as a public park. The Parks' Superintendent in charge of it is also responsible for numerous flower beds in other parts of the town which has done a great deal to improve its attractiveness. In 1974, and again in 1976 and 1977, Whitehaven won the Regional Final of the Britain in Bloom contest.

The most difficult problem confronting the Whitehaven Borough Council was that of decaying and slum property. The rapid expansion of Whitehaven in the second half of the eighteenth century had led to the building of cottages on the gardens of large houses and the creation of dark and dingy courts. There were two efforts to build workmen's cottages outside the township boundary — the three terraces known as New Houses, built about 1788 and numbering some 250 houses, and the hundred cottages on Mount Pleasant, overlooking the harbour, built by James Hogarth about the same date. As the water supply was totally inadequate and refuse clearing fairly rudimentary, sanitation became a problem.

The outbreak of enteric fever in 1862 resulting in nearly fifty deaths had brought a Privy Council Office inspector into the town. His report was blunt and damning and underlined what Rawlinson had pointed out earlier: 'I have no hesitation in asserting that there is no English town with which I am acquainted where the sanitary circumstances (with one or two exceptions) of the inhabitants, and especially of the poor, are in a more disgraceful and degrading condition. The houses of the labouring population (more particularly in the central parts of the town) are crowded together in a way which is scarcely conceivable; the houses themselves are for the most part dirty, dilapidated and imperfectly (if at all) ventilated; they are overcrowded and the cellars are habitually let out as tenements; houses, courts and even streets are without any privy accommodation and where privies are provided they are of the most objectionable kind and generally most objectionable as regards their situation; drainage scarcely exists.'

Between 1862 and 1901 when another outbreak of fever brought another government inspector, much had been done to improve the sanitary condition of the town, and about another 500 houses had been built at Kells, Prospect, Bransty, Sunnyhill, Solway View, Corkickle and Hensingham Road. However, these provided no solution to the slums and it became obvious that a major operation would be required.

Title page of the 1863 report printed by William Smith at the Herald Office, Whitehaven.

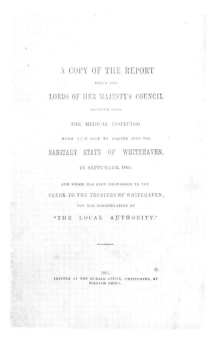

A COPY OF THE REPORT

WHICH THE

LORDS OF HER MAJESTY'S COUNCIL

RECEIVED FROM

THE MEDICAL INSPECTOR

WHOM THEY SENT TO INQUIRE INTO THE

SANITARY STATE OF WHITEHAVEN,

IN SEPTEMBER, 1863;

AND WHICH HAS BEEN FORWARDED TO THE

CLERK TO THE TRUSTEES OF WHITEHAVEN,

FOR THE CONSIDERATION OF

"THE LOCAL AUTHORITY."

1863.
PRINTED AT THE HERALD OFFICE, WHITEHAVEN, BY
WILLIAM SMITH.

In April 1910, the Town Council set up a Housing Committee to see what could be done about the provision of better working-class houses. There was a divergence of opinion about the most suitable site, the alternatives being Bransty, Thwaites Pit and Coach Road. In 1913 it was finally agreed to build eighty houses on Coach Road, but the 1914-18 War intervened before anything could be done.

In the post-1918 period fresh ideas were brought to bear on the housing problem and in 1919 the Town Council began a series of housing schemes which completely changed the town. By 1921 sixty houses had been built at Coach Road with an additional two steel houses in 1925. Sites on Arrowthwaite, Ennerdale Terrace, Basket Road, Woodhouse, Greenbank, Bransty and Hensingham were utilised. By 1941 the Council had erected a total of 1,902 houses. Even this effort was not sufficient to cope with the urgent need for houses and, in 1945, under a scheme initiated by Sir Patrick Abercrombie, an entirely new neighbourhood area, popularly referred to as the Valley Scheme, was proposed by the Council. Building under this scheme was commenced at Corkickle where 260 houses were completed by 1947. The greater part of the scheme lay to the south, at Mirehouse, and here a start was made in 1948. The first 250 houses were ready in 1950, 126 more in 1951 and a further 770 by March 1954. A further 600 were completed by 1956.

In addition to the main Valley Scheme, 126 traditional type houses and 102 prefabs were built at Hensingham between 1946 and 1949 while fifty-one prefabs were built at Woodhouse.

The capital cost of the 3,585 houses built by the Council up to March 1954 was over £4,000,000 and placed Whitehaven well to the fore among the non-county boroughs in the North-West. Over the period 1894-1955 the rateable value of the town had increased from £71,798 to £139,394. At 1 April 1974 it had increased to £2,350,598 due to property revaluations in 1955, 1962 and 1973. By 1967 the Town Council had built its 5,000th house (144 Ullswater Avenue, Richmond) which was officially opened by the Rt Hon Anthony Greenwood, M.P., Minister of Housing and Local Government, on 28 July.

By 31 March 1974, when the Whitehaven Borough Council ceased to function, it had built a grand total of 5,303 houses and twenty-one shops. These were distributed as follows:

Pre-1945:

Coach Road	60 houses
Steel Houses	2 houses
Bransty	392 houses
Arrowthwaite	268 houses
Monkwray	54 houses
Prospect	82 houses
Woodhouse	628 houses
Greenbank	236 houses
Hensingham	202 houses
	1,924 houses

Post-1945:

Hensingham	156 houses
Hensingham and Woodhouse	103 houses
Corkickle	260 houses
Mirehouse	1,791 houses
Homewood and A.P. Bungalows	210 houses
Arrowthwaite D.P. Bungalows	2 houses
Richmond	507 houses
George Street	192 houses
Woodhouse Redevelopment	62 houses
Woodhouse D.P. Bungalows	2 houses
Monkwray A.P. Bungalows	21 houses
George Street — Flats	12 houses

Red Lonning — Houses/Bungalows	72 houses
Duke Street — Maisonettes	4 houses
Bransty A.P. Bungalows	10 houses
Monkwray/Old Arrowthwaite D.P. Bungalows	6 houses
Supported Independency Unit, Mirehouse — Flats	27 houses
Duke Street/Scotch Street	42 houses

	3,379 houses

Pre-1945	1,924 houses
Post-1945	3,379 houses

Total	5,303 houses

Although between 1922 and 1954, when the borough celebrated its Diamond Jubilee, 5,521 persons had been rehoused and 1,600 sub-standard houses closed, there were still some 600 sub-standard houses to be dealt with, most of them in the town centre which the Council had resolved to re-develop. In 1963 a Town Centre Re-development Committee under the chairmanship of Councillor F. Baxter gave consideration to a Central Area Advisory Plan prepared by Mr J. N. Bentham, M.I.Mun.E., the Borough Surveyor and Engineer. This led to a more detailed report, published in January 1965, by Samuel Properties Ltd, for Central Area Re-development.

By this time ideas were changing. Feelings were hardening against the wholesale demolition and rebuilding of town centres and in 1971 yet a third report, *Whitehaven, a new structure for a restoration town*, prepared by Napper Errington Collerton Barnett, architects and planning consultants, Newcastle upon Tyne, was discussed by the Council and accepted as the basis for town centre re-development.

After a pilot study based on conservative work carried out on four properties the first major piece of town centre restoration was carried out over the period April 1972 to September 1973 on seventeen properties on the Church Street-George Street area. On 11 May 1973, the Rt Hon Geoffrey Rippon, Q.C., M.P., Minister of State for the Environment, visited the town and saw what had been achieved. The work was completed at a cost of £180,000, and in Architectural Heritage Year, 1975, the project was given an award by the Civic Trust.

The policy of the revitalisation of town centre property was continued with conservation work on 36-40 Roper Street which was completed in 1974.

Copeland Borough Council accepted the restoration plan for Whitehaven town centre and have carried out the revitalisation of properties in Cross Street, Church Street, Scotch Street and George Street.

In addition to housing consideration has been given to general improvement of the environment. The greater part of the land to the south of the harbour had been occupied by Wellington Pit which had ceased operating in 1933. This was reclaimed by the Town Council and the South Beach Recreation Area was officially opened by the Rt Hon Peter Walker, M.P., Secretary of State for the Environment, on 28 July 1972.

The opportunity was taken at the same time to tidy up the remains of the nearby Duke Pit.

The cost of the reclamation scheme was £107,000.

A thorny problem confronting the Council in the 1950s and 1960s was the provision of a Civic Hall in which concerts and other functions could be held. An architectural competition was held, the top award going to Messrs Pratt and Gray, of London. Government restrictions on

H.M. Queen Elizabeth II signs the
distinguished visitors' book at
Civic Hall, Whitehaven, watched by
the Mayor (Councillor
G. Q. McCartney, J.P.) and Town
Clerk (W. H. J. Browne). Photo by
courtesy of *Lancashire Evening Post*.

H.R.H. the Duchess of Kent being
greeted by the Mayor (Councillor
Mrs F. M. Reed) and the Mayoress
(Mrs. R. Reed) just prior to the
official opening of the Whitehaven
Civic Hall, 3 October 1969. The Lord
Lieutenant (J. C. Wade, Esq., O.B.E.,
J.P.) and the Town Clerk (W. H. J.
Browne) on extreme left and right.
Photo by courtesy of *Barrow News
and Mail*.

building prevented the immediate implementation of the full scheme. The foundation stone was laid on 1 May 1953 by Mr A. Wilson, the borough engineer and surveyor, and the first part, later known as the Dunboyne Hall, was opened on 16 May 1956 by the Mayor, Councillor G. Hanlon, J.P. On 17 October 1956, during the mayoralty of Councillor G. Q. McCartney, J.P., Her Majesty Queen Elizabeth II visited the borough and the hall was the venue for presentations. Her visit is commemorated by a plaque over the door. There was considerable discussion about the size of the main hall and in 1961 the original architects were released from their contract. Three years later Messrs Graham, Roy and Nicholson were appointed architects. The cost of their modified design was £256,570 and the new hall, named the Solway Hall, was officially opened by H.R.H. The Duchess of Kent on 3 October 1969.

The completion of the Civic Hall scheme owed a great deal to the unswerving determination of one man. Writing in the *Whitehaven News* just prior to the official opening the Mayor (Councillor Mrs F. M. Reed) commented: 'I feel I must single out one person who deserves special praise — Alderman William Pritchard — as chairman of the Building and Plans Committee during nearly all the time it has taken to complete the project, his enthusiasm, cheerfulness in spite of many difficulties and disappointments, have been instrumental in giving the town a hall which it can be justly proud. Never can I remember seeing him completely down-hearted and even the greatest setbacks never swayed him from his eventual goal'.

While work was proceeding on the South Beach Recreation Area thought was being given to sports facilities, and in November 1972, the Council was given permission to proceed with a new Sports Centre at a cost of £571,000. The Centre was opened on 27 January 1975 when the cost had reached £650,000, but a fire in an upper gallery on 5 February 1975 put it out of action for a period of more than six months. It was officially opened by Jos. Naylor, Esq., on 24 April 1976.

A multi-storey car park was built at Swingpump Lane at a cost of £670,000. The building was 'topped out' in March 1973. It has accommodation for 580 cars.

H.R.H. Princess Alexandra talking to Mr and Mrs John Gaskell at the official opening of the Royal British Legion John Gaskell Court flats at Sneckyeat Road, 18 May 1978. The flats cost £331,000 to build. Photograph by courtesy of Whitehaven News Ltd.

Chapter 15

The Churches of Whitehaven

The history of the Anglican Church in Whitehaven mirrors the physical growth of the town; the history of other denominations casts an interesting light on the impact of various outside forces.

Owing to the fact that Whitehaven is really a seventeenth century town none of the ecclesiastical buildings is older than the eighteenth century. The Friends' Meeting House (now occupied by the Brethren) was built in 1727 and St James' Church was built in 1753.

St Nicholas

Initially Whitehaven formed part of the parish of St Bees, but there is no reference in the Register of the Priory to a chapel at Whitehaven, although it mentions chapels at Rottington, Weddicar, Ennerdale, Loweswater and Drigg. On the other hand it is interesting to note that on 26 April 1359, Hugh Fleming and Christine, his wife, gave to Master John, rector of the Church of Lamplugh, and Master Richard, of Whitehaven, chaplain, the half-manor of Walton.

It is not specifically stated that Master Richard was chaplain at Whitehaven, but it is not stretching the evidence too far to suggest that he was resident there and conducted services in the neighbourhood of his residence. The first firm evidence we have of the existence of a chapel at Whitehaven occurs in the print of Whitehaven in 1642. This building which was demolished in March 1693, was dedicated to St Nicholas, the patron saint of those who made a living on the great deep, and William Jackson in his 'Papers and Pedigrees mainly relating to Cumberland and Westmorland' argues that the dedication is of considerable antiquity.

As it appears in the print it was a building of forty-five feet by fifteen, having five small windows on the north side, with a bell turret on the west and a cross on the east gable.

As the population of Whitehaven grew the little chapel became inadequate so that in 1687 a scheme was launched to build a new one. Work on it continued until November 1688, when for some reason it was halted. Mr Roger Strickland, the clerk of works, was buried at Whitehaven, 19 August 1690, and work was not resumed until 1691 when Mr Ebenezer Gale took over. It was completed in 1693 at a cost of £1,066 16s 2¼d, and consecrated by the Rt Rev. Nicholas Stratford, Bishop of Chester. It remained a chapelry of St Bees until 1835, when on 11 August the three parishes of St Nicholas, Holy Trinity and St James were carved out of the mother parish of St Bees. In 1745-6 it was enlarged by two wings — the south, used later as a choir vestry, the north as a baptistry. In 1756 an organ was installed which was in use until 1901 when it was replaced by a new instrument. The old Snetzler organ was sold, remodelled and installed at St Michael's, Lamplugh.

After nearly two centuries the fabric of the building had deteriorated and a new church was built of red sandstone from Beggarghyll Quarry, near Egremont. It was consecrated by the Rt Rev. Harvey Goodwin, Bishop of Carlisle, on 31 August 1883. The cost of the rebuilding was met by a gift from Miss Margaret Gibson, in memory of her parents, Robert and Elizabeth Gibson. A stone slab on the north side of the sanctuary commemorated her affection for them. The architect was Chancellor C. J. Ferguson, F.S.A.

St Nicholas Church.

The nave and sanctuary were entirely destroyed by fire on the afternoon of 31 August 1971. The high altar, a fine example of Italian renaissance carving brought from Venice and presented by the Rt Hon. G. A. F. Cavendish Bentinck, P.C., M.P., was lost in the fire as was the altar piece which had come from the earlier church, Matthias Read's 'The Last Supper'. Two other paintings by Read, of Moses and Aaron, survived the fire, have been cleaned and restored and now hang in the tower chapel. The stone doorway of the old church, dated 1693, has been preserved as the inner door of the tower.

Following the fire, consideration was given to rebuilding the nave, but in April 1973, the Diocesan Pastoral Committee decided against this and the congregation which had been worshipping along with Christ Church in the interim was united as the new parish of Christ Church St Nicholas in 1974. The St Nicholas tower was fitted out as an auxiliary tower chapel.

A further move towards the unification of the town centre parishes came when on 24 February 1977, the Rev. Alan J. Postlethwaite was installed as priest-in-charge of the parishes of Holy Trinity with Christ Church, St James and St Nicholas. He was officially inducted as the first vicar of Whitehaven on 30 June 1977.

Interior of St Nicholas Church before the fire of 31 August 1971.

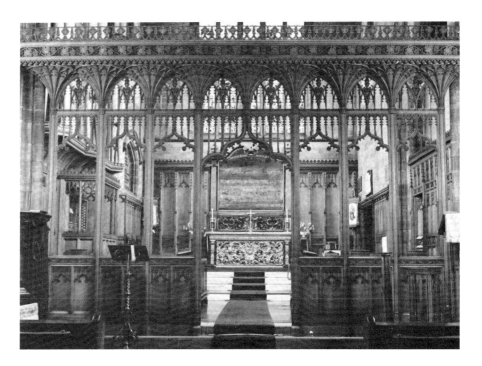

◁ The high altar devasted by the fire. Photo. Peter Hendren.

◁ The main body of the church — a charred shell littered with fallen roof timbers. Photo. Peter Hendren.

The clergy who have served at St Nicholas.are:

Frances Yates, 1693-1720	Charles B. S. Gillings, 1884-1912
Frances Yates, Jr, 1726-38	Frances Ed. Cole, 1913-25
Curwen Huddleston, 1738-69	Sidney G. O. Pugh, 1932-37
Wilfrid Huddleston, 1769-1802	Charles E. Nurse, 1937-48
Andrew Huddleston, 1802-45	Leslie J. Derrett, 1948-54
Frederick Wm. Wicks, 1845-76	William W. Greenwood, 1955-58
John McA. McMillan, 1876-80	T. B. R. Hodgson, 1959-65
Stuart Hall, 1880-83	J. Oliver Forshaw, 1966-76

Holy Trinity Church

Holy Trinity Church was erected by subscription in 1714-15 at a cost of £2,075 and consecrated by the Bishop of Chester on 2 October 1715. It was a plain stone building consisting of an apsidal chancel, nave, aisles and western tower with pinnacles, containing a clock and one bell. Sir James Lowther (1653-1755) contributed £100 towards the building fund and was buried in the church. A very beautiful hand-wrought iron screen, bearing the date 1755, protected his monument. When the building was demolished in 1949 the screen was removed and re-erected as the Duke Street entrance to the grounds of St Nicholas Church.

In the church there were tablets to the memory of five of the clergy who had served there: Rev. John Dalton (1674-1729), rector of Distington and first minister at Holy Trinity; Rev. Charles Cobbe Church (1742-1808), twenty-four years minister; Rev. Thomas Harrison (1782-1840), thirty-two years minister; Rev. Charles Douglas (1833-63), curate; Rev. Thomas Dalton (1805-89), honorary canon of Carlisle, fifty-seven years curate and vicar of the church and thirty-nine years rural dean.

The altar piece was a painting by Matthias Read, a local artist, who was buried in the churchyard. Externally plain, Holy Trinity was a very attractive church inside. In 1935 the parish was united with Christ Church and fourteen years later the building was demolished on the grounds that it was unsafe. Its registers cover the period 1715-1949.

The following were the incumbents:

1715	John Dalton	1840	Thomas Dalton
1729	William Brisco	1889	James Anderson
1745	Thomas Sewell	1902	Frederick Knowles Fell
1781	Charles Cobbe Church	1933-35	Vacant
1808	Thomas Harrison	1935	Became united benefice with Christ Church under G. W. Arnold

Holy Trinity Church, demolished 1949.

St James'

The foundation stone of St James' Church was laid in April 1752 and the church consecrated by the Bishop of Carlisle, acting for the Bishop of Chester, on 26 July 1753. It is a stone building consisting of chancel, nave, aisles and a tower, and a clock and one bell, the cost of erection of which was £3,354. The clock was the work of a local blacksmith. The large iron gates were presented by the Earl of Lonsdale in 1823. In 1865 the pulpit was removed from the centre to the north side of the church. Eight years later the chancel was restored by the Rt Hon. G. A. F. Cavendish Bentinck, P.C., M.P., and in 1886 the church was restored and reseated at a cost of £866.

The fine plaster work on the ceiling is the work of two Italians, Arture and Baggiotti. The decoration is enclosed by two circles. That on the east represents the Ascension and that on the west the Annunciation. The beautiful altar piece — a painting of the Transfiguration of Christ by Guilio Cesare Procaccini (1548-1626) — was formerly in the Escurial, Madrid. It found its way to France and after the Revolution was brought to England. It was presented to the church by William, Third Earl of Lonsdale.

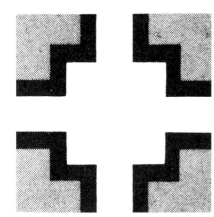

The new logo of the Parish of Whitehaven, designed in 1977.

A new organ was added in 1909 at a cost of £1,500. It was extensively overhauled in 1963 at a cost of £1,430. Structural alterations made in 1921 include a memorial chapel, sacristy, new baptistry and a vestry. There are 1,200 sittings. The registers date from 1753. A new parish hall was built in 1965 at a cost of £12,500.

The incumbents were:

1753	Thomas Spedding	1871	Joseph Bardgett Dalton
1783	John Waite	1878	D. F. J. Macleod
1790	Richard Armitstead	1881	Robert Duncan
1821	William Jackson	1906	John William Hartley
1833	John Jenkins	1931	Reginald Giles Malden
1852	John Robinson	1944	Cyril Godfrey Sheward
1855	Charles A. Perrin	1971	Joseph Hogarth
1867	T. R. Holme	1977	Alan J. Postlethwaite

As indicated above, on 30 June 1977, St James became the parish church for the new parish of Whitehaven.

Hensingham

The Rev. Caesar Caine points out that there are a number of sites in the old and extensive St Bees parish which bear the appellation 'Chapel', and the inference is that at these points there were small chapels where the clergy from the Mother Church of St Bees occasionally ministered. The name Chapel House would seem to indicate such a site. When this chapel fell into disuse is not known.

In 1791 Mr Anthony Benn and others subscribed towards the erection of a church. At first it was only a licensed place of worship, but after being purchased by the Earl of Lonsdale it was consecrated and endowed. Previous to the year 1811 there was no stated minister and no registers were kept. As first erected the church was a mere rectangular building, without chancel or side aisles. In 1843 side aisles were added and at a later date Mrs Bell of the Hollins erected a chancel.

In the old chapel there were seven stained glass windows to the memory of the following: the Rev. James Hare Wake, erected 1865; James Spedding, of Summergrove, died 1863; Mary Dykes Spedding, of Summergrove, died 1870; Thomas Stanley, died 1859; Isabella Millward, died 1874; Elizabeth Wake, died 1875; Mary Claudine Lumb, died 1865.

By 1898 the fabric of the chapel had deteriorated so much that a decision was made to build a new church, but it was not until 1913 that it was built on a site donated by the Earl of Lonsdale.

The new church is a very attractive building in the late Early English style. It has a tower containing a clock and a peal of eight bells, the gift of Mr J. R. Musgrave and his family. The parish hall was built in 1925, the vicarage in 1879-80. The present incumbent, the Rev. William Kelly, was inducted in 1967. His predecessors were:

1811	Charles Church	1910	Charles E. A. Blackburn
1817	George D. Whitehead	1918	E. Freeman
1832	Robert Whitehead	1945	F. M. A. Farrer
1851	John Mordaunt Lowther	1953	Philip Truswell
1865	William Henry Wilkinson	1960	J. Whittaker

Christ Church

From early medieval times to the incorporation of Whitehaven in 1894 the boundary of the township stopped short at Newtown and the area now known as Arrowthwaite, Kells, Woodhouse, Newhouses and Ginns lay outside. For ecclesiastical purposes they lay within the parish of St Bees, and in 1844, on the nomination of the Rev. R. P. Buddicom, the Rev. John Rimmer, M.D., was licensed nominally to the curacy of St Bees, actually as the vicar-designate of a new parish designed to serve the Ginns and Newhouses and the area round about. For a time Dr Rimmer held services in the Newtown Sunday School, but in March

1845, the Bishop of Chester licensed the Glasshouse School, Ginns, for divine service. On 5 August 1845, 'the District of Mount Pleasant' was constituted a separate ecclesiastical parish. A site on Preston Street was purchased for £300 and on 16 October 1845, the foundation stone of Christ Church was laid by Captain J. Robertson-Walker, R.N., of Gilgarran. The building was consecrated by the Rev. John Bird Sumner, Bishop of Chester, later Archbishop of Canterbury, on 29 September 1847.

Dr Rimmer was incumbent for forty years. He resigned in 1883 and was succeeded by the Rev. Stuart Hall who had been vicar of St Nicholas for the previous three years. During Mr Hall's incumbency several alterations were made to the interior of the church. The West gallery was removed, the church reseated, the quasi-chancel formed, the old altar replaced by a new oak one and the entrance removed to the west end. During the vicariate of his successor, the Rev. G. C. Calvert, the choir vestry was built and the old harmonium replaced by a modern organ.

The Town Council's policy with regard to slum clearance moved many of the congregation away from the church and although amalgamated with Holy Trinity parish, and later with St Nicholas, the diminution of numbers led to the closure of the church in 1977, the farewell services being held on 28 May 1977.

The registers of the church comprise only marriages and baptisms and date from 1847 and 1845 respectively, burials being registered at the Cemetery, Christ Church having no burial ground. Christ Church and Holy Trinity parishes were amalgamated in 1935 and the joint parish amalgamated with St Nicholas in 1974 as a preliminary to the creation of a new Parish of Whitehaven in 1977.

The incumbents of the parish have been:

1845	John Rimmer	1931	G. W. Arnold
1883	Stuart Hall	1937	R. Mayall
1888	G. C. Calvert	1941	Vacant
1892	T. S. Cunningham	1942	James Olive
1898	Henry T. Adam	1962	N. S. Dixon
1917	Reginald S. E. Oliver	1973	David Oliver Forshaw
1926	H. C. Joyce		

St Peter's

Throughout the 1920s corporation houses were being built on Arrowthwaite and in the following decade at Woodhouse and Greenbank. People were moved from the overcrowded town centre into these new houses. This caused a decrease in the population of Holy Trinity Parish and an undue increase in that of Christ Church so that in 1935 the parishes of Holy Trinity and Christ Church were amalgamated and a new parish established on Kells.

The preparation for this change had been going on since the time of the first World War. From that time onwards services and Sunday schools had been held in the Mid Street Rooms. In 1920 an old army hut had been acquired and erected on the site of the present vicarage. It was opened for worship on 20 October 1920 by the Bishop of Barrow-in-Furness. The Rev. James Watt was the curate of Christ Church with special responsibility for Kells. The Rev. H. G. Green was appointed curate of the District in 1934 and remained to be the first vicar. He left in 1943. The foundation stone of a more permanent building to replace the 'Tin' Church, as it was known colloquially, was laid in 1938 and the church itself dedicated on 6 September 1939 by the Bishop of Carlisle. It cost £10,000 to build. Present at the stone-laying ceremony in 1938 was Mr H. Leigh Groves of Windermere, who gave £1,000 towards the cost of a vicarage which was ready for occupation in 1940. In the mid-1940s cracks appeared in the walls of the church and in 1948 repairs were started which took fifteen months to complete at a cost of £2,023. The organ, a small manual Walker *Positif*, was dedicated on 16 April 1959.

In 1944 it was resolved to build a parish hall. The site was acquired in

1948 but it was not until 11 September 1965 that the hall was opened and dedicated. The present incumbent, the Rev. Michael R. Braithwaite, was inducted on 22 April 1977.

His predecessors were:

1935	H. H. Green	1951	C. A. W. R. Eckersley
1943	J. H. Vine Hall	1958	E. R. Chapman
		1967	S. Swidenbank

St Andrew's

The growth of the Valley Estate presented ecclesiastical problems and for a time it was supervised jointly by the vicars of Christ Church and Hensingham parishes. Early in 1954 Sunday school services were organised in the Valley schools and from July 1955 to May 1956, the school hall was used for church services.

A new church, dedicated to St Andrew, was consecrated by the Bishop of Carlisle on Saturday 19 May 1956. It was the sixth church or hall-church to be built in the diocese of Carlisle under the Bishop's Three Year Action Appeal for churches in the new housing areas. There have been three incumbents: R. G. Forward, until August 1966; J. A. Ledward, November 1966 until October 1971; and E. F. H. Grimshaw, from June 1972 to date.

Town Mission

The Town Mission on Rosemary Lane seems rather inappropriately named for a building in that area of the town, but its name serves to remind us that it was established in 1862 by a body founded some six years earlier which truly took the whole town as its evangelical objective. The Town Mission Association was inaugurated on 12 June 1856, in the house occupied by Mr John Hamilton in Duke Street. Its first field of activity was defined as being 'from the top of Queen Street, right hand side of Duke Street to the sea', but by 1860 Newtown, Ginns and Mount Pleasant were added to the area of mission work. In October 1862, a room was taken on Mount Pleasant until the Mission was built in the following year. In May 1892, an infant school was added to the premises, and in 1919 they were rebuilt and enlarged at a cost of £500.

On 24 September 1977, Mr Charles Nicholson was inducted as missioner.

Colliery Mission

The mission in the Ginns began with the use of a room in August 1865. When Monkwray School was built in 1876 the Mission moved into the old Glasshouse School building which became known as the Colliery Mission. It became important not only for its impact on the spiritual welfare of the workers and their families living in its immediate vicinity but in times of stress, such as during prolonged strikes, when it was used as a food centre.

A new Colliery Mission was built on a site early in 1960 at a cost of £6,500.

United Reformed Church

The earliest record that we have of Nonconformist preaching in Whitehaven occurs in 1653 when the Rev. Ezekiel Harsnett was sent by the Commonwealth Commissioners to take charge of the old chapel that preceded St Nicholas. He was ejected in 1662 in the purge that followed the Act of Uniformity, when his place was taken by the Rev. Philip Bennett. Where he went is not clear. Before this, however, the Rev. George Larkham, M.A., of Cockermouth, had visited Whitehaven. In his diary, under the date 19 May 1660, he writes: 'I went to Whitehaven to preach. I preached the next day, being the Lord's day, and was mercifully assisted from that text, John VI, 48' ('I am that bread of life'). Larkham was ejected from his church at Cockermouth in 1662 but remained in the area. He and his followers were harassed and persecuted, and he, himself, spent some time in prison for his views. In 1672 the pressure was relaxed a little and the house of Isabella Dixon was licensed as a Presbyterian Meeting House in Whitehaven. Over the next twenty years the number of Nonconformists in Whitehaven increased and we find by a deed dated 23 April 1695, that Elisha Gale, Henry Palmer, William Atkinson, William Feryes and John Shepherd had collected subscriptions and were empowered 'to build a house or chapel in a decent manner, with a handsome gate, etc.' and that it was to be used by Protestant Dissenters from the Church of England, whether Presbyterian or Congregational, according to their way or persuasion.

The baptisms at the chapel for the period 1696 to 1705 are to be found in the St Nicholas baptisms. From this record we see that there were 116 baptisms at the Meeting House, involving sixty-two families, indicating that the congregation was reasonably strong. The building was enlarged in 1749. During the ministry of the Rev. William Rose the membership was about 400, but after his death in 1818 differences of policy arose between the trustees and some of the congregation. The disagreement became so acute that a considerable number seceded, leaving a congregation that was Presbyterian in composition and outlook.

The Rev. Walter Fairlie established in 1822 on the West Strand a Sunday School for children of all denominations which in 1827 removed to Irish Street. In 1845 Mr Robert Barbour, of Manchester, purchased the schoolroom and gave it to the trustees. The church was renovated in 1856-57 at a cost of £800 when a new front in the Gothic style was built. It was again rebuilt in 1905. The ministers who have served the Market Place congregation are:

1688-1704	Roger Anderton	1844-66	Joseph Burns
1704-22	Thomas Dixon	1866-89	George Mackay
1722-25	Lemuel Latham	1890-1915	Matthew Young
1725-56	Ralph Astley	1915-24	John V. McNeill
1765-72	Radcliffe Schofield	1924-30	Arthur A. Smith
1773-1804	James Kirkpatrick	1931-41	E. Hugh Fraser
1812-18	William Rose	1941-48	C. M. Hilton Day
1819-37	Walter Fairlie	1948-55	Henry Osborne
1837-39	Alexander S. Patterson	1955-62	Howard Shapland
1839-41	William Wilson	1964-77	Henry W. J. Powell
1841-44	Matthew Graham	1977-	David H. Roberts

During the eighteenth century the James Street congregation would be best described as Independents — neither strongly Presbyterian nor Congregational, and with no affiliation to any other church or churches. So, in 1755 twenty-seven Scotsmen resident in Whitehaven applied for and obtained what is termed in the ecclesiastical language of the period north of Tweed 'Supply of sermon' from the General Associate Presbytery of Sanquhar. This group met in a store-room in Howgill Street until the church on High Street was built in 1760. This building has been known to generations of Whitehaven residents as 'The Kirk'. It was served by ministers of high intellectual attainments, notably the Rev. William Graham (1737-1801), the Rev. David Williamson (1787-1820) and the Rev. James Howie. In 1895 the two Presbyterian churches were united and the High Street building closed.

It re-opened in 1905 as a Methodist mission. In local Methodist circles it is notable for the number of persons attending it who became lay preachers or entered the ministry. Owing to slum clearance it lost its congregation and was closed on 31 December 1965. It is at present used as a furniture store.

Selina, Countess of Huntingdon (1707-91) was for a time a follower of John Wesley, but eventually broke with him and formed a separate denomination called the Countess of Huntingdon's Connexion. She founded a college for training ministers at Trevecca, and at the time of

WHITEHAVEN CONGREGATIONAL CHURCH
1874 — 1969

FINAL SERVICE
SUNDAY, 31st AUGUST, 1969, 10-45 a.m.

Whitehaven Congregational Church
order of final service, Sunday
31 August 1969.

her death there were sixty-four chapels in the Connexion which later became merged into the Congregational Union.

In 1780 Joseph Whitridge, of London, a member of a Bootle family, built and endowed a chapel in his native village for the Connexion and the movement reached Whitehaven in 1783. Within ten years it was strong enough to build its own home and on 15 December 1793, Providence Chapel, Duke Street, was opened with Mr Thomas Cook as pastor. In 1819 Mr Cook resigned and the property was procured for the use of those who had seceded from the James Street chapel. After undergoing considerable alteration and enlargement it was ready for occupation towards the end of that year and the Rev. Archibald Jack commenced his ministry. Those who broke away from the James Street congregation retained for a time the name by which those who shared their beliefs had been known for the past two centuries — Independents — and Providence Chapel became known as the Independent Chapel. The change of name to Congregationalists came with the move to the new church on Scotch Street in 1874.

The building was again enlarged in 1838, during the remarkable ministry of the Rev. Joseph Helliwell. In his diary under the date 1 August 1838, Helliwell writes: 'We had a meeting *this morning at 5 o'clock* for the purpose of returning thanks to Almighty God for the final liberation of the Slaves. The attendance was good — about 120 — and the meeting was a very joyful one'. Thirty years later the building was described as 'Dark, drafty, ill-ventilated, and unsightly', and on 9 October 1872, the foundation stone was laid of a new building in the Gothic style which was opened on 3 November 1874. It was built of concrete with a stone front, the lower portion of which was an arcade with granite columns. It had a square tower with a spire. The cost of erection was £10,500. The architect was Mr T. L. Banks, who also designed the Lowther Street Methodist Church.

Following World War II the congregation declined and on 1 May 1969, the decision was taken to merge with the Presbyterian Church as from 1 September 1969. The final service in the church was held on 31 August 1969. The re-union of the two congregations was marked by services on 7 September 1969, conducted by Prof. the Rev. John Marsh, C.B.E., M.A., Ph.D., D.D. At a national level discussions had been going on between the Congregationalists and the Presbyterians for a union of the two churches which came into effect in 1972, and on 11 October 1972, Dr Marsh conducted the Thanksgiving Service which marked the national union of the two churches and the formation of the United Reformed Church.

The church in Scotch Street was sold to the Whitehaven Corporation and the proceeds of the sale applied towards the building of a new church hall which was formally opened by Mr John H. Hocking on 23 June 1975.

The ministers who served at Duke Street were:

1819-34	Archibald Jack		Henry Sanders
1835-39	Joseph Helliwell	1859-65	William Place
	James McFarlane	1866-74	Alexander Galbraith

and at Scotch Street:

1874-76	Alexander Galbraith	1932-49	Clifford W. Hutchings
1877-96	Alexander Nairn	1950-53	William Kitching
1897-1911	A. O. Lochore	1953-57	Andrew F. Simpson
1912-26	Herbert Stowell	1957-64	Philip Doddridge
1927-32	John R. Palmer		Humphreys
		1965-68	Peter de St Paer

Society of Friends

Although George Fox, the founder of the Society of Friends, was frequently in Cumberland, there is no evidence that he visited Whitehaven, and it was not until 1716 that ground was acquired in Sandhills

Lane for the building of a meeting house, and not until 1727 that it was erected. The Friends continued to use it until 1931 when it was sold to the Brethren. At present the Friends use 41 Irish Street as a Meeting House.

The Brethren

The Brethren movement originated in Ireland in the early part of the nineteenth century and spread from there to the continent, the British dominions and the United States. Associations were formed in Dublin in 1828 and in Plymouth in 1830. From the latter arose the popular name *Plymouth Brethren*. In Whitehaven the Brethren movement began as a result of a meeting held in a room belonging to a Mr William Brown, of Bransty, on 5 February 1854, and meetings were held there for three years until the accommodation began to be too small. After that use was made of the Forester's Room in Fox Lane. A leading figure in the Brethren in Whitehaven in the third quarter of last century was George Wightman Brown (1814-71), father of Dame Edith Brown (1864-1956), founder of the Ludhiana Christian Medical College. The movement continued to grow gradually and at the beginning of the century use was made of the Friends Meeting House in Sandhills Lane which was purchased in 1931.

Methodist Church

The Methodist Society with its classes and leaders had come into existence in 1742, and its founder, the Rev. John Wesley, visited Whitehaven several times, but the work for Methodism had been begun by two Methodist preachers, Joseph Cownley and Christopher Hopper somewhere between 1747 and 1749. Cownley, who seems to have been most closely associated with the early beginnings of the work in Whitehaven, has been described by Wesley as 'one of the best preachers in England'. In 1751 Sir James Lowther gave the Society a plot of land in Michael Street for the erection of a chapel, but it was not for another ten years that it was built and opened. In 1763 Whitehaven was created a separate circuit. The building was damaged by subsidence in 1791 and use was made of Mr Hogarth's chapel on Mount Pleasant which continued as a Methodist chapel for some time after the Michael Street chapel was repaired and re-opened in 1795.

The first Sunday School in Whitehaven was opened in that year in connection with the Michael Street chapel, just fifteen years after Robert Raikes had started the Sunday School movement in Gloucester.

The chapel was entirely rebuilt on its original site in 1818 and continued in use until it was superseded in 1877 by the present building in Lowther Street, erected at a cost of about £10,000. A schoolroom built in 1882 cost another £2,000.

The introduction into English Methodism of open-air revival meetings caused a split and the formation in 1812 of a group known as Primitive Methodists. Locally the movement made itself felt by 1823. A meeting place was acquired in Fox Lane which remained in constant use until the new chapel was opened in Howgill Street in 1859. From 1828 until the 1850s use was also made of the Mount Pleasant chapel. A large schoolroom was built adjoining the Howgill Street chapel in 1878, and there were further extensions in 1903. The chapel was closed in 1940 on the amalgamation of the three sections of the Methodist church.

Open air services were held at Kells by members of the Primitive Methodists in the late summer of 1914 and in the following winter services were held in a cottage. A society of six members was formed, and for six years these cottage services continued. In 1920 an army hut was purchased, removed and re-erected; it was opened in April 1921 as a place of worship. Locally it was known as *Sandy's Mission*. It was replaced by a brick structure on 13 April 1921.

Several references have been made to the chapel built on Mount Pleasant by James Hogarth. It was to have been consecrated as an Anglican chapel by the Bishop of Chester on 14 August 1789, but although the bishop arrived in Whitehaven he was dissuaded from consecrating the building by the Earl of Lonsdale. It was used temporarily by the Methodists while the Michael Street Chapel was being repaired. Later it was taken over by the Primitive Methodists until their new chapel was built in Howgill Street. For a time it was used as a candle factory but it gradually fell into decay.

About 1885 Canon Dalton, of Holy Trinity Church, established the West Strand Mission which under his oversight was carried on vigorously. He employed a missionary to conduct and to visit the neighbourhood. After the Canon's death his successor carried it on for a time but was unable to continue for lack of funds. The Mission was taken over by the Wesleyan Methodists, but when the premises on the West Strand was acquired by the Town Council in order to extend the electricity works, a new home had to be sought and Mr L. Borrowdale and Mr J. Chisam bought the Hogarth Chapel. Owing to the delapidated condition into which it had fallen it required £1,000 spent upon it to make it serviceable. It was opened on 27 September 1899, with Mr G. E. Dutson as missioner.

James Hogarth's philosophy set out on a small, rare broadsheet dated 20 March 1788.

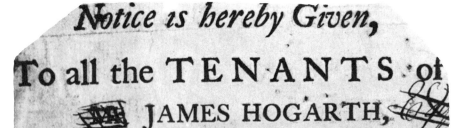

Notice is hereby Given,

To all the TENANTS of JAMES HOGARTH,

THAT he is fully determined no idle, disorderly Persons, who bring up their Children without SCHOOLING and WORK, shall dwell in his Premises.

Therefore all who are conscious that they merit that Character, (and are determined to continue in their present Habits of Life) would do well to provide themselves Houses elsewhere; for under him they must not remain.

But for the Encouragement of

The RELIGIOUS, INDUSTRIOUS, MODEST, and WELL-BEHAVED Poor of his Tenants,

HE will erect a CHARITY SCHOOL, and find their Children both EDUCATION and BOOKS, gratis; and, off School-Hours, find Employment both for them and their Mothers, at his Manufactory; and also a commodious and convenient CHURCH to accommodate them on the LORD'S DAY; which he will insist on all his Tenants frequenting, or otherwise they must depart from his Premises.

WHITEHAVEN, 20th March, 1788.

[J. WARE & SON, PRINTERS.]

Owing to slum clearance in the area it served, its congregation gradually fell away so that it was closed in 1954 and demolished to make way for a canteen for Crosthwaite School.

Hogarth ran a weaving factory on Mount Pleasant and built a large number of houses there to accommodate his work people. He established a charity school for their children and gave the house in Queen Street to the Whitehaven Dispensary that was occupied by that institution until it moved to Howgill Street. He died 13 March 1796 and was buried in a vault under the tower of the chapel.

Methodism in the time of John Wesley was a benevolent autocracy and when, after Wesley's death, Alexander Kilham demanded the complete democratisation of the church courts, he was expelled and in 1797 founded the Methodist New Connexion. When the Connexion first made an impact on Whitehaven is not clear, but it is evident from a circular issued at the time of the building of their chapel in Catherine Street in 1836 that prior to that date they had been meeting in a warehouse in Duke Street. In 1907 the united Methodist Free Churches and the Methodist New Connexion joined forces to become the United Methodist Church. The Catherine Street chapel was closed in June 1934 following the union of the three Wesleyan, Primitive and United Methodist Churches.

The first Wesleyan Methodist Chapel at Hensingham was built at West View in 1856. It had a seating capacity for 150 worshippers and was also used as the Sunday School. It is now a private house.

A new chapel with seating for 250 was opened on 17 March 1902. There is a Sunday School alongside with accommodation for 150 children. The building was designed by Mr Arthur Huddart and cost £1,852.

When Methodism first made its impact on the North of England its organisation was based upon Newcastle-upon-Tyne but it was not long before Cumberland and the Isle of Man were created a separate circuit. In 1778 these two areas were split and over the next century Carlisle, Workington, Cockermouth and Maryport became autonomous circuits. By the time that the Lowther Street church was built the pattern was set which continues to the present time. Circuit ministerial staff have varied between three and four with the Superintendent minister responsible for the oversight of the Lowther Street congregation.

The ministers at Lowther Street over the past century have been:

1873-74	Thomas Harding	1912-14	J. H. Cartwright
1874-77	Samuel Taylor	1914-15	E. Lightwood Smith
1877-78	Thomas Nicholson	1915-19	T. R. Pickering
1878-81	William Mearns	1919-23	J. Cannell Harrison
1881-84	Edward J. Smith	1923-28	S. Swithenbank
1884-87	Caleb Foster	1928-32	G. H. Bancroft Judge
1887-88	Richard Butterworth	1932-37	J. G. Penman
1888-90	John Priestley	1937-41	Frederick Taylor
1890-93	Richard Stevens	1941-47	J. Angell James
1893-96	William G. White	1947-53	William Teague
1896-1900	Charles Swannell	1953-61	William Winchurch
1900-01	Enoch Biscombe	1961-66	William A. Copley
1901-03	Fred Hilton	1966-70	William H. Topliss
1903-06	B. Charles Barker	1970-74	Arthur Candeland
1906-09	Edward Murphy	1974-78	Norman B. Fishburn
1909-12	Joseph Parson	1978-	Leslie D. Cox

Roman Catholic Church

The suppression of the monasteries by Henry VIII and the Reformation of the Church in England were followed in due course by Acts designed to root out the teaching of the Roman Catholic Church and to keep its adherents in subjection.

In the following two centuries Roman Catholic priests and laymen suffered martyrdom for their beliefs. Although the penal laws against

Nonconformists were suspended in 1671-72 Roman Catholics were not among those who could apply to have a building licensed as a place of worship. When Catholics met it was in secret. Mass and other ecclesiastical functions were celebrated in private houses with doors closed and sentinels posted. Means of support for priests were exiguous and precarious.

The Jacobite rebellions of 1715 and 1745 did not ease the situation, so that although Father Francis Rich came from St Gregory's, Douai, in 1706, to establish a mission in West Cumberland it is doubtful if the cause gathered any great strength until the latter half of the century. The only substantial Catholics in Whitehaven in 1723 were Samuel Bowman and his wife Eleanor. On 30 May 1761, Charles Conner bought a house in Duke Street which ran through to a narrow lane leading off Catherine Street. The back part of the house was turned into a chapel, the passage acquiring the name Chapel Lane. As the congregation grew more and more of the ground floor was taken over.

Father Gregory Holden enlarged the chapel in 1824. His work in settling a strike in 1831 and his heroic self-sacrificing labours among the poor during the dreadful cholera epidemic of 1832 made a great impression upon the town, and the Earl of Lonsdale made available a site on Coach Road for the first church there. This church, dedicated to St Gregory, was erected in 1834 and is now used as a school canteen.

Father Holden left Whitehaven in 1854 for Cleator where he had already founded a mission and died there in 1859. The Duke Street

Funeral Card — Fr Holden.

PRAY FOR THE SOUL OF FATHER HOLDEN.

Sacred to the Memory of the

REV. WM. GREGORY HOLDEN,

(Late Pastor of Saint Bega's Catholic Church, Cleator.)

Who Departed this Life on Saturday the 8th of January, 1859;

AGED 70 YEARS.

Protestants admired him as well as Catholics, for his philantrophic spirit, his amiable disposition, and his readiness at all times to do all in his power to console the afflicted. About the year 1838, he caused the chapel at Coach Road, Saint Gregory's, to be erected; while it was in course of erection his exertions were very great. He likewise built Saint Bega's chapel. This neat edifice, situated at Cleator, was commenced about 1849, and completed about 1852. To the poor he was always a friend. He gave to every one who asked him for assistance. Not only to the poor of his own congregation did he extend his charity, but also to the needy of other religious persuasions.

property continued to be used as a school until St Begh's was built, when the school was moved into St Gregory's.

Father Holden was followed by Father Maurus Shepherd and in 1860 by Father E. G. Lynass. During the incumbency of the latter, the foundation stone of a new church was laid by Bishop Dorian in 1865 and the church was opened for worship on 29 October 1868. Dedicated to St Bega, it is built of stone in the Decorated English style, consisting of an apsidal chancel, clerestoried nave, lateral chapels and sacristy. The sanctuary and the two side chapels are separated by carved screens. The roofs of the nave and aisles are of open timber work and those of the chancel and side chapels are divided by timber ribs into panels. It was designed by Mr Edward Welby Pugin and originally had a belfry surmounted by an ornamental metal cross. Unfortunately this had to be removed in 1931. The exterior is built of white stone walling with red stone dressing. The west door entrance is lined with alabaster. The chief benefactors were the Earl of Lonsdale, the Bishop of the diocese, Mr J. G. Dees of Floraville, and Mr Francis Charlton of Northumberland.

The centenary of the opening of the church was celebrated by special services on 15 and 16 September 1968, conducted by Archbishop Hyginus Eugene Cardinale, Apostolic Delegate in Great Britain.

The school chapel of SS Gregory and Patrick, in Quay Street, was erected in 1890 and is served from St Beghs.

The priests in charge of the parish were:

1706-25	Francis Rich	1818-54	Gregory Holden
1725-26	William Hewlett	1854-60	Thomas Maurus
1726-27	Maurus Buckley		Shepherd
1727-30	Dionysius Wm.	1860-73	Benedict Lynass
	Huddleston	1873-87	James Benedict Rowley
1730-31	Wilfrid Witham	1887-91	Gregory Murphy
1731-35	Paul Allanson	1891-92	James Dunstan Breen
1735-47	Bede Hutton	1892-94	Leonard Hoseph Davies
1750-51	Anselm Eastham	1894-1914	Gregory Murphy
1751-59	Robert Daniel	1914-24	Simon Benedict Finch
1761-61	Anselm Bolas	1924-30	Sebastian Cave
1761-64	Philip Jefferson	1930-32	Hubert Michael Caffrey
1764-74	Benet Catterel	1932-34	Ambrose Agius
1774-75	Bede Newton	1934-38	Edmund Whiriskey
1775-76	Ambrose Wareing	1938-47	Anselm Lightbound
1776-79	Maurus Chaplin	1947-49	Wilfred de Normanville
1780-80	Boniface Taylor	1949-55	Brendan Minney
1781-81	Joseph Crook	1955-77	Vincent Fogarty
1781-1818	James Johnston	1977-	Luke Waring

St Mary's, Kells

As more and more houses were built on Kells the need for a mass centre became apparent, and on 27 November 1927, a temporary chapel dedicated to the Blessed Virgin, and called St Mary's, was blessed and opened by the Rt Rev. Thomas Wulston Pearson, O.S.B.

The chapel was served by Fr Urban Butler, O.S.B., and Fr Van Thiel, O.S.B., monks of Downside Abbey.

As the district developed, a school for 230 infants and juniors was built at St Mary's.

The parish of St Mary's was canonically erected as from 8 May 1942, and Fr Augustine Kervin, O.S.B., a monk of Belmont, was appointed the first parish priest and took up residence at High Road with an assistant priest.

Fr Kervin was appointed parish priest of Mount Carmel, Redditch, in 1949, and was succeeded by Fr Paulinus Lyon, O.S.B., who nursed the parish through the difficult days of World War II and the building restrictions which followed. His zeal and energy were rewarded on

19 December 1961, when a new church, built at a cost of £40,000, was blessed and opened by the Rt Rev. T. B. Pearson, Ph.D.

Fr Lyon was parish priest until 1978 when he retired to the presbytery at St Begh's.

Interior of St Mary's Church, Kells.

Fr Lyon, O.S.B., celebrating mass.

St Benedict's Mirehouse

The growth of the Valley Estate presented problems for the Roman Catholics as well as for the Anglicans. It soon became apparent, from the numbers involved in travelling, that a Mass centre would have to be found on the estate. The Valley School was used for services from July 1955 until May 1958, when use was made of the Labour Rooms and the Calder Club. Services were conducted by two priests from St Begh's, Fr Philip Jackson and Fr Bernard Chambers.

In 1961 the Bishop sent Canon Matthew McNarney, D.D., to be priest in charge and to found a new parish. After just one year Canon McNarney, had erected a temporary church which was opened on Palm Sunday, 1962. The church was dedicated to St Benedict. Canon McNarney left in 1963 and was followed by Fr Edward Shields who became the first Parish Priest. In 1965 he initiated the building of the presbytery on a site adjacent to the church.

In 1972 Fr Michael Taylor was appointed the new Parish Priest. The parishioners made known to him their strong desire for a permanent church in which to worship. On 29 September 1974, Canon McNarney returned to cut the first sod for the church. He died on 12 February 1975, and the foundation stone for the church was laid on 2 March 1975, by the Rt Rev. T. B. Pearson, Bishop of Sinda.

The church, designed by Cassidy and Ashton Partnership of Preston, and built by Border Engineering (Contractors) Ltd, was solemnly opened and consecrated by the Rt Rev. Brian Charles Foley, Bishop of Lancaster, assisted by the Rt Rev. L. P. Hardman, Bishop of Zomba, and Bishop Pearson.

Fr Taylor moved to Kendal in 1978 and was followed as Parish Priest by Fr David Murphy of Penrith.

St Benedict's Church, Mirehouse.

The Sisters of St Paul

The congregation of the Sisters of St Paul was founded in England in 1847. Their foundress, Genevieve Dupuis, known as Sister Zoile, was born in Paris in 1813 and later taught near there and Chartres before coming to England at the request of Father Tandy of Banbury. Bishop Ullathorne of Birmingham exercised a profound influence over the development of the community.

The Sisters came to Whitehaven on 2 May 1870. The first community comprised Sister Aloysius Bowen, the superior, Sisters Agatha Dunbar, Flavia O'Dwyer, Canice Bray, Marie de Lourdes Stanley and Agnes Gertrude Gilhooley. Probably three of these taught in the newly opened all-age school in the former St Gregory's Church.

The first convent was attached to the Presbytery at Coach Road and there the Sisters lived in cramped conditions until the purchase of No.3 Corkickle (St Anne's) at the beginning of this century. It was extended in 1966 by the purchase of the adjoining Congregational manse.

Teaching has been the chief work of the Sisters in Whitehaven. This was especially important in 1870 when there were few Catholic secular teachers available. They also look after the sacristies, take charge of some of the sodalities and visit the sick and distressed of the parish, living up to their motto: *Omnibus Omnia* (All things to all people).

Superiors at St Anne's Convent, Whitehaven, 1870-1978:

Mother Aloysius Bowen (First Superior 2.5.1870)	Mother Fintan Collins
Mother Agatha Dunbar	Mother Teresa Berchmans Tierney
Mother Mary Joseph McArdle	Mother Veronica McCourt
Mother Magdalen Hipwell	Mother Elizabeth Hughes
Mother Mary of the Cross O'Farrell	Mother Rose Columba McCarthy
	Mother Juliana Donnelly

The Pentecostal Movement

The Pentecostal movement originated in America about 1900. It was brought to Europe by Pastor T. B. Barratt, a Cornishman, who served as a Methodist missionary in Oslo. Under Barratt's ministry at All Saints', Sunderland, several people received the baptism of the Holy Ghost and the movement spread throughout the country. It was brought to Whitehaven by a Miss Walker, of Lytham, when working as a district nurse at Kells. This led to cottage meetings at the home of Mr Tom Richardson, Hill Top Road, and Mr Harry Smith, Bentinck Row, Ginns, alternately, in 1918. In 1920 the Tangier Hall (over the old Coffee Shop) was rented for regular Sunday and week-night services, with Mr Harry Smith as presiding elder and Mr Edward Richardson as assembly secretary. When the Co-operative Society acquired the property for development, the Assembly moved to the old Labour Hall, Fox Lane, in November 1927, before transferring to a more suitable hall in the old Fibre Mill, Catherine Street.

In April 1956, Messrs J. Kitchin and Son transferred business from Irish Street to Roper Street, and the Assembly purchased the empty warehouse which was converted into a Mission Hall, and officially opened in August 1957, by Mr John Carter, General Secretary of the Assemblies of God in Great Britain and Ireland, to which the Whitehaven Assembly is attached. There are now some 600 Assemblies in the United Kingdom.

From 1924 to 1928 student pastors from Hampstead Bible School had oversight of the congregation. From then until 1977 local brethren have administered its affairs. Mr H. McAllister was Overseer from 1932 to 1945, Mr H. Postlethwaite from 1945 to 1956, Mr J. L. Armstrong from 1956 to 1968, and Mr R. Matthews from 1968 to 1977. In July

1977, Pastor John Perkins was inducted as the local Assembly's first full time minister.

In 1978 the Assembly bought the former Christ Church Parish Hall.

Of the three large Pentecostal bodies in Britain, the Elim foursquare Gospel Church has the most centralised form of government. It owes its origins to the movement founded by Barratt and the Pentecostal Missionary Union established in 1909, and in particular to the work of George Jeffreys, who was trained in one of the schools established by the Union, but preferred to become an evangelist rather than a missionary. Elim began in 1915 as a revivalist agency, but gradually found itself establishing its own churches. It practises baptism by immersion but the keynote of its teaching is to be found in I Corinthians, Ch. XII, in its emphasis on the baptism of the Holy Spirit and the gifts of the Spirit of which the gift of tongues is one.

The Elim movement made its first impact on Whitehaven in a series of revival meetings held by the Rev. George Canty, of Gloucester, in the Civic Hall.

His work was consolidated by the Rev. Ronald Clark and meetings were held in the YWCA until October 1961, when a church was built on George Street at a cost of approximately £3,500.

A youth deliberately set fire to the building on 26 August and extensive damage was done. This was repaired and the church extended in 1970 at a cost of £2,067.

The ministers who have served at Whitehaven are:

	1960 Ronald Clark	1965-71	John Cave
1960-63	F. Taylor	1971-72	A. O. Johnstone
1963-65	W. J. Allen	1972-78	S. C. Cain

Eric Gaudion was inducted 14 January 1978.

There were some 350 Elim churches in Great Britain in 1968, the number has now grown to 420.

Y.M.C.A.

The Young Men's Christian Association was founded in Whitehaven in 1883. In 1902 it acquired its present premises in Irish Street. Substantial donations towards the purchase of the building were made by Lord Lonsdale and the Whitehaven Coal Company Ltd. Mr H. W. Walker gave generously towards the cost of alterations.

Y.W.C.A.

The Young Women's Christian Association bought the Bethel Mission, New Lowther Street, about 1940.

This Mission was first opened in 1824, re-opened in 1869 and rebuilt in 1907. It was closely linked with the Congregational, the ministers and deacons of that church taking an active part in the organisation of the Bethel.

Salvation Army

The Salvation Army began with revivalist services in London in 1965, conducted by William Booth who, with his wife and other helpers, formed the Christian Revival Association, later renamed the East London Christian Mission. Booth used the phrase 'salvation army' in a leaflet published in 1878 and the expression caught on and was soon accepted as the name of his organisation. Its influence spread beyond London to become world-wide.

It reached Whitehaven in October 1885, when the first officers were Sarah Morton and Sarah Ann Hugill. The Whitehaven Corps, which is listed as No.73, first met in a room over the Tangier Street Coffee Shop and then in a room in the Market Place. The Band was formed in 1894.

By the end of the century it had acquired the former Congregational Chapel in Duke Street as its meeting place.

It continued to operate from Duke Street until 1937 when the former Catherine Street Methodist Chapel became available. In time the fabric of the Catherine Street building began to show signs of decay. It was demolished and a new headquarters built on the site which was opened in October 1971.

The former Catherine Street Methodist Chapel which was used by the Salvation Army from 1937 until 1971.

Chapter 16

Whitehaven Theatres

Howgill Street Theatre playbill, 1756.

The history of the theatre in Whitehaven is a fascinating study. The story commences about 1736 when John Hayton opened his Assembly Rooms in Howgill Street and later built an annexe which was used for theatrical performances. The exact date of the first theatrical performance there is still obscure. The earliest play-bill in the Whitehaven Library which bears a date is for a performance of a comedy called *The Suspicious Husband* on 14 January 1756. From the point of view of theatrical history this play-bill is extremely interesting. Among the actors named on it is James William Dodd who 'commenced acting at the early age of sixteen, at Sheffield'. As Dodd was born in 1740 it is possible that Whitehaven not Sheffield was the scene of his debut. Also on this bill there is an actor called Darby, later known as Thomas Ryder, who was also commencing his career as an actor. He afterwards achieved considerable fame in comedy both in Dublin and in London. In 1767 a building in Albion Street, known as Watson's Assembly Rooms, was fitted up as a theatre, but was probably eclipsed by the opening of the Roper Street Theatre in 1769 which was modelled on the theatre at Bath. Curiously enough the earliest surviving copy of a play-bill relating to the Roper Street Theatre — for Wednesday 22 November 1769 — is also for a performance of *The Suspicious Husband*.

With the first publication of *The Cumberland Pacquet* in 1774, there is a constant source of reports on local theatrical activity. A typical season was that which began on 7 November 1776, when *The School for Wives* and *The Virgin Unmask'd* were presented, under the management of Messrs Heaton and Anatin. This season lasted until January 1777, during which time the theatre was open three days a week. Productions in Whitehaven during this season included *The Runaway* which, we are informed, was written by 'a Lady', and ran for two hundred nights at Drury Lane. Later there was *Alzuma, or The Conquest of Peru, She Stoops to Conquer*, which was accompanied on the same bill by 'a new Music Farce, called *The Rival Candidates*, and *The Foundling, or School for Guardians*. This last comedy was followed, in the same programme, by *A Christmas Tale*, which must have been the forerunner of our modern pantomime. The characters included Faladel (the Gentleman Usher). Boneron (the Good Magician) and Nigromant (the Evil Magician), with Various Good and Evil Spirits comprising, without more specifications, a Jesuit, Poet, Glutton, Gamester, Actress, Woman of Quality and Attorney. Scenes in *A Christmas Tale* included the Fiery Lake, Nigromant's Castle, the Enchanted Laurel and, as the advertisement informs us, 'the Whimsical Transformation of Faladel into an Owl'!

Two members of this company, Messrs Austin and Whitlock, were responsible for the next theatrical season in Whitehaven, after their successful re-opening of the Theatre Royal in Chester. After a brief visit in the beginning of 1778 the Company moved on to re-open the theatre at Newcastle, but returned in December when, it is interesting to note, they advertised their performances as being 'By His Majesty's Servants', the designation reserved for those who played in Theatres Royal. After this visit the theatre was known as the 'Theatre Royal'. As a result of this change in status the classics could be performed at Whitehaven without subterfuge; nevertheless the entertainment offered was generally mixed. In strange juxtaposition are found *King Lear* and the musical dramatic

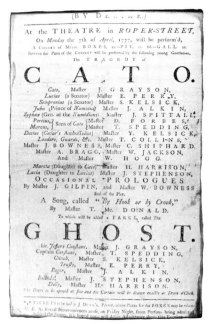

Playbill for production of *Cato* at Roper Street Theatre, 7 April 1777, by pupils of Mr H. Ward's school.

A late Victorian theatre programme announcing Charles H. Hawtrey's touring play 'Private Secretary' direct from the Globe Theatre, London.

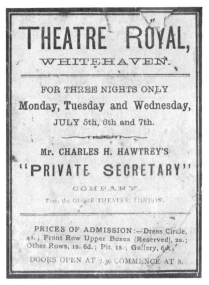

entertainment of three acts called *The Maid of the Oaks*, or *Fete Champetre*, written by General Burgoyne.

Another early play-bill in the Whitehaven Library relating to the Roper Street Theatre is dated 7 April 1777, and refers to a performance of *Cato* by the pupils of Mr Ward, a schoolmaster in Howgill Street who was a theatrical enthusiast. Audiences in those days were fickle and sometimes rough. The travelling players were not always well liked and in some cases often despised. They were often treated badly; for instance, about 1780 a group of players applied for a licence to re-open the theatre. They were advised to obtain the consent of the local landowner, the Earl of Lonsdale, but received no reply. Assuming that silence meant consent they opened the theatre. Alas, it did not and the manager and leading actor were thrown into Penrith gaol by the irate Earl.

Keeping on the right side of the law was only one of the difficulties confronting a theatrical manager in those times. Rivals were quite unscupulous and one well-known manager is known to have hired a shorthand writer to take down a successful rival's play. He then changed the title and the characters' names and produced the play on his own stage with himself in the leading part.

The early nineteenth century newspaper reports are frequently very blunt. One of the most lively occurs in the *Whitehaven Gazette* for 17 February 1823, which records the close of Mr Alexander's season. At his leave-taking the manager suggested that the reasons for the failure of the season lay in the trade depression of the period and the exhorbitant rent of the theatre. The newspaper accepted these but suggested others in addition. 'Whitehaven', it avers, 'has been accustomed to good performers, and it will not pay to see inferior ones. The company that has just left us was not only weak in point of talent, but deficient in numbers; scarce any play could be got up without the most gross doubling of parts — nay, we have seen one man play six different characters in the course of one night. This was not only harassing to the performers but particularly disagreeable to the audience.'

Mr Alexander had followed the highly successful Mr McCready as manager of the theatre and comparison was inevitable. Anyone who wishes to obtain a more detailed picture of Whitehaven's Theatre Royal at this time should read Graham Sutton's *North Star*.

On 21 December 1837, the Whitehaven Cricket Club had a special evening when the plays performed were *Wonder: a Woman keep a Secret* and *Raising the Wind*. To mark this occasion one poster was printed on silk. The second title is interesting since Williamson Peile, the then treasurer of the Whitehaven Playground and Mr Paumier, manager of the theatre, were the first two Whitehaven people to make an ascent in a balloon.

Many famous names were associated with the Whitehaven Theatre throughout the nineteenth century, and almost a century after it had opened, it was subjected to internal re-construction and re-opened on 1 February 1869. The interior was somewhat remodelled in 1870-71. It was closed in 1909 for a further overhaul and re-opened on 26 August of that year, after enlargement and internal re-construction.

Audiences, however, were as finicky as before, and Donald Wolfit records in his autobiography *First Interval* how, in 1922, a Whitehaven audience gave him 'the bird'. But the end was not far off, and in the 1930s the Theatre Royal closed never to re-open. For a time it was used as a store by the *Whitehaven News* but it was demolished in 1960 to allow for an extension of the printing works and in 1978 underwent radical alterations and became Michael Moon's second antiquarian bookshop.

Chapter 17　Education

When Whitehaven received its charter of incorporation a School Attendance Committee was set up, but its powers were strictly limited and it was not until 1903 that the Whitehaven Education Committee was established to co-ordinate the activities of the church schools which had strenuously opposed all efforts to establish a local School Board.

Most of the local schools were operating in old buildings. Piper's Marine School had been built in 1818, St James' National School in 1824, St Nicholas' School in 1846 (and enlarged in 1874), Trinity National School in 1852, and St Begh's Roman Catholic School opened in 1868 used a chapel built in 1834. St James' Infant School was built in 1875, and the Earl of Lonsdale School on Monkwray, in 1876. The only two new schools were St Patrick and St Gregory's Infant School in Quay Street, built in 1889, and Crosthwaite Memorial School, Rosemary Lane, which had been opened in 1901 to replace the old Refuge School in the Market Place.

The ability to levy a rate for educational purposes led to a gradual improvement in school provision. The old Marine School was sold and the money realised used in 1908 to purchase the site of the County Secondary School, built in 1908. The St Nicholas' Schools were closed in 1911 when the Council built the Irish Street Schools at a cost of £20,000. The Earl of Lonsdale School was enlarged and modernised in 1922, two new Roman Catholic Schools were provided at Coach Road in 1926 and 1927, and a new junior and Infant School was built at Bransty in 1930.

Kells Infants School was opened on 30 June 1938, by Lord Eustace Percy.

Since 1946 the Town Council has been relieved of its educational functions by the County Council. In the three decades that have elapsed since the transfer of powers an extensive school building programme has taken place. Kells Secondary Modern School was opened in 1951; the Valley Junior and Infants Schools in 1952; Whitehaven College of Further Education in 1955; St Mary's R.C. School, Kells, extended 1957; Hensingham Junior School opened 1959; SS Gregory and Patrick R.C. School 1960; Overend Secondary Modern School 1960; St James' Infants School extended 1961; Hensingham Infants School extended 1965; and St James' Junior School rebuilt 1965. Jericho Infants and Junior School was built in 1969 at a cost of £77,000.

Secondary education was reorganised on a comprehensive pattern in September 1966. A new Grammar School to replace the one on Catherine Street, built near Overend Secondary Modern School, was occupied in August 1968, and officially opened by Prof. Henry Miller, M.D., F.R.C.P., Vice-Chancellor Designate of the University of Newcastle-upon-Tyne on 17 March 1969. The school and a new house block for Overend School cost £685,162.

Richmond Secondary Modern School moved from Irish Street into the former Grammar School building in January 1969.

A new Roman Catholic comprehensive school to replace St Begh's Secondary Modern School and St Cuthbert's Secondary Modern School, Cleator Moor, called St Benedict's High School was built at Richmond with access from Red Lonning. The first part, completed in April 1971 at a cost of £251,290, provided accommodation for 550 pupils. It was

officially opened by the Rt Rev. Brian Charles Foley and dedicated by
the Rt Rev. J. Hodkinson, Abbot of Belmont, on 13 October 1971. An
extension, costing £200,000 and providing accommodation for a further
350 pupils, was officially opened by the Rt Rev. T. B. Pearson, Bishop of
Sinda, on 11 July 1977. This allowed St Cuthbert's to be closed and the
pupils to be transferred to St Benedict's.

In January 1975, Cumbria Education Committee's Planning Sub-
Committee put forward a scheme of educational reorganisation which
was designed to cope with two problems:

(1)   to meet the Government's demand for the introduction of a fully
comprehensive system of education, and

(2)   to deal with the problem arising from the declining number of
children of school age.

After prolonged public discussion, the scheme as finally accepted by
the Minister of State for Education was for:

'One mixed school for pupils 11-18 on the Hensingham campus, with
sixth formers joining the school at 16+ from Lillyhall and Ehenside
Schools, and subject to the views of the governors, from St Benedict's
R.C. School'.

The suggested date of implementation was September 1981, 'subject to
finance being available within the County budget for the relevant
building programmes'.

As a result of this scheme of re-organisation Kells Secondary Modern
School was closed in June 1978, and the pupils transferred to Overend
and Richmond Secondary Modern Schools. The scheme visualises Richmond Secondary Modern School being phased out by 1981.

Chapter 18   Whitehaven potteries

William Gilpin (1657-1724), Sir John Lowther's steward, became interested in the possibility of using local clays to make good quality pottery and tobacco pipes, and in 1698 sent for a Staffordshire expert to make trials which seemed to prove hopeful. He also made enquiries about the Fulham and Lambeth potteries. The scheme to make pottery did not materialise and Aaron Wedgwood settled at his trade in the parish of Dearham, near Cockermouth.

What is clear from the Lowther estate rentals is that a pipehouse was built on a piece of property known as Hodgson's Croft and let to Abel Robinson. He held the property from 1698 to 1701, and in the latter year a second pipehouse was built. Abel Robinson was followed by John Boulain from 1701 to 1704, and then the house was rented by Thomas Birch from 1704 to 1713 when he bought it outright for the sum of £30 3s 0d. Birch seems to have come to Whitehaven in 1701 to take over the second pipehouse which he relinquished in 1704 to Thomas Terry who worked it for two years. How long Birch carried on after 1713 is not clear but probably for quite some time as a Caleb Birch, pipemaker, is listed in the 1762 census. Pipe-making as a trade went on until the 1850s.

Nothing is known of what happened about pottery making over the next forty years, but in 1740 Sir James Lowther granted a seven year lease on part of a building known as the Gin House to Thomas Atkinson, potter. Atkinson's lease was cancelled four years later because 'he had made nothing of the premises for nearly two years', but he is still referred to as a potter when his daughter was baptised in 1749.

The lease of the Gin House passed to John Hudson who continued as lessee until 1781. The Gin House gave its name to the neighbourhood round about which became known as 'the Ginns'. It lay within St Bees parish and the registers for the period 1763-1799 contain the names of

▽ Milk jug, made for the Friendly Sawyers Society, 1820. The transfer has been applied in reverse.

▷ Milk jug, showing the transfer as it should be.

Pottery savings bank with Free Trade insignia, made for Isaac Sloan, c. 1840.

thirteen persons described as potters: Robert Lowther (1763); Michael Young (1779); Jacob Low (1779); James Mallet (1780); Philip Wilson (1781); Jeremiah James (1783); George Johnson (1786); John Hodgson (1790); Towson Lowther (1790); William Noble (1791); John Coulthard (1793); James Young (1797); and John Trousdale (1799). Six of these fall within the last decade of the century and may indicate that the industry received an impetus following the building of the Newhouses in 1788.

The oldest surviving piece of pottery is a jug with naval scenes and sentiments made for Daniel and Mary McIntosh and their son, John. McIntosh had fought under Admiral Duncan at Camperdown in 1797. Whether it was actually manufactured locally is not absolutely certain. Daniel McIntosh is buried in Holy Trinity churchyard.

A directory for 1811 shows that there were six dealers in pottery in Whitehaven at that time. Only one can be identified as a manufacturer — Henry Richardson. He had taken over the Hudson pottery and was running it in conjunction with a copperas works in the Ginns. By 1829 the business had passed to his son John, and by 1847 to John Kitchin who had started as a pottery and china dealer in 1821.

In 1813 John Goulding and John Tunstall obtained the lease of some land adjoining the old glass-house for the erection of a pottery. They took John Trousdale into partnership. Goulding died in 1821, and by 1847 the business had been taken over by Edward Lewis who was operating in 1864.

In 1819 a third pottery made its appearance. It was known as the Whitehaven Pottery, and was run by Woodnorth, Harrison, Hall and Co. It stood on Pottery Row, on the site now occupied by the abattoir.

They advertised themselves as manufacturers of 'blue printed, blue painted, enamelled blue and brown, lined upon and under the glaze, blue and greenedged — fine and common cream colour, black, purple, red and rose coloured, printed, and in a great variety of fancy coloured, printed and embossed ware', and declared that their products were 'equal, if not superior to the Generality of Staffordshire Ware'.

The Woodnorth of this company is the Peter Woodnorth later associated with the Ladypit Pottery which was still working in the 1850s. The Hall of the partnership is presumably the Ralph Hall of Burslem who became the father-in-law of John Wilkinson. John Wilkinson who is described in a directory for 1829 as a manufacturer of 'white and coloured delf' had taken over control of the Whitehaven Pottery. Near him John Trousdale was making black pottery and John Richardson brown and black.

There was yet another pottery which is noted in Pigot's directory for 1828-29: 'Francis Davis (semi-china), High Pottery, Scotch Street'.

Reform Bill mug, 1832. Made at Wilkinson's Pottery.

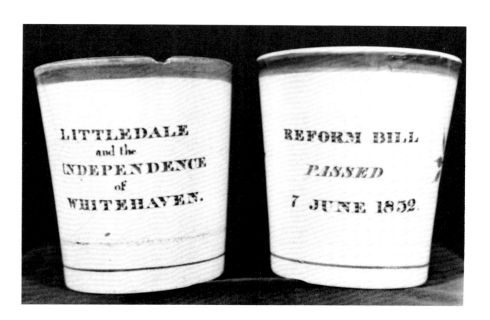

Composite piece consisting of base plate, tobacco jar, inkstand, chalice and candlestick, one of a pair made for the Great Exhibition, 1851.

Richardson's pottery and the copperas works stood on a site behind Bentinck's Row, now used by the Corporation as a storage yard.

John Wilkinson (1797-1868) was the son of Randle Wilkinson, of Tunstall, who died 25 May 1837, aged seventy-nine. About August 1822 he married Mary Hall, daughter of Ralph Hall, of Burslem, an earthenware manufacturer who made a considerable number of pottery figures.

Wilkinson's was by far the most outstanding local pottery, and in Mr Brown Harrison, foreman from 1850 onwards, it possessed a craftsman of considerable ability. John Wilkinson resided at the pottery until his death in 1868. His widow carried on the business until she died in 1877 aged eighty. Some fragments of pottery recently excavated at Coulderton include one bearing her own trademark. On her death the management of the firm passed to her youngest son, Randle, who maintained it until the 1880s when it closed. Randle Wilkinson ran a wholesale pottery store in Roper Street for some years and in 1923 moved to Tangier Street. He eventually retired to Brampton where he died on 17 September 1925, aged eighty.

It is obvious from a report of the local celebrations at the time of the coronation of Queen Victoria at the Whitehaven potteries were at that time giving employment to more than 150 people.

There are in the Whitehaven Museum two pieces of pottery which indicate the unsophisticated pleasures of the period. The entire workforce of the Whitehaven Pottery had gone on an outing to Ravenglass. The record of the episode is preserved on a large meat plate, part of a dinner service made to mark the occasion, and reads:

Presented to
Mr John Parker of Grove

by the WORK PEOPLE of the
WHITEHAVEN POTTERY

for his Courtesy towards them
on their

VISIT TO RAVENGLASS

June 10th, 1850

The other piece which marks the occasion is a puzzle jug presented to John Whinneray, the landlord of the King's Arms, at Ravenglass. How they travelled is not clear as the Furness Railway was not opened until the following month.

John Patman, an excise officer, came to Whitehaven in 1829. The nature of his work caused him to be transferred, first to Newcastle, and later to County Donegal, Ireland, where he died. His widow and family then returned to Whitehaven where the eldest son, John, became a clerk, or accountant, to John Wilkinson, at the Whitehaven Pottery. Later, a younger son, Frederick (1825-80) served his apprenticeship to Mr Wilkinson. For a number of years he had a shop on King Street selling pottery and glass but eventually he took over the Brown Pottery. Frederick Patman died 26 August 1880, aged fifty-five, and was succeeded by his nephew, John Atkinson Patman. The latter died at 13 Meadow Road on 23 October 1910, aged fifty-seven.

The business was carried on by Patman's foreman, John Thornber, but closed down about 1915.

The Ladypit Pottery was sold in 1830 to a firm operating under the name of Bell and Jackson. Watson Bell, the son of George Bell, mariner, was apprenticed to Peter Woodnorth on 18 February 1817, for seven years, as a hollowware squeezer. In 1847 the Ladypit Pottery was in the hands of Ralph Smith, 'maker of cane and Rockingham ware', but it was out of action before 1864.

Chapter 19

The twentieth century including local industries

Industrially, the opening decades of the twentieth century found Whitehaven in a very vulnerable position. The economy was poised on one heavy industry — coal mining — and that industry was wracked by strikes and dogged by disasters. The numbers employed in the pits varied from 2,181 in 1900 to 3,800 in 1927, but the general economic depression of the late 1920s and 1930s was being felt in Whitehaven in common with the rest of Cumberland. In October 1935, the worst blow of all fell — the pits were closed. There seemed little hope of revival. The industrially hard hit parts of the country were euphemistically designated 'Special Areas' and Commissioners were appointed. One of these saw little hope for West Cumberland and favoured emigration. Fortunately there were men of a more stubborn cast of mind who believed in the possibility of the economic recovery and in 1935 the Cumberland Development Council was formed with Jack Adams, a local trade union organiser, as its first secretary.

The zest with which he threw himself into the task, coupled with the whole-hearted backing of the Council, and of Mr Frank Anderson, the Member of Parliament for the Division, slowly turned the tide. In 1937 the pits were re-opened. Alongside the efforts to rehabilitate the old

Sekers Silk Mills.

basic industries of West Cumberland went negotiations to establish new ones.

In 1938 Mr N. T. 'Miki' Sekers and his cousin Mr T. L. de Gara established a silk factory at Hensingham which moved into a new specially designed building in the following year.

The first year was spent manufacturing high class silk and rayon fabrics for the fashion trade.

Between 1939 and 1945, the company was engaged in Government contract work, weaving parachute silks. Understandably, therefore, only a very small part of production capacity could be devoted to developing fashion fabrics.

By 1947, however, the company was well established in the Haute Couture markets supplying high class fabrics to most of the great fashion houses, amongst whom were Edward Molyneux and Bianca Mosca in England and Christian Dior in France. From then on the dazzling collection of silks, lames, satins and colour woven fabrics set fashion trends throughout Europe.

In 1955 the company went public and in 1960 produced its first range of furnishing fabrics. This first collection was only two years later awarded the coveted Duke of Edinburgh Prize for Elegant Design. The company gained further Design Awards in 1965 and 1973 and are now acknowledged leaders in this field.

The mill manufactures a wide range and variety of fabrics for use in the dress, furnishing and upholstery markets. There are plains, stripes and checks, traditional and modern designs, soft silky fabrics and rough textured weaves.

Following the acquisition in April 1974 of the whole of the issued share capital of D. Landau & Sons Ltd, a Merchanting Division has been established and the range of fabrics now includes a variety of cotton prints and velvets.

New weaving shed at Sekers showing shuttleless looms.

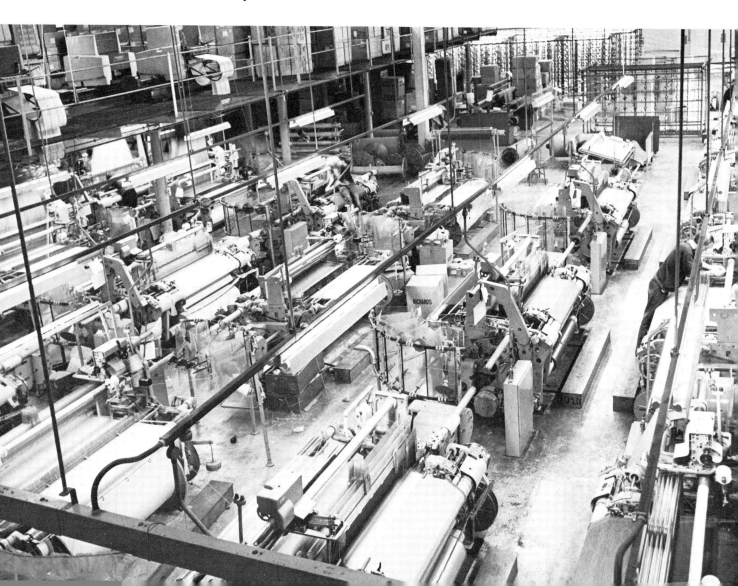

The interior of the theatre at Rosehill.

In 1975 the name of the parent group was changed from West Cumberland Silk Mills to Sekers International Ltd in keeping with its international image. With the recent acquisition of London Drapes International, the additional service of making and fitting curtains and drapes can be offered by the Sekers group.

Over the last few years the factory has been modernised and enlarged to cope with an increasingly diversified production and now employs approximately 250 personnel, some of whom work at the combined showroom of Sekers and Landau at 300 Regent Street, London, W.1.

Various countries provide the factory machinery — France the Jacquard equipment, Germany and Switzerland the looms, which include the latest shuttleless models. Equally, the raw materials do not come from only one source, but from wherever the right yarns can be found.

Mr Sekers interests were not confined to the factory. He added enormously to the cultural attraction of the district by building what has been termed 'a jewel box theatre' at Rosehill. In this he had the support, among others, of his fellow West Cumbrian industrialists. At the beginning of September 1959, Dame Peggy Ashcroft read a specially written prologue, and the standards set on the opening night have been maintained.

On 27 and 28 July 1962, Princess Margaret and her husband, Lord Snowdon, stayed at Rosehill and attended performances at the theatre, and on 21 October 1964, Queen Elizabeth, the Queen Mother, attended a concert there. Mr Seker's work for the arts was not confined to Whitehaven, and in recognition of what he had done in that direction he was awarded an M.B.E. in 1955. He became chairman of the London Philharmonic Orchestra Council, was involved with the Glyndbourne Arts Trust, Chichester Festival Theatre and opera trusts. His interests extended to the continent. He was granted a knighthood in 1965.

Following a heart operation in 1970 he retired as managing director, but in 1971 started a second career as a design consultant, forming M W Design Associates. He died while on holiday on the continent in 1972.

The Rosehill Theatre has been renamed the Sir Nicholas Sekers Theatre.

Marchon Products Ltd

On 6 December 1939, Frank Schon and Fred Marzillier registered Marchon Products Ltd and occupied an office in London. Initially, the company conducted only merchanting operations, frustrated when their offices were destroyed by enemy action. They decided to move to Whitehaven and in 1941 began manufacturing firelighters on a small scale at Hensingham near to Whitehaven. These firelighters were made from sawdust and naphthalene and, although not too successful at first, were gradually improved in quality.

In those early days, Frank Schon was the driving force and Fred Marzillier took care of the finance and administration of the business. Frank Schon had acquired, while working on the continent before the war, a thorough knowledge of the production and the uses of synthetic detergents and had an ambition to develop the manufacture of detergent and toiletry chemicals through his own company.

Firelighter output continued to increase and the company took over the Guinea Warehouse and other small properties in Whitehaven. In 1943 came a major step forward when Marchon moved into part of its present cliff-top site at Kells. The land had previously been occupied by the Ladysmith Pit coke ovens, and contained a number of old process buildings. The profits from the sale of firelighters was invested in plant and equipment and the sulphation of fatty alcohols — the key process in the production of toiletry chemicals — was started. That first process plant was run successfully for many years and was not finally closed down until 1977.

Marchon works.

During the difficult formative years, Schon's entrepreneurial abilities were matched by Marzillier's skill in controlling cash-flow and in setting up an administrative system which stood up to the ever-increasing demands of a rapidly expanding business, and with the end of the war, Marchon was able to begin expanding on an even larger scale. The closing down of Ordnance factories in the area freed qualified technicians who joined the Marchon organisation and formed the nucleus of a technical team.

With the closing of the Ordnance factory at Sellafield, twelve miles south of Whitehaven, a great deal of plant and a number of buildings came on to the market. Marchon bought two large buildings and a small laboratory, which were re-erected on the Kells site, where they remain still today as operational units.

The main thrust over the first two or three post-war years was the ever-increasing production of surface-active agents. Apart from toiletry preparations supplied to most leading manufacturers, Marchon developed large sales of surface-active agents and emulsifiers for the textile industry, for leather processing and for foodstuffs.

In 1949, Mr Schon returned from a whirlwind American tour with files of valuable reports — including the drawings for a jet spray-drying tower. The company built this spray tower and began to produce spray-dried powder detergents. The experience gained on that tower led to the first contract with a major international company for the manufacture and packaging of heavy duty detergent powder.

With the comfort of a major contract and the cash generated by the ever-expanding shampoo and toiletries business, by far the most important operation at that time, a second and much larger spray drier was built, and the packing room expanded. This enabled the company to seek manufacturing and packing contracts which it still holds to this day. At that time, the company purchased all its raw materials from outside sources, many of which were necessarily overseas, and it became apparent that to embark on a full scale programme of technical and manufacturing development, the company would have to become more self-sufficient.

It was equally evident that that sort of development could be undertaken only if a much larger market for the company's products were assured. It was in these circumstances that Marchon first contracted to supply detergent bases and foaming agents, intermediates and raw materials to some of the country's largest manufacturers. This decision led, in the early 1950s, to a decision to manufacture at Whitehaven an essential detergent ingredient, sodium tripolyphosphate and for this phosphoric acid was required. The standard 'wet process' route to phosphoric acid — which involves reacting sulphuric acid and phosphate rock — was chosen. The second stage in the manufacture of tripolyphosphate involved the purification of the acid, its neutralisation, drying and calcining, and suitable processes for all these stages were developed at Whitehaven.

At the same time, the possibility of manufacturing the major raw material for toiletries production — fatty alcohol — (by hydrogenating lauryl laurate produced on site) was also critically examined and the decision was taken to start manufacture in Whitehaven.

This was a major step forward for the company and brought it into the field of 'high-pressure' technology for the first time. The plant was officially opened by Sir Henry Tizard on 22 June 1954 and produced some 5,000 tonnes per year of a badly needed raw material. The decision to manufacture sodium-tripolyphosphate and fatty alcohols at Whitehaven meant that the company was no longer totally dependent on others for its major raw materials, and it provided the base for further rapid expansion.

With the continuing growth in demand for detergents, the need for additional quantities of sodium tripolyphosphate became apparent. The continuous production of sodium tripolyphosphate demanded large

H.R.H. Princess Mary visits Marchon,
30 March 1954.

tonnages of sulphuric acid, and with the decision to expand the tripolyphosphate plant came the need for further quantities of sulphuric acid to
a degree which could not be easily met by outside purchases and therefore the on-site production of sulphuric acid became essential. Sulphuric
acid was, and is, an important raw material in almost every industry. In
the early 1950s some three-quarters of the United Kingdom's sulphuric
acid production was based on imported elemental sulphur coming mostly
from America. During that period difficulties were experienced in
obtaining supplies of sulphur from the United States and this led to such
a nation-wide sulphuric acid shortage in 1950-51 that H.M. Government
encouraged the development of sulphuric acid manufacture from
indigenous raw materials. It was known that there were substantial
deposits of mineable anhydrite (anhydrous calcium sulphate) available in
the country, and the manufacture of sulphuric acid and cement from
anhydrite by a process originally developed in Germany had been carried
out by ICI at Billingham since 1930. By a happy coincidence huge
deposits of anhydrite were known to exist underneath the Marchon site
and the idea of building an anhydrite sulphuric acid plant at Whitehaven
was thus conceived early in 1951. Sir (then Mr) Harold Wilson was then

133

H.R.H. the Duke of Edinburgh visits Solway anhydrite mine, 24 November 1955.

President of the Board of Trade, and his Department sponsored the project. The finance, some £3 million, for the original project which included the development of the anhydrite mine and the construction of the first two kilns and acid plants, was largely provided by the Treasury in the form of a loan.

The new plant, later to be called Solway Chemicals, was appropriately enough inaugurated by Jack Adams (later Lord Adams of Ennerdale) who had assisted the company to a large extent in its formative years. The anhydrite mine was opened on 11 January 1955 by Sir Robert Chance the then Lord Lieutenant of Cumberland, and the Sulphuric Acid Plant by His Royal Highness the Duke of Edinburgh on 24 November 1955.

When in the middle of 1955 the first two kilns came on stream production started at an annual rate of 90,000 tonnes each of H_2SO_4 and cement which was quickly increased to well over 100,000 per annum, thus handsomely exceeding the design capacity.

This was followed by the opening of the second Phosphoric Acid Plant which increased capacity to some 40,000 tonnes of P_2O_5 per annum, and allowed the production of sodium tripolyphosphate to reach a level of 45,000 tonnes per annum by the mid-1950s.

Whilst this large scale development was proceeding on the inorganic side of the business, the organic side was not neglected. Plants for the manufacture of other essential detergent raw materials were also commissioned, particularly the methyl ester and alkylolamide plants, used as thickening and foam-boosting agents in shampoos and in liquid and powder detergents.

Marchon Products Ltd as a subsidiary of Albright & Wilson Ltd 1955-68

In late 1955, Albright and Wilson acquired Marchon Products Ltd and all of its subsidiaries as part of Albright and Wilson's own programme of expansion.

The purchase made sources of additional finance available to Marchon for its continuing development. Marchon received its first Queen's Award to Industry for Export Achievement in 1966.

Inorganics

Further expansion of sulphuric acid manufacture was announced in May 1962 when Lord Fleck, the then Chairman of ICI Ltd, inaugurated the building of the third kiln. This increased the capacity by a further 70,000 tonnes each of sulphuric acid and cement per annum. On 7 May 1965, further expansion were announced by Mr Schon. Harold Wilson, then the Prime Minister for the first time, came to Whitehaven and inaugurated the building of Kilns 4 and 5. These were commissioned on 7 January and 21 May 1967 respectively, and together boosted capacity by a further 160,000 tonnes each of acid and cement. By now, Solway Chemicals was becoming one of the largest sulphuric acid producers in the United Kingdom.

With an ample supply of sulphuric acid now available, phosphoric acid capacity was rapidly increased using the 'wet process' for the third plant (with a capacity of 80,000 tonnes of P_2O_5 per annum), and the new Kellog-Lopker process (which had been piloted at Whitehaven) for the fourth production unit (with a capacity of 85,000 tonnes of P_2O_5 per annum). These units were commissioned in December 1961 and November 1968 respectively. Both the original phosphoric acid plants were phased out of production.

During this period a completely new technology for producing sodium tripolyphosphate, involving spray-drying techniques, was introduced and by the end of 1968 production capacity had reached the following levels:

Sulphuric Acid	350,000 tonnes per annum
Cement	350,000 tonnes per annum
Phosphoric Acid	165,000 tonnes of P_2O_5 per annum
Sodium Tripolyphosphate	170,000 tonnes per annum

The increase in tripolyphosphate production brought with it an increased demand for calcium phosphate or phosphate rock as it is popularly known. Phosphate rock was imported from Casablanca and initially it was shipped in chartered vessels, but the firm gradually acquired its own fleet — the *Marchon Trader* (built by Austin and Pickersgill in Sunderland in May 1957), the *Marchon Enterprise* (built by Clellands of Wallsend in November 1961) and the *Marchon Venturer* (also built by Clellands, in February 1962). For a number of years these vessels were able to keep pace with developments but by 1965 it became obvious that, if the factory were to continue to expand, greater flexibility in transportation, discharge and handling were required.

Long term developments for the harbour failed to materialise for a number of reasons, and the problem was overcome by ferrying phosphate rock, brought from Casablanca in 20,000 tonne or larger bulk carriers to the harbour in the company's own smaller vessels and the specially built barge, the *Odin*. This method has proved very successful and continues to the present day.

Organics

In the late 1950s a plant was built to sulphonate purchased alkylate using SO_3 gas from Solway. This gave Marchon a greater degree of flexibility in the sulphonation of alkyl benzenes and the sulphation of

Marchon Venturer, built by Clellands in February 1962.

fatty alcohols (both essential intermediates for surfactant production). These two operations are the basis on which the company's business has been expanded.

In 1957, a new plant was commissioned for the manufacture of methacrylic monomers and polymers for use as viscosity control additives in lubricating oils. This was immediately followed by one for the production of sodium and potassium toluene and xylene sulphonates (other essential detergent raw materials).

By the early part of 1962, a decision was taken to expand fatty alcohol production from 5,000 tonnes per annum to 20,000 tonnes, to meet the rising demand for this important raw material, both in the U.K. and overseas. In 1964, a new plant was commissioned using a new technique in which fatty acids are converted directly to fatty alcohols. At the time this was a radical step to take, and the soundness of the decision has been proved over and over again.

Overseas

During the period 1955-68, developments overseas played a major role in expanding the company's interests and activities.

In 1963, a fatty alcohol plant and associated processes based on Whitehaven technology was built by the engineering company constructors John Brown at Volgodonsk in the U.S.S.R. and a similar factory was commissioned the following year at Shebekino. Both plants were steered through their early days by the same team of engineers and technicians from the Marchon Works.

Anticipating the U.K's. joining the Common Market, Marchon gained a foothold in Europe by forming an Italian subsidiary — Marchon Italiana SpA on 20 November 1956. Production of detergents and toiletries began on 20 March 1961 and the operation was an immediate success. The plant has steadily expanded since then and continues to grow.

Frank Schon, Baron Schon, of Whitehaven (1976).

A new subsidiary, Marchon France was formed on 11 June 1968 and production commenced in December 1969. This move into France further strengthened Marchon's position in Europe.

Management

The period 1965-68 was a period in which major changes in management occurred. Soon after the take-over of the company by Albright and Wilson Ltd, Mr Marzillier retired from his executive directorship. For the conspicuous part both he and Mr Schon had played in the economic rehabilitation of West Cumberland, in 1961, both were elected freemen of the Borough of Whitehaven.

In 1964, Frank Schon became Chairman of the Cumberland Development Council, and the North Regional Economic Planning Council. In 1966, he was elected to the Industrial Reorganisation Corporation. He was awarded a knighthood in the Queen's Birthday Honours List of 1966.

On 5 May 1967, Sir Frank Schon resigned from the Board of Albright and Wilson Ltd and from his position as Chairman and Managing Director of Marchon Products Ltd and Solway Chemicals Ltd.

In the New Year's Honours List of 1972, he was made a baron, taking the title Lord Schon of Whitehaven in the County of Cumbria.

His successors were the then Sales Director Mr Otto Secher and Financial and Administrative Director Mr Peter Baines. Mr Baines became Managing Director and Mr Secher the Chairman. Mr Baines was also appointed to the Board of Directors of Albright and Wilson as Commercial Director soon afterwards.

The Marchon Division 1968-75

On 1 April 1968, as part of a continuing Albright and Wilson reorganisation, three major U.K. subsidiaries — Albright and Wilson (Mfg) Ltd, Associated Chemical Companies Ltd and Marchon Products Ltd — ceased to trade under their old names and began to operate under the parent company name of Albright and Wilson Ltd. They adopted the following divisional names:

OLDBURY DIVISION

ASSOCIATED CHEMICAL COMPANIES DIVISION

MARCHON DIVISION

In September 1970, the control of the Division became the responsibility of Mr Otto Secher and he, on retirement in 1971, was succeeded by Dr D. A. A. (Danny) Fagandini, who earlier had been largely responsible for the growth of Marchon Italiana.

In a further reorganisation effective from 1 February 1972, the Marchon Division became responsible for the agricultural business of the Associated Chemical Companies Division (including Farm Protection Ltd), and its chrome chemicals and other business became the responsibility of Oldbury Division, renamed the Industrial Chemicals Division.

The Marchon Division was given additional responsibility in January 1973 when Albright and Wilson (Australia) Ltd, Albright, Morarji and Pandit of India, Polyphos in South Africa, Albright and Wilson Ltd in Ireland and the overseas marketing companies in Europe came under the control of Whitehaven.

The Marchon Division was further reorganised into a number of profit accountable units based largely on geographical areas as follows:

WHITEHAVEN

EUROPEAN

AGRICULTURAL PRODUCTS

AUSTRALIA

Mr Martin D. Rowe was appointed Chairman of the Whitehaven Sector, Dr Giorgio Mira of the European Sector, Mr W. H. (Bill) Coates of the Agricultural Products Sector and Mr George James of the Australia Sector. Mr John R. Wills was appointed to succeed Dr Fagandini as Divisional Managing Director in August 1973.

As part of a further expansion programme in Europe, it was announced on 12 Decmeber 1970 that Marchon Italiana's second plant was to be built at Frosinone near Rome and it came on stream on 12 July 1972.

The announcement that Marchon was to build a new plant at Alcover in Spain was made on 8 September 1970. The plant was commissioned in November 1972 and has quickly expanded.

The Division received its second and third Queen's Awards to Industry for Export Achievement in 1966 and 1975.

Inorganics

In the late 1960s the rising cost of production of sulphuric acid and cement from anhydrite was becoming a serious cause for concern, and an in-depth study by Mr Wills produced a clear recommendation that sulphuric acid be produced via the sulphur-burning route. The main reason for this recommendation was that the anhydrite route was both labour and capital intensive, and because it was largely mechanical, maintenance costs were escalating at an uncontrolled rate.

These factors alone were more than sufficient to shift the economic balance in favour of sulphur-burning and in August 1971 the decision was finally taken to change over progressively to sulphur burning.

Number one burner was built to place kilns one and two and started up on 1 March 1973 with a capacity of 200,000 tonnes per annum. Number three kiln was replaced with the second sulphur burner on 28 November 1975 increasing the capacity for sulphuric acid via the sulphur route to 375,000 tonnes per annum. Six months later the third sulphur burner came on stream again boosting the capacity by a further 175,000 tonnes. By this time, all five kilns had been replaced and sulphuric acid capacity had been increased to over half a million tonnes per annum. The Whitehaven site became the largest single-site producer of sulphuric acid in the U.K.

An announcement was made on 12 December 1973 that £3.2 million was to be invested in a new plant for the production of 40,000 tonnes per annum (as P_2O_5) of purified phosphoric acid for use in industrial phosphates manufactured in Albright and Wilson factories, and for sale.

The process to be used was a new one developed within the company and known as the Marchon/Oldbury or M.O. process. The process also produced a by-product suitable for use in fertiliser manufacture.

Organics

This period saw the commissioning of a new continuous SO_3 plant for the sulphation of fatty alcohols and ethoxylated alcohols (another important raw material which has been manufactured on site since 1952) and for the sulphonation of alkyl benzene using liquid SO_3 (initially purchased and then manufactured on the new Solway plant). The emphasis swung away from the chlorosulphonic acid and oleum routes. Over the years, chlorosulphonic acid had been used to produce the higher quality toiletries products, and oleum for detergent powders. Now both could be manufactured using one source of SO_3 and by the same processing units. The plant was expanded in several phases, and eventually replaced the company's very first production unit.

On 10 March 1975, the company announced that it was to invest £1.35 million on a plant for the production of a new range of inter- mediates (imidazoline betaines) to be used for the manufacture of specially mild surfactants.

The Detergents and Chemicals Group 1975-77

On 8 December 1975, the Marchon and Industrial Chemicals Divisions of the Company were merged into the new Detergents and Chemicals Group which was then organised in six sectors:

AGRICULTURAL
AUSTRALIAN
DETERGENTS
ORGANICS
PHOSPHATES
SPECIALITIES

each with an executive committee whose chairman reported to the Managing Director of the Detergents and Chemicals Group — Mr John Wills.

The Detergents and Chemicals Group was much the largest organisational entity within the company and had responsibility for seventeen factories* — ten in the U.K. and seven overseas, in addition to a network of sales offices.

In April 1976, Albright and Wilson announced that they had agreed to acquire 50% of the equity in a South African chemical concern now known as Marchon-Paragon Holdings (Pty) Ltd. Ultimately, a selected range of Albright and Wilson's products will be manufactured in South Africa for sale to the detergents and toiletries and other industries. In January and April 1976, new overseas marketing companies were floated in Germany and Denmark respectively, joining the existing companies in Austria, Belgium, Sweden, Finland and Holland.

In mid-1976, a new sodium tripolyphosphate plant was commissioned at Whitehaven, lifting capacity to 250,000 tonnes per annum and making the Marchon Works the largest single-site producer of this material in the world.

On 31 March 1977, a new Sports and Social Club building on the junction of the Coach Road and Corkickle was formally opened by Mr J. C. Wade, the Lord Lieutenant of Cumbria. It cost £185,000 to build and equip.

On 5 April, the largest investment in Albright and Wilson's history was announced, a £19.5 million expansion at Whitehaven for the construction of two new plants — a 160,000 tonnes per annum (P_2O_5) phosphoric acid plant and an 80,000 tonnes per annum (P_2O_5) purified phosphoric acid plant.

In 1977, the total number on the payroll at the Whitehaven Works was 2,250

In 1977, the Company acquired 45% of the equity of the Singapore based manufacturing company, now known as UIC-Marchon (Pte) Ltd and purchased Josen Chemical Company of Malaysia, the only phosphorus chemical producer in south east Asia.

The Managing Director's Office 1977-

The Detergents and Chemicals Group was disbanded on 1 June 1977. As a result the six sectors reported directly to a newly formed Managing Director's office in the Company's headquarters in London.

Mr John R. Wills was appointed Commercial Director of Albright and Wilson Ltd.

---

* Barton, Bourne, Whitehaven, Oldbury, Widnes (Anne Street), Widnes (West Bank), Stratford, Rainham, Kirkby, Portishead and Dublin, Castiglione, St Mihiel, Frosinone, Alcover, Yarraville and Box Hill.

'Marchon' became known as the Marchon Works of Albright and Wilson Ltd. It manufactures materials for the Detergents and Phosphates Sectors of the Company, and is the headquarters of the former. It is also the base for the Corporate Engineering, Commercial and Buying Departments.

The Chairman of the Marchon Works is Mr Martin D. Rowe, formerly Production Director of the late Detergents and Chemicals Group.

A further change in the management of Marchon came in July 1978 when the Government gave the go-ahead for the acquisition of Albright and Wilson Ltd by the American combine Tenneco Incorporated.

H. Edgard and Sons (London) Ltd

Another firm that came to Whitehaven during World War II was H. Edgard and Sons. They had been civil and military tailors and riding habit manufacturers in Chelsea since 1850, but they became victims of the blitz and had to find new accommodation. In 1940 they came to Whitehaven with a nucleus of key workers and found a temporary home in the old Fibre Mill in Catherine Street where they began to train local labour in the manufacture of military, naval and air force uniforms. In all over 100 different types of uniform are made. In 1947 they took over the Romney Pram Factory in Cart Road, off Preston Street, where they have a staff of about 450, mainly women, many of whom have been with the firm for a very long time.

In October 1970, a subsidiary factory, employing 100 people, was opened at Clifton, Workington.

In 1973 the share capital of the company was acquired by Francis Sumner (Holdings) Ltd.

Interior of Edgard's factory.

Cumberland Curled Hair Manufacturing Company Ltd

The factory of Cumberland Curled Hair Manufacturing Co Ltd, was established in 1945 at Tower Works, Whitehaven, by Mr K. A. Oppenheim, whose family had been in the curled hair trade since 1833. Curled hair is used for bedding and upholstery purposes.

As the business expanded, the original premises were not large enough and the factory was transferred to Richmond Hill in 1951. In 1964 they again moved to bigger premises at Silloth Airfield where they are at present operating. In 1959 they took over a public company namely, John Fraser and Sons Ltd, also producing curled hair, and this production is now amalgamated with that of Cumberland Curled Hair Manufacturing Co Ltd at Silloth.

A subsidiary company, namely Cheri Foam Ltd, was established in 1960 for the production of polyurethane foam, and this company is also operating in a separate building at Silloth, producing the foam from its prime stage of liquids and converting it to shapes and sizes.

In 1977 Mr Oppenheim retired and the Cumberland Curled Hair Manufacturing Co Ltd was acquired by C. H. Industrials Ltd of Coventry.

Beacon Mills

Mr John Pattinson who had two water mills at Eamont Bridge wanted to extend his business and in 1878 built the 'Clint' Steam Mills at Penrith, taking into partnership Mr H. C. Pattinson and Mr Henry Winter, both of Penrith.

In 1885 the business was again expanded and Mr John Pattinson removed to Whitehaven and occupied the Barracks Mills in Catherine Street. In 1889 the steamer *Margaret* was built, a few years later the *Clint*, and after that the *Busk*, to bring the firm's grain from Liverpool to Whitehaven.

In 1889 there was a dissolution of partnership, Mr John Pattinson retained the Whitehaven portion of the business and took into partnership his son, Mr John William Pattinson. In 1906 the firm was turned into a limited company and in the following year the Beacon Mills were built on the old shipbuilding site.

In 1949 the property was sold to Quaker Oats Ltd who employed about 130 people. Between 1960 and 1970 the pattern of the market and consumer demand changed and after a two-year study the company closed the Whitehaven mill in February 1972. The building was demolished in 1975.

Beacon Mills and its founder John Pattinson, c. 1908.

West Cumberland Farmers Trading Society Limited

Among the more mature business organisations in Whitehaven is the West Cumberland Farmers' Trading Society Ltd. It began in 1911 when a small group of farmers decided to form a group-buying organisation to enable them to improve the quality of the feeding stuffs they required and to obtain the financial advantages of bulk purchases.

Their Society was registered under the Industrial and Provident Societies Act, and a Committee of Management was appointed to supervise its affairs. Membership increased steadily and with it the range of commodities that were handled.

In 1919 the directors personally guaranteed the bank to the extent of £10,000 and appointed Mr John Wade as the Society's general manager and secretary. Three years later the first branch was opened at Cockermouth; and in 1932 Mr John C. Wade became general manager and secretary on the death of his father. By that time the Society had nine branches.

Within thirteen more years the number of branches had grown to thirteen, the Society had absorbed the Cumberland Egg Packers Ltd and annual sales passed the £1,000,000 mark for the first time. In 1952 sales exceeded £4,000,000 and in the following year the North of England Seed Growers Ltd and Lothian and Border Farmers transferred their business to the Society. Next year sales passed the £6,000,000 mark and the number of branches reached eighteen. In 1956 South West Farmers Ltd transferred their business to the Society and the firm of Hutchinson and McCreath Ltd was acquired. Sales exceeded £8,000,000 and there were twenty-one branches.

By 1963 sales exceeded £18,000,000 and six more branches had been opened. In 1964 the Yorkshire Farmers Ltd was absorbed with the result that in 1968 sales had reached £30,131,565. During 1977 J. R. Holland (Wholesale) Ltd of Newcastle became part of the Society's Produce Division. By this time the Society had operating points in thirteen towns in Scotland and thirty-four in England, stretching from Montrose in the north to Lincoln in the south on the easter side of the country, and from Paisley to Ormskirk on the west, and the annual turnover was more than £120,000,000.

At the present moment the Society has more than 21,000 members and, as has been indicated, covers a very large part of northern England and southern Scotland. Its services, both in the supply of requirements and in the marketing of produce, are continually expanding.

In 1967 Mr John Wade relinquished personal day-to-day control of the Society's affairs in order to devote more time to policy planning and to the overall development of the Society.

He was succeeded as General Manager and Secretary by Mr John E. Clark. Mr Clark retired in 1975 and died in May 1977. That month saw the retirement from the Board after long and distinguished service of Mr Harry Grice, of Bootle, and of Mr Alfred Watson. Mr Grice had been a director of the Society for forty-five years, vice-chairman for nine and chairman from 1969 to 1975. Mr Watson was vice-chairman of the Yorkshire Farmers when the two Societies merged in 1964 and had been a director of that Society since 1947.

Mr Frank James was acting General Manager until the appointment of Mr N. E. L. Hill.

The present chairman of the Society is Mr J. L. Blackley, J.P., of Berscar, Closeburn, Dumfriesshire.

Smith Brothers (Whitehaven) Limited

The family bookbinding and printing business known as Smith Brothers was started in 1880 by Charles James Smith, Adam Smith and Thomas Aird Smith. Originally they operated from an old brewery building on

Scotch Street, later taken over by the tannery, but the factory soon moved to a new building on the North Shore and was incorporated as a limited company in 1900. Shortly after World War II the Company expanded its activities by extending the North Shore site, followed by the leasing of the Ivy Mill, Hensingham.

They became a subsidiary of Peter Dixon (Holdings) Ltd, the Grimsby-based manufacturing company in 1963. Production capacity was increased by moving into premises at Richmond, Hensingham (previously occupied by Cumberland Curled Hair manufacturing Company Ltd) and two factories were occupied at Salterbeck Trading Estate, near Workington. One of these, housing the gravure printing plant, was totally destroyed by fire in 1970, but was soon replaced by a fine purpose-built factory.

Mardon Packaging International acquired the Company in 1973, since when there has been major expansion, particularly at Salterbeck — where most of the Industrial Estate is now occupied by Smith's factories. The vast range of flexible food packaging already produced has recently been supplemented by the manufacture of polyethylene film for Smith's own use: medical packaging and heat transfer paper — and these latter two products have achieved notable success in the export market. In addition to selling direct to twenty-six countries, Smiths now control a flexible packaging company in Miami, Florida, to gain a foothold in the vast American market.

New office accommodation has been built at the Head Office in Hensingham, and a new factory, costing £3,000,000 is in course of construction at Hensingham which will become operational in 1980. More than 1,000 workers are now employed at the various local sites.

Egremont Tubes Limited

Another subsidiary of the Mardon Packaging Group is Egremont Tubes Ltd.

The Company was first established in August 1965, at Cleator Moor in the old Market Hall building, when it was known as Scandinavian Thermotex Developments Ltd. The Market Hall was destroyed by fire in 1968 and the Company moved to Chapel Street, Egremont.

In 1969 they moved into the former Cumberland Curled Hair Manufacturing Company's building at Richmond which was already occupied by their Associated Company, Smith Brothers (Whitehaven) Ltd. An extension to the factory was completed in May 1977 and a further extension added in 1978.

The Company is concerned in the manufacture of composite containers for use in the building trade and automobile industry and also high quality work for leading Scotch whisky distillers. The extension has been built to allow for an expansion of the cardboard cable reel manufacturing business. There are about 160 employees.

James Leslie & Sons

In view of the way that Whitehaven has expanded in the past half century no account of local industry would be complete without some reference to local builders.

James Leslie started as a builder in Burnley in 1886 and by 1910 the business had become James Leslie and Sons. He came to Whitehaven in 1919 with his two sons, Robert and Jeffrey, to build the Whitehaven Corporation's first Council estate of sixty houses on Coach Road. From there they went on to become the most important building contractors in West Cumberland, particularly in the inter-war years. Mr Jeffrey Leslie left the business in 1927, but Mr Dalton Leslie, the grandson of the founder, who had begun to work for the firm in 1926, was made a partner in 1939.

Coach Road council houses under construction, 1919-20.

In all they built over 2,000 Council houses and a similar number of private houses at Whitehaven and Workington, in addition to doing commercial and industrial building in various parts of the county.

In Whitehaven, in addition to building several schools and the Kells Methodist Church, they built houses at Bransty and Kells for the Corporation and developed private housing at Midgey, the Loop Road, Church Hill, Victoria Road, Tower Hill and Leathwaite. At Workington the main private development was on the Laverock Hall estate and the Calva Brow estate.

A brochure issued in 1938 indicates that the houses on the Victoria Road estate were being offered at prices varying between £485 and £775, at Midgey between £585 and £850. On the Laverock Hall estate prices varied between £400 and £850, and at Calva Brow between £485 and £650.

Mr Dalton Leslie retired in 1972 and his yard and the remaining ground on the Leathwaite estate were taken over by Messrs J. and W. Robson Ltd.

J. & W. Robson Ltd

Messrs J. and W. Robson Ltd was established by the brothers John and William Robson after they had served their time with Leslie's. They set up on their own in 1953 and over the next few years established a reputation as housebuilders. Since 1960 they have made a major contribution to housing development at Whitehaven with their Hillcrest estate where 330 houses have been built.

In addition to the housing development they built the Goodwil Supa-Sava store on Hillcrest which cost £250,000 to build and equip, and a further £100,000 to stock. The store, which was opened on 2 June 1977, has been promoted by a group of local businessmen who have other stores at Hensingham, Cleator Moor and Hensingham.

They are rapidly completing the Leathwaite estate which they took over from Messrs J. Leslie and Sons in 1972.

Mr William Glasson

The other local builder who has added materially to the stock of private houses in Whitehaven is Mr William Glasson who started in business in 1958. After building some houses at Kells and St Bees he started building houses with a wide panoramic view over the Solway at Rannerdale Drive, Ash Grove, Beech Grove, Rosemary Close and Sycamore Close, where in all seventy-five houses have been erected. His next development will be at Low Moresby and at Rheda.

Border Engineering Contractors Ltd

Border Engineering Contractors Ltd was founded in 1920 at Carlisle by Mr David Johnston, a former R.E. officer who had won the M.C. in the First World War. After his death in 1947 he was succeeded by his son, Mr Dudley Johnston. From small beginnings it has expanded into one of the best known firms of building and civil engineering contractors in Cumbria. It now has a staff of around 700 and an annual turnover of about £7m.

In 1923 a branch office was opened at Whitehaven which became the headquarters of the Company because of the accumulation of plant there. A large yard on Coach Road was bought in 1952 and after the reorganisation in 1960 a new office block was erected there in 1961.

Contracts are undertaken throughout the North of England and South of Scotland. The range of work done is very large. Roads, bridges, reservoirs, sewerage schemes, gas mains, water mains and reclamation schemes are among the civil engineering work undertaken.

Types of building work done are also very comprehensive and include commercial and industrial buildings of all sorts and buildings for government departments and local authorities. The first building contract was for a council housing scheme at Thornhill, Egremont. After this, larger contracts were undertaken and these included the building of the Queens Cinema, the Empress Ballroom and the Swimming Baths at Whitehaven and the Ritz Cinema, Workington.

Following the formation of the West Cumberland Development Company in 1937 work was begun on the Solway Industrial Estate at Maryport and the Border Engineering Contractors Ltd built the first three factories there. They also built the West Cumberland Silk Mills at Hensingham and the Cumberland Cloth Company at Siddick. The Company has built a number of factories on the Lillyhall Industrial Estate at Distington and the industrial estate at Brampton.

The Company has diversified its interests by buying land and building private houses in several parts of the county. In Whitehaven it built a small estate of thirty-four houses called Queen's Close, on the Cleator Moor Road, and then began the Fairfield Estate, opposite the Silks Mills (220 houses) and High Meadows (300 houses) near the Loop Road.

After being associated with another plant company for many years, a new venture was started in 1968 with the formation of B.E.C. Plant Ltd. This subsidiary now operates some £1m worth of plant and machinery in the contractors' plant fields.

The Company is now controlled by three area managers, two working from Whitehaven and one from Carlisle. These are backed up by four service departments which cover estimating, quantity surveying, buying and costing. Office and finance work is controlled by the Finance Director who is also Secretary of the Company.

Thomas Milburn Ltd

The building trade in Whitehaven is the one aspect of industry in which individual enterprise has flourished most notably and the most interesting example is the success of Mr Thomas Milburn. Born in 1939 he left school at the age of fifteen to start work as an apprentice bricklayer with John Laing Construction Ltd. In 1962 he launched out on his own. His turnover in that first year was £4,000. He soon had enough orders to employ three ex-Laing workmen.

His first major contract came with the building of St Bega's Church of England School at Eskdale for £30,000. It was opened in December 1969. After that came a twenty-four unit flatlet complex at Moorclose, Workington, the building of the Cleator Moor Civic Hall, opened 6 October 1971, the Distington Crematorium ('one of the most beautiful buildings in West Cumberland'), opened February 1974. He built Phase I

Distington Crematorium, February 1974. 'One of the most beautiful buildings in West Cumberland'.

of the Port Haverigg development, an estate of thirty-five private houses at Bleach Green, part of the Pow Beck Court complex at Mirehouse, an estate of thirty-nine houses and bungalows at Cleator Moor which were sold to the local authority.

The firm has also been involved in improvement schemes to council houses on five estates (Kells, Greenbank, Moresby Parks, Siddick and Carlisle) affecting some 700 houses.

They have built a £200,000 extension to St Benedict's High School at Red Lonning, an extension to the Egremont Tubes factory, and is at present working on a new factory for Smith Brothers (Whitehaven) Ltd estimated to cost £3m. The firm's annual turnover has increased from £3m in 1974 to about £4¾m in 1978. The work-force totals 300 including forty-five office staff.

Newtown Foundry

In 1807 Edward Perry, merchant, acquired a piece of land in Newtown on which to build a foundry for the manufacture of iron and brass commodities. He went bankrupt in 1812 and in 1813 the foundry was reconveyed to the Earl of Lonsdale. It was let to various people until 1896 and in 1899 was acquired by Messrs J. Stout and Sons Ltd.

The foundry makes a wide range of castings — in cast steel, s.g. iron, alloy irons and grey iron, also non-ferrous castings.

In 1976 new electric induction melting equipment was installed. The foundry is the only one in Cumbria producing cast steel and s.g. iron. It has about twenty-five employees and in August 1978 was taken over by the Kirkbride Engineering Co Ltd.

Cumberland Motor Services Ltd

The Cumberland Motor Services Ltd was founded by Mr Henry Meageen at the end of the 1914-18 War, when he purchased six second-hand double-decker buses that had seen war service. The scheme swept on to success and extended to Egremont, Cleator Moor, Frizington, Workington, Maryport, Carlisle and Penrith and south to Millom.

Typical early Cumberland charabanc
on a day's outing.

Bransty Arch, demolished 10 March
1927 to allow freer flow of traffic
along Tangier Street.

Early Cumberland Motor Services
bus.

Bus stations were built at Workington (the first in England), Whitehaven, Keswick, Maryport and other places. Repair shops, fitted with modern plant were erected. In 1941, at the time of the death of the founder, the Company had a fleet of 178 vehicles, employed 500 workers and carried between fourteen and fifteen million passengers. In 1967 the number of vehicles had increased to 197, employees to 820 and the passenger load to twenty-six million. In 1948 the control of the Company passed to the British Transport Commission. The Company plays an important part in the industrial life of the community carrying workmen from their homes to their places of employment, but in recent years the rapid increase in the ownership of private cars has reduced its traffic. The number of vehicles has fallen to 162, workpeople to 540 and the passenger load to seventeen million for the year 1977.

Robert and Henry Jefferson, Wine Merchants

The oldest business house in Whitehaven is that of Robert and Henry Jefferson which has been established in the same premises for more than two centuries.

It owes its inception to Robert Jefferson (1704-79) who came to Whitehaven from Aikton, near Wigton, and in 1746 married Martha Skelton. His obituary describes him as 'many years a captain in a ship in the Virginia trade, and much respected as an honest man'. In common with most sea captains of the period, he traded as well as commanding his ship.

He had four children: Thomas who died in 1770 aged twenty-one; Robert who died in New York in 1783 age thirty-one; Henry (1750-1827); and Mary who died in 1787 aged twenty-three.

Henry, who lived at 4 Cross Street, followed in his father's footsteps and became a master mariner. In 1775 he was master of the snow, *Gale*, 200 tons, built at Whitehaven in 1758, and trading with Virginia. Five years later he married Ann, the daughter of Robert Tweedie of Antigua. He had two sons, Robert (1785-1848) who appears to have been born in Antigua and Henry (1800-77), baptised at Holy Trinity Church, who gave their names to the business. There were two other children, Margaret and Thomas. Robert lived for a time at Keekle Grove before buying Springfield on the death of John Ponsonby in 1841. Henry lived for some time at Hensingham House and then built Rothersyke. Primarily they were wine importers, but their interests tended to be widely spread. Their imports were carried in their own vessels.

In the second decade of the nineteenth century these were the *Thetis*, 161 tons, launched by William Wilson at Whitehaven in 1817 and the *Doris*, 133 tons, launched by Thomas and John Brocklebank in 1818. In the following decade they purchased the *Lady Shaw Stewart*, 181 tons, launched by Brocklebanks in 1827.

They brought cargoes of rum, sugar and molasses from the West Indies and wine from Portugal and Spain. A considerable portion of the sugar shipped to Whitehaven came from the Yeaman estate in Antigua owned by the Jeffersons and it was from that estate that they imported their famous rum. Another speciality was their East Indian Sherry which they shipped to the West Indies and back in their sailing ships in butts and hogsheads before bottling. It was contended that the voyage improved the flavour.

In 1834 they bought the *Derwent*, 220 tons, from Jonathan Fell at Workington, but lost the *Thetis* which foundered at sea off Cape Finisterre after striking a sunken wreck in May 1837. Two passengers and one of the crew were lost. Later they acquired the *British Queen*, launched in 1838 by Lumley Kennedy and Co, a Whitehaven shipbuilding company in which the Jeffersons were partners.

Typical Jefferson advert —
Cumberland Pacquet, 6 September 1808.

Archangel, and Swedith PITCH ;—Yellow and Amber ROSIN.
Apply to SMITH and LEDGER, Liverpool.

BOTTLES and WHISKY.
ON SALE, 300 Grofs of WINE and PORTER BOTTLES.—12 PUNCHEONS of WHISKY.—Apply to
HENRY JEFFERSON and SON.
Whitehaven, 20 Aug. 1808.   (34)

CURATE WANTED.
WANTED immediately, a CLERGY-

Later they had the *Patna*, 362 tons, launched by Brocklebanks in 1842, the *Antigua*, launched at Whitby in 1858 and the *Ehen*, 301 tons, built for them by Lumley Kennedy and Co in 1863.

The following note on the *Thetis* is illuminating: 'Left Montego Bay, Jamaica, 10 December 1828, arrived Whitehaven 11 December — sixty-two days; distance by log 5,917 miles. Crew: Captain, mate, carpenter, cook, three seamen and two boys. Cargo: rum twenty hogsheads, forty-five puncheons, thirty-one tierces; sugar twelve hogsheads, one barrel, eighty-six tierces; limejuice twenty-one hogsheads, four pipes, one puncheon; coffee thirty-five barrels, twenty tierces; pimento sixty-five bags; molasses seven puncheons; ginger ten barrels; fustic fourteen tons; timber sixty-five logs of mahogany, one log of cedar, and twenty-two spars of lancewood'.

The round trip Whitehaven-West Indies, often referred to as the 'Sugar Colonies', took five or six months and with luck two trips a year could be made. Many vessels, outward bound, carried tobacco hogsheads filled with coal, if no other cargo could be obtained, but the export of all kinds of goods was of great importance.

Both Robert and Henry Jefferson played an active part in local politics. Henry supported Matthias Attwood at the Reform Election in 1832, but his opinions underwent a change and at the time of the Corn Law agitation he became a supporter of the Liberal party. He was one of the supporters of the Town Bill and advocated the adoption of the Local Government Act. He was a member of the Town and Harbour Trustees and a magistrate. He was one of the promoters of the Whitehaven Junction Railway of which his brother Robert became chairman. He died suddenly when attending a meeting of the Board of Guardians.

The business interests of the brothers Robert and Henry Jefferson were not confined to the wine and spirits business. They were interested in shipbuilding and railway development — as has been indicated — and were trustees of the Whitehaven Joint Stock Bank.

The main organisation of the business in the second half of the nineteenth century descended on Robert's son, Henry (1824-96) who succeeded to his father's share of the enterprise, although his interests in time became equally wide as his parents . . .

He became a trustee of the Joint Stock Bank, senior trustee of the Whitehaven Savings Bank, a trustee of the Whitehaven and West Cumberland Infirmary, a Governor of St Bees Grammar School and a director, and later chairman, of the directors of the Cleator and Egremont Railway.

Lieut. R. Jefferson, Commanding The Whitehaven Troop W. & C. Y. Cavalry.

Lieut. J. H. Jefferson. Whitehaven Troop W. & C.Y. Cavalry.

In 1858 he was appointed a magistrate, made a deputy lieutenant in 1879 and in 1890 served as High Sheriff of the county.

He was married twice: first to Miss Mary Harris, of Greysouthen and later to Miss Maria Watts Gordon, of Dumfries. On the death of his uncle he was joined in the business by his cousin Robert Jefferson, of Rothersyke. The latter died unmarried and on his demise Rothersyke was bought by Lord Leconfield.

Henry's son Robert (1857-1942) lived for a time at Rosehill before he inherited Springfield. He carried on the family business at Lowther Street and maintained the family tradition of community service.

He was appointed a magistrate in 1891, was for nineteen years deputy-chairman of the Whitehaven Bench and chairman for twelve years. He was also a county alderman.

He joined the Westmorland and Cumberland Yeomanry in 1885 and became the first commanding officer of the Whitehaven Troop which he and his brother Hugh raised in 1896. He retired from the Yeomanry in 1901 with the rank of honorary major.

At one time he was one of the leading steeplechase riders in the county and rode his own horses to victory in many events in the North of England. An injury received while riding his gelding, Balcary, at Carlisle caused him to retire from steeplechasing. He was the founder and for thirty-three years president of the Hound Trailing Association.

He died on 31 May 1942 and the management of the business passed to his son Henry (b. 1896) who had entered it in 1920 and received a thorough grounding before being made a partner in 1924. Henry Jefferson served in the First World War with the Cumberland and Westmorland Yeomanry and later with the 5th Dragoon Guards. Like his father he served for many years on the Cumberland County Council.

He has two daughters, Constance and Elizabeth, who are both active in the business. In May 1970 Elizabeth Jefferson was awarded the Master's Certificate of the Wine and Sprits Trade Association.

Chapter 20

Famous personalities

Archbishop Edmund Grindal, 1519~83

Portrait of Grindal from Strype's biography.

Edmund Grindal was born in the parish of St Bees in the year 1519, but whether he was born at St Bees itself or at Hensingham, as stated by his biographer John Strype, is difficult to say. His elder brother Robert (d. 1658) occupied what William Jackson is convinced is the ancestral estate at the village of St Bees. That there were Grindals at Hensingham is proved by the burial record of another Robert Grindal, of 'Hensingham', which is recorded in the St Bees register under the date 14 January 1587.

Grindal went to Cambridge in 1536 where he graduated M.A. in 1541, the same year as Edwin Sandys, whose forebears came from Rottington. Both were men of a similar outlook with a strong puritan strain in their characters. Both went into exile during the reign of Queen Mary. On 21 December 1559, Sandys was consecrated bishop of Worcester and Grindal bishop of London. Owing to his sympathy with the puritan clergy Grindal found his position as bishop of London a difficult one. The diocese of London was the chief centre of puritanism and, as the Queen and Archbishop Parker wished to bring them into obedience to the Act of Uniformity, Grindal was not the best man to achieve this, so that when the Archbishop of York became vacant in 1560 he was promoted and Sandys followed him as bishop of London. Grindal's life may well have been happier had he remained at York, but on the death of Parker in 1575 Cecil urged the Queen to offer the see of Canterbury to Grindal. At this time the Queen's policy required a leaning towards puritanism and Grindal moved south, Sandys taking his place at York. Almost as soon as he had been appointed the royal policy changed and the Queen and Grindal found themselves at odds. The subject that caused the Queen's greatest displeasure was prophesyings or the meetings of the clergy for the exposition and discussion of scripture. In 1577, on his refusal to suppress the 'prophesyings' he was suspended from his jurisdictional but not from his spiritual functions. These were restored to him in 1582, but in the previous year he had been troubled by a cataract on his eyes and it became obvious that he must resign. Before the arrangements were made he died in his house at Croydon on 6 July 1583. Previously, in April 1583, he endowed a free grammar school at St Bees and made bequests to Pembroke Hall and Christ's College, Cambridge and Queen's College, Oxford.

James Ray

Little is known of the life of James Ray, a native of Whitehaven, apart from the fact that he had certain military leanings. As a youth he served with the Hanoverian forces against the Earl of Derwentwater in 1715. When, in 1745, he learned of the Young Pretender's impending attack on Carlisle he was of a sufficiently militant turn of mind to join the Duke of Cumberland and to follow him throughout the rest of the campaign to the final battle at Culloden.

He appears to have kept a diary of his experiences, for he published a small pamphlet entitled *The Acts of the Rebels, Written by an Egyptian: Being an Abstract of the Journal of Mr James Ray, of Whitehaven: Volunteer under the Duke of Cumberland.* This was followed by *A Compleat History of the Rebellion.*

The bibliographical history of *A Compleat History of the Rebellion* is extremely interesting. Some years ago Mr R. C. Jarvis made a study of it while doing some research into printers' ornaments of the mid-eighteenth century provincial presses as part of a wider study of the anonymous pamphlet literature of the period. As a result he came to some conclusions about the different editions which he published in *Notes and Queries*, September 1945.

The first edition of this book was 'Printed for the Author by Robert Whitworth', of Manchester. The peculiar condition of the tail-piece used led Mr Jarvis to make the date of publication 1747 and he says: 'On

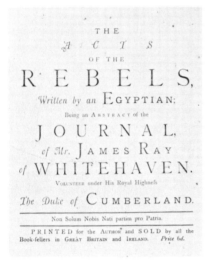

THE
A C T S
OF THE
R E B E L S,
Written by an EGYPTIAN:
Being an ABSTRACT of the
J O U R N A L,
of Mr. J A M E S R A Y
of W H I T E H A V E N.
VOLUNTEER under His Royal Highness
The Duke of CUMBERLAND.

Non Solum Nobis Nati partim pro Patria.

PRINTED for the AUTHOR and SOLD by all the
Book-sellers in GREAT BRITAIN and IRELAND. *Price 6d.*

Title page of *The Acts of the Rebels.*

looking through Ray for some internal evidence in conformation of this later date one is surprised to find an account of the execution of the last of the rebel lords, which took place on Tower Hill in the April of 1747 — surprised, that is to say, that a work containing such an account of incidents which took place in 1747 should have remained so long dated as 1746.

'Although it is not possible, by reason of space, to report in detail the result of close collation of the various editions, it can be said that Ray's History does not appear to have been set up again from the original 'copy' after Whitworth's Manchester edition.'

The York 1749 edition was set up by John Jackson direct from Whitworth; the Bristol 1750, printed by Samuel and Felix Fairley, was set up from the York of 1749; the York of 1754 from the Bristol 1750; the York of 1755 from the 1754; and Robert Browne's London edition of 1758 from one or other of the York editions of 1754 or 1755. 'All this can be shown by the study of certain literals and other misprints.'

Mr Jarvis's study of other contemporary accounts of the Rebellion has proved that, despite a long held opinion to the contrary, Ray's account of the Rebellion is not entirely his own work. 'He writes a unique and obviously genuine story of his own adventures and then perhaps like so many others before him — and since — he seems to have suffered at the hands of his editors. Very likely it is they who pad it and spin it out and will not let him say a word of his own. A genuine story — first hand and first class — has been overlaid and interlarded with a whole lot of second rate, secondhand stuff.'

A Compleat History of the Rebellion is a straight forward history written largely from the point of view of one who has served in the campaign. *The Acts of the Rebels* is a much slighter piece, written in a pseudo-scriptural style, on the lines of 'The Book of Kings', rendered peculiarly amusing by a half-chapter on the evils of tea-drinking added to the last chapter of the first edition by some bright spark in the printing works and apologised for by Ray in the second edition.

James Ray is recorded in the 1762 census as living in Howgill Street, but whether this is the same person as the author of the *Compleat History* is not clear. If it is he lived to a ripe old age for the *Cumberland Pacquet* for 11 November 1789, has an advertisement for the sale of the 'house in Howgill Street, heretofore the property of Mr James Ray. Also Pew No.3 in the James Street Chapel'.

Dean Swift

Portrait of Dean Swift.

Jonathan Swift (1667-1745), Dean of St Patrick's, Dublin, and the author of *Gulliver's Travels*, was the son of Jonathan Swift, Steward of the King's Inns, Dublin, who died leaving his wife in straitened financial circumstances. These were ameliorated by the kindness of Godwin Swift, but the poverty of his early days left its mark upon him.

When he was about a year old an incident occurred which calls for more careful examination than it has hitherto received, because it raises a spate of questions. In an autobiographical fragment Swift wrote: 'His nurse, who was a woman of Whitehaven, being under an absolute necessity of seeing one of her relations, who was then extremely sick and from whom she expected a legacy and, being at the same time extremely fond of the infant, she stole him on shipboard unknown to his mother and uncle and carried him with her to Whitehaven, where he continued for almost three years. For, when the matter was discovered, his mother sent orders by all means not to hazard a second voyage till he could be better able to bear it.

'The nurse was so careful of him that, before he returned, he had learned to spell; and by the time he was three years old he could read any chapter of the Bible.'

This prototype of Robert Louis Stevenson's 'Cummie' is a complete mystery. We have no indication of her age or how she came to be employed as a nurse in Dublin. Was she a slip of a girl or a mature woman? What were her domestic circumstances? Who was the sick relative in the background whose extreme illness brought her back to Whitehaven in a hurry? The St Bees parish registers for the period around 1668 are in too bad a state to afford any clue.

This is a pity because she must have moved in a circle which had some sort of education and she herself must have had a reasonable education, for Swift implies that it was she who taught him to spell and encouraged him to read.

Neither do we know where Swift stayed during those early years, but a local tradition links his name with the Red Flag, an old public-house on Prospect adjoining which was a bowling green. Its position is clearly shown on Matthias Read's famous sketch of Whitehaven in 1738, and both house and green were in existence in 1690, but whether they were in existence twenty or so years earlier is not clear.

If Swift's nurse took up residence at the Red Flag, or bowling green house, she would be in touch with the more affluent and influential members of the community who spent their leisure time there.

Whatever may have happened to Swift after his return to Dublin to sour his disposition there is no evidence that his sojourn in Whitehaven was an unhappy one.

Evelyn Hardy, in her book *The Conjured Spirit*, says that Swift's nurse was Irish not Cumbrian, but that she was married to a Whitehaven man.

Denis Johnston *In Search of Swift*, says that Jonathan Swift the elder may have been dead at least ten months, if not more, before the birth of his putative and celebrated son. He insists that there is a reprehensible amount of mystery about the place and circumstances of Swift's birth and about his to-ing and fro-ing to England as an infant.

Petrus Pindarus, Secundus

John Wolcot (1738-1819), who wrote under the name of 'Peter Pindar', was one of the prominent satirists of the eighteenth century. He is of special interest to us because of 'A Commiserating epistle to James Lowther, Earl of Lonsdale, 1791', which he wrote attacking the Earl for his treatment of the townspeople.

Mining operations in the George Street and Michael Street area had caused a subsidence and damaged some property. Not unnaturally the owners wanted compensation, but his Lordship retaliated by closing the coal pits, thereby forcing the claimants to waive their demands.

Wolcot had many imitators; one, C. F. Lawler, wrote under the same name; others under very similar names, such as Peter Pindar junior, Peter Pindar minimus, Peter Pindar the elder, and Peter Pindar the younger.

An interesting pamphlet was acquired by the Whitehaven Public Library some time ago, entitled *An Irregular Poetical Epistle to the Right Honourable James, Earl of Lonsdale, Viscount Lonsdale by Petrus Pindarus, Secundus, Gent.*, privately printed in 1794. It was occasioned by the seizure of a theatrical company as vagrants and the imprisonment of the manager and the leading actor. The writer attacks the Earl very strongly and bitterly for his high handedness and describes him as:

> Cumberland's King —
> The God, omnipotent, of poor Whitehaven!
> Who, with a nod, their earth can'st shake,
> An make their tott'ring houses quake,
> Whene'er the Pigmies teize;
> Who, with the waving of thy hand,
> Their weather-cocks can'st all command,
> And bind their swelling seas.

Who, if the puny rogues complain,
Can'st bring pale famine's meagre train,
Beneath thy dreadful banners;
And more to prove thy deep control,
Can'st fairly lock up all their coal,
And starve 'em into manners!

The writer concludes with the lines:
. . . Thine, is a nobler spirit, which in HELL
Its actions glorious, in this world, may tell;
Til Lucifer, grown jealous at thy fame,
Shall kick thee back again to earth and shame;
Ev'n to Whitehaven — where they restless soul
Shall seem to labour in thy pits of coal;
But harmless then; and doubly, trebly pain'd
To see MILLENIUM — PARADISE REGAIN'D!
To see that down-trod spot, that injur'd town,
Rise into happiness — to peace renown;
Another wonder of the world, they blood,
A LOWTHER , MILD, BENEFICENT AND GOOD!

The author in this piece of invective, quite unparalleled in our local literature, is unknown, but surmise connects the work with the name of Isaac Littledale, a local merchant, who was later to stand as the Reform candidate in Whitehaven's first Parliamentary election.

John Roach, 1748-1819

Of all the maritime and seafaring people associated with Whitehaven, the only person who has left a published account of his adventures is a humble seaman named John Roach.

Born in Whitehaven in 1748, Roach seems to have had an innate love of the sea. At the age of eleven he was apprenticed to Captain John Steele of the *Leviathan* of Workington. On Christmas Eve, 1762, the *Leviathan* was wrecked off Dublin and our youthful Argonaut joined Captain Falcon, of the *Heart of Oak* of Workington, to finish his apprenticeship.

Three years later an urge to see the world sent him aboard the *Hawk*, commanded by Captain Falcon's brother, Michael, who took him to St Petersburg. The Falcon family were among the pioneer shipbuilders at Workington where at least three generations were actively engaged in the trade.

In the following year Roach sailed to Norway. Still unsated, he joined a French sloop bound for Dunkirk, via Waterford, but was once more nearly drowned when a storm drove them ashore at Balbriggen. Even this did not deter him, for he immediately joined the *Earl of Chatham* of London, which was bound for Jamaica. On his return he re-entered the Irish coal trade for six months, but tiring of this, he shipped from Dublin to Bristol, where he joined the *Jane*, a slaver, which picked up 500 negroes on the Guinea coast and then sailed for Jamaica.

After several adventures in the neighbourhood of Jamaica he was engaged by Captain Woodhouse, of the sloop *Betsey*, to go with him to the Bay of Honduras. During this voyage he was informed of the Captain's true intention — to go up the Isthmus of Darien for mules and horned cattle. About 10 April 1770, they arrived at Nombre de Dios. The Captain got what he wanted, but sailed off without paying the Spaniards.

On arrival at Cheriqui Lagoon, Roach was sent ashore with five negroes to collect firewood, but was captured by natives who made him a slave. After two-and-a-half years' servitude he escaped into Spanish territory. Here he was taken for a spy and for long, weary years he languished in various Spanish prisons before ultimately being sentenced to life imprisonment in the mines of Old Spain.

When, eventually, he was put aboard a vessel bound for Europe he contracted paralysis on the voyage and was put ashore at Havana. At the end of a year he was sent with other English prisoners to Jamaica, when whence he found his way back to Whitehaven.

For reasons which I need not enter here, it is almost impossible to obtain corroborative evidence of Roach's narrative, but a statement published in the *Cumberland Pacquet* of 10 June 1783, seems to indicate that his contemporaries did not disbelieve his tale.

On his return to Whitehaven Roach wrote up the story of his adventures and his little book ran to two editions which were published by Francis Briscoe, a local printer. But what happened to him in the thirty-six years which intervened between his return and his death on 20 May 1819 is not known. The local press briefly recorded his death in the workhouse at Workington at the age of seventy-eight.

An edition of his book was also published at Dumfries.

Dr William Brownrigg

Dr William Brownrigg, physician and chemist, was born at High Close Hall, Plumbland on 24 March 1711, where his father was agent for the estate. After studying medicine at London for two years he completed his medical education at Leydon, graduated M.D. in 1737 and published an elaborate thesis, *De Praxi Medica ineunda*. Entering upon practice at Whitehaven, he became interested in the gaseous exhalations from the coal mines in the area.

In 1741 he forwarded several papers upon the subject to the Royal Society and was elected a Fellow, but his papers were not published, at his own request, as he intended to prepare a complete work. He had a laboratory erected at Whitehaven and as a result of his friendship with Carlisle Spedding, Sir James Lowther's mining engineer, was supplied with a constant stream of methane or firedamp from the mines and this was fed into furnaces over which he managed to secure considerable variations of heat.

In this he anticipated the National Coal Board by over two centuries.

His papers brought him into communication with Sir Hans Sloane, Dr Hales and other eminent men. With their advice and help he undertook to prepare a general history of the damps, the outline of which Hales read and submitted to the Royal Society in 1741.

He learned to foretell explosions in the mines by the rapidity of fall of the barometer and was often consulted by proprietors of collieries.

An extract from the essay, read before the Royal Society in 1741 *On the Uses of Knowledge of Mineral Exhalations when applied to discover the Principles and Properties of Mineral Waters, the Nature of Burning Mountains, and those Poisonous Lakes called Averni*, was published in *Philosophical Transactions* as an appendix to his paper on *Spa Water*. In it he endeavours to prove that the distinguishing qualities of most mineral waters depend upon a particular kind of air, which forms a considerable part of their composition, and that this air differs in no respect from choke-damp.

Sulphurous waters he also shows to depend for its special qualities on a kind of firedamp. He had a remarkable prescience of the importance of these gases and came very near to being a chemical discoverer of the first rank.

He was probably the first person acquainted with the acid nature of fixed air, or carbonic acid gas. A visit to Spa was subsequently made the occasion of some experiments on the air given off by spa waters. These are reported in *Philosophical Transactions* and for this work Brownrigg received the Copley medal of the Royal Society. He showed that this gas was destructive to animal life. He also proved that the same gas was the solvent of various earths in the water and that when these had been precipitated from it they could be redissolved after again dissolving the gas in the water.

In several particulars his researches were parallel with those of Priestley, Black and Cavendish. His later observations are given in *Philosophical Transactions.*

In 1748 Brownrigg published a valuable book *On the Art of Making Common Salt,* and an abridgment of this, by W. Watson, F.R.S., was inserted in *Philosophical Transcactions.* He was the first to give any account of platinum, or as it was variously known at the time – platina di pinto, juan blanco or white gold. The specimens upon which he experimented were brought to England in 1741 by a relative, Charles Wood, who had been an assayer in Jamaica. Brownrigg presented them to the Royal Society together with an account of their properties.

In 1771 he published his *Considerations on the Means of preventing the Communication of Pestilential Contagion and the Methods by which it is conveyed from one Person to another.* In 1772 Benjamin Franklin visited him at the family home at Ormathwaite, near Keswick, an incident that is indicative of Brownrigg's international standing.

In 1783 he and his friend Dr Joshua Dixon established the Whitehaven Dispensary that was the forerunner of the hospital service.

He died at Ormathwaite on 6 January 1800 and is buried in Crosthwaite Church.

William Litt

William Litt, the youngest of the four sons of John Litt, was born at Bowthorn on 8 November 1785. His father, who later moved to Netherend, Hensingham, was a man of considerable standing, holding the lucrative officer of Commissioner for the Inclosure of Waste Lands, as well as being engaged in agricultural and mining pursuits. The children had all the advantages which flow from a liberal education and even as a boy William was distinguished by his literary attainments.

At one time his parents intended that he should be educated for the ministry, but as his interests were all on athletics and field sports of all descriptions, the idea was quietly dropped and the boy grew up at Netherend, taking such part in the life of the farm as suited his inclination or convenience.

At that time wrestling was the favourite recreation of the Cumberland peasantry and into this he entered with energy and enthusiasm. He won a famous bout on Arlecdon Moor on 26 October 1811 against Tom Nicholson, at that time the most outstanding wrestler in the county.

The stake money was sixty guineas – at that time the largest sum that had ever been contended for in any ring in the north.

He moved in a literary circle which included the 'Gentle, gifted, eloquent M'Combe; Wilson Ledger, the manly and independent editor of the Liberal *Gazette*, when Liberalism was a dangerous doctrine; Todd, the "Leander", whose name was once so familiar in the Poet's corner of our newspapers, a powerful satirist, a man of great genius and a true poet, with all the excitability and eccentricity of his order'.

Litt himself was a frequent contributor to the pages of both the *Pacquet* and the *Gazette,* but more especially of the former and his verse was of a high standard.

About this time he launched out in business as a brewer but found it easier to get orders than to extract money from his clients and within a short time lost the money he had invested.

Litt's father died in 1819, but his large speculations had latterly been less successful than usual and he had been heavily involved in an expensive Chancery suit. In consequence, the Netherend home was broken up and William, who had married in 1817, was left to his own resources.

In 1823 he published *Wrestliana, or an Historical Account of Ancient*

Poem by William Litt. Written for the Anniversary of the Birth of the Rt Hon The Earl of Lonsdale, 29 December 1825.

and Modern Wrestling, a book which attained great popularity through-out Cumberland and Westmorland and which was favourably reviewed by Professor Wilson in *Blackwood.*

The success of *Wrestliana* encouraged Litt to write a novel, *Henry and Mary,* which was published in 1825. Although it has the merit of illuminating the life of West Cumberland in the latter part of the eighteenth century, its composition was too hasty to meet the unqualified approval of the critics and Litt lost interest in his literary pursuits.

In 1832 he migrated to Canada where he died in 1847.

Joseph Hodgson

Joseph Hodgson — *Putty Joe.*

Joseph Hodgson, known colloquially as 'Putty Joe' from the fact that in his latter years he was an itinerant glazier, was one of Whitehaven's real characters. Born in Whitehaven in 1810, his father died when he was only two years old. His mother was left with four young children, but, despite her extreme poverty, she strove to get Joseph the elements of education. Learning did not come easily to him and when his mother married again his step-father saw to it that he and his eldest brother were taken to work in William Pit where the boys earned fivepence a day for minding trap doors.

In 1850 he published a *Memoir* of his various itineraries through the United Kingdom in which he described his early experiences. Pit work was hard and hazardous and Hodgson returned to it only as a very last resort. There was an explosion in William Pit in which fifteen men were killed, from which his 'brother Thomas and one Peter Hine were the last two men got out with life'.

Later he and a William McCullock were discharged from their job as plasterers and went to work at William Pit, but 'in course of a few weeks the pit fired or exploded, when he with thirty-one more human beings and eighteen horses were also killed'.

On a previous occasion Hodgson was engaged in leading coal to the shaft when he got caught between a basket and the horse's hindquarters. Four hewers 'immediately came to my assistance and raised the basket up warily off my back and gathered me out from amongst the horse's legs, kindly bearing me up, until I recovered my breath and presenting me with some liquid from a bottle, and soon as I recovered from my

Two of Joseph Hodgson's many publications.

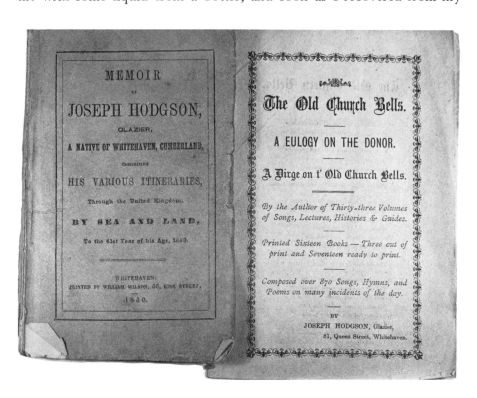

dilemma, I walked towards the pit shaft; but when I ascended near to the surface, the pit exploded at the place of my misfortune and killed the four men that so recently saved me from strangling'.

He spent many years tramping the countryside, eking out a bare existence as a packman and seller of broadsheets. Many of these sheets he wrote and published himself. The quality of his poetry, however, was not very high. His *Poem on the Tay Bridge Disaster* recalls the great McGonigal:

> O'er Scotland now a gloom is cast
>   by the disaster in the Tay,
> When all the passengers and train
>   Were in a moment call'd away.
> All the tickets were collected
>   At St Fort station in the train;
> Three minutes after all were drowned
>   And sank beneath the stormy main . . .

In 1875 he published *Greenhowe's Cemetery*, a description of the new cemetery on the Low Road with an account of some of the people buried in it. At the end of the pamphlet there is a list of his other publications.

William Thomson, D.D., F.R.S.

William Thomson, D.D., F.R.S., was born at Whitehaven on 11 February 1819, the eldest son of the family of seven of John Thomson. His grandfather was William Thomson, believed to have been a minister of the Scottish Church with some connection with Bridge of Allan in Stirlingshire; but what little evidence there is on the subject goes to show that in later life he lived and died in Glasgow where he was buried with some of his children.

John Thomson, with a brother Robert, and two sisters Jean and Margaret, were brought up by their father's brother Walter Thomson, in Whitehaven. Not a great deal is known about Walter Thomson but he was sufficiently well-off to set his nephew John on a road which led to success.

John in his old age was of middle height, of spare build, reserved temperament and of regular habits. It is related of him that he always rose at 6 am; and indeed his last illness, which culminated in his death at the age of eighty-seven, was caused by a fall in treading on and tripping over a cat in the dark early one morning. His strength of will and purpose had stood him in good stead in business and in his position of Chairman of the Whitehaven Magistrates which he occupied for many years. Ample evidence exists of his taking part in the corporate life of the town and of the esteem in which he was held by fellow citizens.

He married Ann Home, daughter of Patrick Home, one of the claimants to the Earldom of Marchmont and Barony of Polwarth.

Their eldest son William received his earliest education at a small academy in Whitehaven under the Rev. Archibald Jack, the Congregational Minister who subsequently became Chairman of the Educational Union.

In 1831, aged eleven, he was sent to Shrewsbury and from there went on to Oxford where he graduated B.A. in 1840 and M.A. in 1844. In 1842 he published a treatise *Outlines of the Laws of Thoughts* and was ordained deacon, taking priest's order in 1843. His growing reputation as a logician led the authorities of Queen's College to recall him in 1847 to act as college tutor. In 1853 he was chosen Bampton lecturer taking as his subject *The atoning work of Christ*. These lectures attracted great attention.

On the question of academic organisation, Thomson was strongly in favour of reform and wrote a pamphlet *An open college best of all* (1854).

In 1855 Thomson contributed a paper *Crime and its excuses* to *Oxford Essays* but by 1861 he had parted company with Benjamin Jowett and the newer school of broad churchmen and in answer to their opinions edited a volume of essays, entitled *Aids to Faith*, which contained a contribution by himself on *The Death of Christ* which was a popular restatement of his Bampton lectures.

In the latter year he was created Bishop of Gloucester and in 1863 Archbishop of York. In 1861, also, his sermons preached in 'Lincoln's Inn Chapel' were published while in 1870 the second edition of his *Life in the light of God's word* appeared.

The only occasion in his latter life when he came back to Whitehaven was to perform the official opening of the Public Library in 1888.

He died at Bishopthorpe on Christmas Day, 1890.

Anthony Benson Pears

Anthony Benson Pears was born at Whitehaven in 1853 and after leaving school was apprenticed to a draper following that occupation until, in 1881, he was compelled by ill-health to abandon it. Later he took a responsible post at the Whitehaven Tannery where he remained until 1906 when failing health caused him to retire.

He travelled extensively on the Continent and much of what he saw is reflected in his verse and prose. He died at Cockermouth on 31 October 1929 at the age of seventy-six.

E. R. Denwood says of him: 'But the verse of A. B. Pears is the work of a man whose thought and speech are coloured by much study of philosophical and religious speculation and it is into his own heart and mind rather than into any visible phenomena that he looks for the answers to the questions he would fain understand. The average man or woman is satisfied with the apparent reality of things as they are or as they seem to be, and the poet who would disturb their equanimity and faith in the rightness of established things will never have many readers.

'It is always easier to pluck the flowers than to dig out the roots of things; hence the popularity of the superficial poets — the Kiplings, the Masefields and the Newbolts, whose philosophy is as shallow as is their message. The men and women who make us think too strenuously are never acclaimed by the crowd.'

A collection of A. B. Pear's verse was published in 1920 under the title *Short Swallow Flights of Song*. The quality of his poetry can be judged from his *God and Nature*.

> Because I may not see God's face,
> And all his mighty purpose trace,
> Because I may not see the end,
> To which the lines of being tend.
>
> Because in the intricate plan,
> Which points from monad up to man,
> The kindred sequence silent stands,
> Like lingering touch of parting hands.
>
> Must I deny creative skill,
> Wisdom unerring, and unfaltering will
> If in the type the abstract lives,
> No form, but still a shadow gives.
>
> If but the shade of God I see,
> Must I deny infinity,
> The shade the substance half reveals,
> The ultimate it half conceals.

John H. Pears

Anthony Benson Pears had a younger brother, John, born at Whitehaven in 1861. In his fifth year he graduated from the dames' school which he attended to a small private school run by a despotic character who believed in the constant application of the cane. Before Pears was rescued from this 'long narrow torture-chamber at the summit of a winding flight of stairs' his nerves were wrecked, his health spoiled and his vision permanently injured. Fortunately he was transferred to Ghyll Bank School and of John Nixon he later wrote: 'I shall always revere the memory of that kind and efficient teacher to whose influence I owe so much'. At this school he was given an interest in religion, politics and literature, subjects which were to have a profound influence on his life.

Later he took a keen interest in the public life of Cockermouth and was five times Chairman of the Urban District Council there. He became a Justice of the Peace and was for many years a local preacher in the Methodist Church.

Lord Lawson

Jack Lawson, Lord Lawson of Beamish.

John James Lawson, better known as 'Jack' Lawson, was born at 5 Dobsons Buildings, Albion Street on 16 October 1881, and in the spring of 1883 was taken by his parents to a larger house at Kells. There the family lived until about 1889 when they moved to Flimby and thence in the following year to Bolden Colliery, Co. Durham.

At the age of three he was sent to the Earl of Lonsdale's School on Monkwray where he got the beginnings of his education. By the time he was twelve he was at work in the pit.

In 1907 he was given an opportunity to go to Ruskin College and there spent two years. In 1919 he was elected Labour M.P. for Chester-le-Street and represented that constituency until 1949. During his parliamentary career he held offices of Financial Secretary to the War Office, 1924; Parliamentary Secretary, Ministry of Labour, 1929-31; and Minister of State for War, 1945-46.

The story of the early part of Jack Lawson's life is told in his very expressive autobiography, *A Man's Life*, which was first published in August 1932 and which has several times been reprinted. No one has yet produced an anthology on 'Mothers' but when it does appear his description of his mother will be a necessary inclusion. It is one of the most vivid prose passages of its kind to be found anywhere.

Two years later he published his only novel, *Under the Wheels*, which was well received. One critic said of it: 'His miners, if crushed beneath the wheels of industry, are none the less living human beings with human needs, relationships and aspirations. And although he makes his attitude abundantly clear on every page he always writes in terms of art rather than of propaganda or criticism.'

Similarly, when *Peter Lee* appeared in 1936: 'He writes with force and common sense and he brings to his task a fund of humanity and of information that lightens the book even though it is so closely packed'.

Five years later Lawson published another mining biography, *The Man in the Cap*, a life of Herbert Smith.

In 1945 he published *Who Goes Home? Broadcasts and Sketches*, a short series of essays which deserve to be much better known if only for the tribute he pays to books in 'What books have meant to me'.

Lord Lawson died 3 August 1965.

Ann Raney Coleman

From a local standpoint the most fascinating event of the 1970s was the publication of *Victorian Lady on the Texas Frontier*, the journal of

Ann Raney Coleman, edited by C. Richard King. Born on 5 November 1810 and baptised at St James' Church, Whitehaven, 17 December 1811, Ann Raney was the second child of John Raney, a Whitehaven merchant and his wife Ann Barker. Her father had inherited £50,000 and four properties on the death of his father. Her mother had had a dowry of £3,000 on the occasion of her marriage. Her mother's eldest brother, Richard Barker, owned a tallow factory and had West Indian shipping interests. Her mother's sister, Elizabeth, married William Bowes, a prosperous Whitehaven shipbuilder, while another sister, Margaret, married Thomas Hammond, a ship-broker.

Ann Raney received a gentle upbringing and moved in a very affluent circle. Part òf John Raney's inheritance was a share in the banking house of Hope, Raney, Johnstone and Co which went bankrupt in June 1826, bringing ruin to him and to his family.

The family moved to Liverpool where John Raney engaged in a business venture which failed. As a result he and his younger son, John, went abroad to Texas to start a new life. George Alexander, the elder son, was in the merchant navy and went on to command one of the Brocklebank ships. On 14 February 1832, Mrs Raney, Ann and the younger daughter Mary, who was then a little over sixteen, sailed from Liverpool for Texas. Before they arrived John Raney, junior, had died. They settled eight miles from Brazoria but the climate or living conditions were against them. Ann succumbed to an illness of several weeks' duration. John Raney's health gave way and he died. His wife died nine days later. Mary became ill but recovered.

On 14 February 1833, exactly one year from the day that the family had sailed from Liverpool, Ann married John Thomas at Brazoria. Mary married a Major Samuel Hoit on 10 April 1834. Mary's husband was an alcoholic and died not long after their wedding. She was not long a widow, she married Major Benjamin Harrison, a son of President William Henry Harrison.

With the outbreak of the Mexican War of 1836 the Thomas's had to abandon their plantation and flee to Louisiana. John Thomas died in 1847 and Ann married a Mr Coleman whom she divorced some eight years later. Major Harrison died and Mary married a Mr Smith. She died 10 June 1853 and her husband three months later, leaving a daughter Alice who had been born in 1850.

Ann had three children by her first husband: Edmond St John Hawkins, George Alexander and Victoria. Both boys died young, the death of Edmond being particularly grievous to his father.

Ann's marriage to Coleman was a disaster. She describes him as 'unjust and cruel' in his treatment of her. After her divorce she was forced back on her own resources and she had to eke out a livelihood as a peripatetic housekeeper and teacher until 1887 when, at the age of seventy-seven, she was awarded a tiny pension of eight dollars a month.

She died ten years later in March 1897. During that period she wrote for her niece, Alice Smith, the story of her life and adventures.

This unsophisticated account, telling of her childhood in Cumberland and life in America where she survived the Mexican War of 1836, the privations and difficulties of frontier life in a country where medical knowledge and medical care was primitive and life in Texax during the Civil War when the town of Lavaca where she was then residing was bombarded and destroyed by the Unionist Army, makes compelling reading. The American side of the story has been closely researched by the editor. The journal, the original of which has been purchased by Duke University Library, has been described as 'the greatest find in Texas history for years', still requires some research on the early years to clarify the history of the Raney family and the events leading up to John Raney's bankruptcy. According to the will of John Raney, senior, who died in 1811, his son inherited property in the parishes of Ponsonby, Torpenhow, Arlecdon, and Distington, a dwelling house in Marlborough Street, and a warehouse in Queen Street.

John Fletcher Miller

John Fletcher Miller (1816-56), the eldest son of William Miller, was born at 7 High Street on 20 June 1816. William and his elder brother Joseph were tanners carrying on the business which their father, George Miller, had established half a century earlier. The Millers were Quakers and John was sent to the school at Kendal on which John Dalton and his brother Jonathan had left such a strong mark. At that time it was under the management of Samuel Marshall. There he soon showed a keen interest in science, particularly medicine.

His desire, which was fully supported by his parents, was for a career in medicine but his health became impaired to such a degree that it became impracticable. Instead, he turned his attention to literature, the natural sciences and languages.

In the hope of benefitting his health he left England in October 1837 for Sydney, New South Wales, where he remained for several months, returning home by way of Valparaiso, Chile, reaching England in January 1839.

At the age of fifteen he had begun a meteorological register which was continued, almost without interruption, until the day he died.

In 1844 John Fletcher Miller began at his own expense a very extensive series of experiments 'On the Fall of Rain in the English Lake District'. Early in 1846 he extended his observations to the mountains and the paper he wrote was read on his behalf by a Col. Sabine at a meeting of the Royal Society on 18 May 1848 and published in *Philosophical Transactions, Part I*, in the following year.

In all he contributed five papers on rainfall in the Lake District to the Royal Society and was elected a Fellow in 1850. One of his papers contrasts the rainfall in the Lake District with that in the mountains of India, and the following points emerge from his studies:

> '1. That we have a tropical fall of rain in the temperate zone and that in some portions of the Lake District the annual quantity occasionally amounts to 180 inches.

> '2. That the fall in a single month at several stations in the Lake District in very wet seasons considerably exceeds thirty inches, as was the case at Seathwaite, Gatesgarth and Langdale Head in December 1852.

> '3. That the maximum fall in twenty-four hours is nearly seven inches and in forty-eight consecutive hours ten inches nearly.

Anti-slavery movement notice. John Fletcher Miller's father was a strong supporter of the movement.

C U M B E R L A N D   P A C Q U

NEGRO SLAVERY
IN THE WEST INDIES.

A PUBLIC MEETING of the Inhabitants of Whitehaven will be held in the FRIENDS' MEETING HOUSE, Sandhills Lane, on FRIDAY Evening the 22d of October, 1830, to consider the Propriety of petitioning Parliament to pass a Law forthwith for the early and utter Extinction of a System of Bondage, which has too long been suffered to outrage the Feelings and disgrace the Character of a Christian People: and also to establish an ANTI-SLAVERY SOCIETY for Whitehaven and its Vicinity.

Mr. WILLIAM MILLER has consented to take the Chair at Seven o'Clock precisely.

These quantities, expecially the annual fall, are, it is believed, unprecedented, except on some of the mountain ranges of India.

'4. The maximum fall of rain is found at or above 2,000 feet above sea level, above which elevation the quantity rapidly diminishes.'

To obtain the results he required he maintained thirty-five rain guages in different parts of the Lake District. Looking after them entailed making frequent walks of twenty or thirty miles over rough country. On one occasion he covered seventy miles within twenty-four hours.

In 1850 he built an observatory which was a notable landmark on Wellington Row for a long time.

He was a member of several learned societies. He became an Associate of the Institute of Civil Engineers in 1851, was a Fellow of the Royal Society, Doctor of Philosophy and Master of Arts of the University of Gottingen, Fellow of the Royal Astronomical Society and a corresponding member of the Literary and Philosophical Society of Manchester.

In mature life his early desire to become a doctor revived and in 1855 he considered entering Guy's Hospital, but his health failed and he died at Whitehaven on 14 July 1856.

His records are preserved at the Whitehaven Library. As Dr Lonsdale says of them: 'His calligraphy is strikingly beautiful and much more consonant with the work of the engraver's art than the penmanship of a man of science furnishing figures and other details respecting the weather'.

Dame Edith Brown

Edith Brown (1864-1956) was born in the Bank Buildings, Coates Lane (now the Whitehaven Club). Her father, George Wightman Brown, manager of the Bank of Whitehaven, was a leading figure in rhe Whitehaven Brethren. He died as a result of an accident when his carriage was upset travelling from Keswick.

Edith left Whitehaven at the age of seven and was educated at Manchester High School and Croydon High School before going to Girton College, Cambridge, where she took an honours degree which she followed with a medical diploma at Edinburgh and then graduated M.D. at Brussels.

On 17 October 1891, she and Ellen Farrer, both recruits of the Baptist Zenana Mission, sailed for India as medical missionaries. Edith Brown was a woman of deep convictions whose stiff training was the best kind to fit her for an unknown future in which she would be required to take such independent action as would ultimately profoundly affect the thought and outlook of India's women.

She was stationed at Ludhiana, in the Punjab, as a junior missionary and began to study Urdu which was essential if she was to make contact with the native population.

During the first year at Ludhiana she learned that the three essentials of missionary work are patience, patience and patience.

Eventually she had a mental vision of a Medical College from which a constant stream of hospital assistants, dispensers, nurses and midwives would issue carrying healing to the unnumbered women of their own nationality whose need cried aloud for help. She persuaded the Surgeon-General of India of the soundness of her idea and gained support for it at a conference of women medical missionaries held at Ludhiana in 1893.

An appeal was circulated in the British Isles for gifts of money, bed-linen, quilts, invalid comforts and household necessities, nothing could be too much, nothing too humble to contribute towards the work of the College. The College opened on 4 January 1894 with four Christian medical students and two dispenser students.

Dr Edith Brown, photograph taken just before leaving for India for the first time.

Dame Edith Brown, D.B.E., M.A., M.D., M.C.O.G., Founder and first Principal of Women's Christian Medical College, Ludhiana, India.

Herbert Wilson Walker.

The teaching staff consisted of Edith Brown, a Miss Balfour and two part-time lecturers, Miss Allen and Miss Caldwell. In 1898 the first wards of the Memorial Hospital attached to the College were opened and six years later the Government offered financial help to the College as it was now recognised that the work being done was beneficial to the Province.

In 1909 the first non-Christian students were admitted and the work of the College was broadened. Two years later Dr Brown was awarded the Silver Kaiser-i-Hind Medal. In 1915 women students transferred from the Government College, Lahore, to Ludhiana, which was then recognised as the Women's Christian Medical College, with which was incorporated the Punjab Medical School for Women.

In 1922 Dr Brown was awarded the Gold Kaiser-i-Hind Medal and in 1931 her work in India was recognised by King George V when Dr Brown was created a Dame Commander of the British Empire. She visited Whitehaven in 1938 when she was given a civic reception and spoke about her work in India. She died in Kashmir, 6 December 1956.

Herbert Wilson Walker

Herbert Wilson Walker (1875-1934), business man, educationalist and philanthropist, was one of the most outstanding figures in the life of Whitehaven in the first half of the present century. Although locally he is primarily associated with the tannery, his influence was pervasive and touched all walks of life.

The origins of the tannery go back to the eighteenth century. In 1749 Sir James Lowther sold a plot of land, thirty yards fronting on to Scotch Street and thirty-eight yards backwards to Charles Street, to Israel Younghusband, linen draper. In 1761 Younghusband sold the plot to Gabriel Griffith who became bankrupt in 1764, possibly because involved on the fringes of the How, Younger and Wilkinson debacle of the previous year.

His assignees sold the land to George Miller who used it as the site of a tannery. In 1858 the tannery was conveyed to William Walker and it was successfully maintained by the Walker family for the next century. About 1900 the business was taken over by William Walker's two sons, Arthur and Herbert Wilson. At that time the firm was still run as a private concern, but it subsequently became William Walker (Whitehaven) Ltd. In addition to the Whitehaven tannery the family also had a tannery at Workington and re-opened the tannery at Maryport formerly conducted by Messrs Williamson.

Mr Arthur Walker died in 1921 and Mr Herbert Wilson Walker became managing director and chairman of the company. He became well-known far beyond Whitehaven because he had financial interests in tanneries at Warrington, Liverpool, London, Leeds and elsewhere. The Whitehaven tannery was expanded by taking over the old workhouse on the other side of Scotch Street, the two buildings being linked at first floor level. In time that bridge became a landmark dominating the view up Scotch Street, just as St James commands the view up Queen Street.

Following the death of his brother he took over the interests in the Whitehaven Colliery Co and later became chairman. Mr H. W. Walker had a long distinguished career on the Whitehaven Borough Council from 1904 until 1924. He was elected an alderman in 1912 and served as Mayor 1913-15. First as vice-chairman and later as chairman of the Finance Committee, he proved a shrewd and far-seeing custodian of the public purse and was responsible for putting the town's electricity undertaking on a sound financial footing.

He was Mayor during the opening year of the First World War and had all the additional burdens that that crucial time imposed. When the Derby recruiting scheme was introduced he was one of the few Mayors who realised that unless exemptions were made the mines and other works would be stripped of workers essential to the production of

Bridge linking both parts of the Whitehaven Tannery.

munitions and as a result of representations, miners and others were sent back to their work.

He was appointed a Justice of the Peace in 1916 and served on the Cumberland County Council from 1917 until 1922.

Even when he retired from the Council he was not entirely free from involvement in local affairs. In 1927 a heavy poor law precept threatened to send the general rate soaring up to 24*s* (120p) in the £. To prevent this Mr Walker lent the town £6,000 free of interest to enable the rate to be kept down to 20*s* (100p). The money was repaid when the financial pressure eased. It would be interesting to know what his spirit thought of the rate levied in 1962-63 which was 28*s* (140p) in the £.

He was a progressive educationalist and took a keen interest in the Whitehaven County Secondary School, now the Whitehaven County Grammar School to which he gave an Exhibition and a Scholarship. One of the four houses in the school bears his name.

He was interested in the old Whitehaven Infirmary in Howgill Street and when Whitehaven Castle became the Whitehaven Hospital the Walker family took a keen interest in the new institution. In 1924 Mr Walker made a gift to it of £10,000, spread over six and a half years, while his mother paid for the X-ray apparatus and bequeathed £1,000 to it. He also took an active part in the management of the Hospital.

Many of his benefactions were done quietly and anonymously. Only a few close friends were aware that it was he who had anonymously bought Whitehaven Castle on 11 August 1920 and presented it along with £20,000 to the community for use as a hospital.

Mr Walker was lord of the manor of Keswick and Castlerigg. Originally his Wasdale estate included Scawfell and several adjoining mountains. Having been an enthusiastic rock-climber in his early life, he sold these for a nominal sum to the Fell and Rock Climbing Club which in turn gave them to the National Trust.

He was a strong supporter of the Methodist church and in 1927 gave £10,000 for church extension purposes. As one of his great contemporaries, Mr William H. Wandless, said at the time of his death:

> 'He was a Puritan in training and outlook: clericalism was anathema; he gloried in his Methodist traditions. To see him in the pew after a hard week's work listening to a young local preacher was proof of his devotion to Methodism.
>
> 'His charity was boundless and he dispensed it graciously. The secret of this was his ideal that he was given wealth as a stewardship for which he had to render an account. He could not tolerate either waste or extravagance. He was thorough almost to the point of obstinacy in all that he did. The things that he believed in he supported lavishly.'

Mrs Walker, a daughter of Mr P. T. Freeman, of Keswick, continued to take an interest in local affairs although a more active part in community life was played by his son William who served for some years on the Whitehaven Town Council, as a councillor and alderman on the Cumberland County Council, as a Deputy Lieutenant of Cumberland and as a magistrate from 1960. His daughter, Claribel (now Mrs Curwen), also has a long record of service to the county as a councillor and an alderman, and as a magistrate since 1934.

The Whitehaven Tannery was closed in 1958 and the buildings demolished to make way for redevelopment of that part of Scotch Street.

Lord Adams

Mr H. W. Walker's death came at an unfortunate time in the history of Whitehaven. In the aftermath of World War I had come a national economic depression which was felt locally in the decline of the iron ore industry and in a series of crises in the coalfield.

In 1933 the Whitehaven and District Industries Development Committee published a brochure calling attention to the industrial potential of the area but it was soon realised that the effort required a broader

Lord Adams.

base and the Cumberland Development Council was formed with John Jackson Adams as its secretary. His appointment was the catalyst that brought prosperity back to Cumberland and completely revolutionised its industrial pattern. No account of the period would be complete without acknowledgment of the debt we owe to him. His achievements were publicly applauded on 1 January 1949 with the announcement that the King was to confer upon him a Barony. He became Lord Adams of Ennerdale.

John Jackson Adams was born in Arlecdon in 1890. His father died in an accident in a local iron ore mine when Jack was four years of age. In consequence his schooling was cut short at the earliest possible date so that he could help to augment the family income, at first in farm service and later in the iron ore mine where his father had died.

In 1910 he migrated to New Zealand in the company of men who later became members of the New Zealand cabinet. On his return to Cumberland in 1914 he flung himself with zest into local politics. In 1919 he led eleven others in an attack upon the twelve sitting members of the Arlecdon and Frizington Urban District Council. The result was the establishment of the first all-Labour council to be elected in this country with Jack Adams as Chairman. Through the I.L.P. he met many people who would be of assistance to him in later life.

He had married Agnes Jane Birney in 1914. Their only child, Thomas, born in 1923, died when only a few days old and the cause of this tragedy and its subsequent effect upon his wife's health led him to take an increasing interest in health matters. After his election to the County Council in 1919 he became a member of the County Health Committee. From 1922 he served as vice-chairman to Lady Mabel Howard for whom he had a great admiration and with whom he forged a bond of friendship. After her death in 1945 he became chairman of the Committee. He had been elected a County Alderman in 1931 and was appointed a magistrate in 1934.

He became General Secretary of the Winding Enginemen's Union and moved to Workington in 1921 for the convenience of his work. He had the unusual distinction of still being a member of the Arlecdon and Frizington U.D.C. while gaining a seat on the Workington Borough Council. His forthright character and pungent wit won him friends and enemies in probably equal numbers. He served on that Council from 1923 until 1931. While in Workington he fought hard in the Labour cause, assisting the late Tom Cape, M.P., in a number of tough election battles. Through the local authority he was interested in the building of the Maternity Wing of the Hospital endowed by the late Miss Thompson. While he was chairman of the Health Committee the infant mortality rate fell from 150 to sixty deaths per thousand and maternal mortality and infectious diseases in similar proportions.

As the 1920s became the 1930s, the dole queues lengthened. Living standards sank. Thousands were undernourished. Strikes and social unrest were everywhere in evidence. In 1933 Jewkes and Winterbottom drew attention to the depressed industrial situation in the North West and in the following year the Ministry of Labour published its report on the industrial conditions in certain depressed areas. The report led to the appointment of a Commissioner for the 'Special Areas' as they became known.

It was against a background of 15,000 people in employment in West Cumberland and 18,000 out of work that Jack Adams was invited to accept the post of secretary to the newly formed Cumberland Development Council. Within a short time he and Mr J. R. Williams, manager of the *Whitehaven News* and chairman of the Development Council publicity sub-committee had produced *Wonderful West Cumberland*, a glossy brochure extolling the merits of the area. With the establishment of the West Cumberland Industrial Development Company Ltd, with himself as General Manager, later Director, he was ready to build factories to let and set off in search of clients. In his efforts to secure the maximum support from Whitehall he was ably supported by both West Cumberland M.P.s, Tom Cape and Frank Anderson. In the story of West Cumberland's economic recovery Anderson is a man whose part has never been fully acknowledged.

The economic rehabilitation of West Cumberland was not, as Adams himself readily admitted, the work of one man, but of men of all parties and of no party who came together to pool their intellectual and other resources, to discuss problems, to advise and suggest solutions. That such men could work with him is a measure of the loyalty that he could evoke and of the earnestness of their desire to see West Cumberland flourish. It was a stirring and truly marvellous decade.

His first success was the re-opening of the Whitehaven coal mines in 1937 with help from the Nuffield Trust for the Special Areas. The first new factory established was at Millom. The first major new development at Whitehaven was the opening of the West Cumberland Silk Mills.

During this period when the economic structure of the area was undergoing close investigation and when reports for government departments and commissions had to be prepared with the greatest care, Jack Adams encouraged his associates on the Development Council and Development Company to take full advantage of the facilities and services available through King's College, Newcastle upon Type, and the University of Durham. Reports covering a very wide field flowed from his office to help and advise the Government and industrialists with regard to all aspects of life in the area. Foremost among these was the industrial survey produced by Prof. G. H. J. Daysh in 1938 and revised in 1951.

To acknowledge the opportunity which this work had afforded the University, the Senate conferred on him in 1948 the degree of M.A. (Honoris Causa).

World War II brought problems and difficulties but overall increasing prosperity to West Cumberland. After the war he had to find ways of taking up the slack produced by the closure of certain war industries at Drigg and Sellafield. In this he was fortunate. His own party was in power in Westminster and as Deputy Regional Controller of the Board of Trade he had the chance to put into operation some of the provisions of the Distribution of Industry Act of 1945, particularly those sections dealing with grants for basic services and the clearing of derelict sites. He retired from that post in 1948 and was awarded the O.B.E. By that time the groundwork had been laid for the building of the Windscale and Calder Works of the Industrial Group of the United Kingdom Atomic Energy Authority at Sellafield. The Windscale Works were built 1948-52. The Calder Works were officially opened by Her Majesty Queen Elizabeth on 17 October 1956.

In 1949 he was elevated to the peerage as Baron Adams of Ennerdale, the first Cumberland-born man to be so honoured since 1797. In the following year he was made a Freeman of the Borough of Workington and in 1953 Whitehaven likewise paid tribute to the great work he had done for the community. By that time more than £35m had been spent on industrial schemes alone and the number of people gainfully employed in West Cumberland had increased from 15,000 to 60,000, with 75% or more in light industries.

He retired in November 1959 and died on 23 August 1960.

His bluntness startled many people but behind the brusqueness was a sense of humour, well exemplified by the notice over his desk in his office at 30 Roper Street which read 'DAILY PRAYER: Oh Lord, help me to keep my big mouth shut until I know what I'm talking about'.

West Cumberland was fortunate that he talked to such good purpose.

Thomas Blackburn

Thomas Blackburn was born at Hensingham vicarage on 10 February 1916, the son of the Rev. C. E. A. Blackburn. The family moved to

Northumberland in 1918 so that they were far away from Whitehaven when the clash of personalities between father and son developed which played havoc with the younger Blackburn's youth. His childhood was spent in an atmosphere of savage Victorian paternalism that was not mitigated by his experiences at preparatory and boarding school.

However, at the age of sixteen he discovered poetry although, as he himself has said: 'Poetry is poetry. It is not a form of remedial therapy. It made life significant but it did not at that time help me to adjust to society'. It took him a long to adjust. He wrote a wry account of his early life in his autobiography *A clip of steel* (1969).

He taught in grammar schools and was Gregory Fellow at Leeds University for two years before becoming Principal Lecturer at the College of St Mark and St John.

His first collection of poetry was published in 1951 since when nine other volumes have appeared in addition to his *Selected Poems* (1972). His *Robert Browning: a study of his poetry* first published in 1967 was reprinted in 1974. A musical drama, *The Judas Tree* written in 1966, has been performed at the cathedrals of Edinburgh, Liverpool, Southwark and Washington.

He is the compiler of *45-60: an anthology of English poetry* (1960), and has been involved with others in the compilation of other anthologies.

Blackburn has been acclaimed as 'among the most technically accomplished poets of his generation' and, as a critic in the *Sunday Times* remarked when *The Next Word* was published in 1958: 'His concern is with the deepest experiences of mankind'.

An enthusiastic rock-climber in his spare time, he is proud of having introduced Chris Bonnington to the sport.

His home is in Putney.

Chapter 21

Whitehaven Artists

A great deal of attention has been paid to the maritime, commercial and industrial history of Whitehaven; much less so to aesthetics. Thanks to the work of the late Brian Crossland we are beginning to appreciate and to find out something about the architectural history of the town. We are now, also, beginning to realise something of the contribution the town has made to the manufacture of ceramics and to the art of painting.

The first professional painter to take up residence was Matthias Read (1669-1747), a Londoner who came to Whitehaven about 1690. He may have come here along with Jan Van Wyck who was commissioned to paint two pictures for Sir John Lowther, one of them a view of the town from the sea. He was befriended by William Gilpin (1657-1724), steward to Sir John Lowther, and encouraged to copy paintings at The Flatt and at Gilpin's own home, Scaleby Castle.

Read taught Gilpin how to handle a pencil and how to mix colours with the result that he not only became a reasonably capable amateur artist, but also enthused his son, Captain John Bernard Gilpin (1701-76) who became patron and tutor to a number of young artists in the Carlisle area. Two of the Captain's children became interested in art: William (1724-1802), rector of Boldre, wrote extensively on the subject, and Sawrey (1733-1807) was apprenticed to Samuel Scott, the marine painter, but developed considerable talent in equine subjects. He became an R.A. in 1797 and president of the Incorporated Society of Artists in 1774.

Read became a popular figure in Whitehaven where his work was in considerable demand. He did altar-pieces for St Nicholas Church and Holy Trinity Church in Whitehaven and for St Andrews in Penrith. He painted several views of Whitehaven. One, executed about 1710, is in the Whitehaven Museum, another done about 1720 is in the Carlisle Art Gallery. His most famous work: *A Bird's Eye View of Whitehaven*, painted in 1738, was engraved by Richard Parr. Three versions of the painting exist, one at Holker Hall and two which have been sold recently in London.

His interest in art was carried on by his nephew, Joseph Hinde (d. 1783), concerning whom we know little except that he too copied some of the paintings in The Flatt and, on the death of Sir James Lowther in 1755, arranged for the transfer of the entire collection of 144 paintings from The Flatt to Holker Hall.

Joseph Hinde had a brother, Henry, who was also a painter.

Ten years before Matthias Read died, a child named Strickland Lowry (1737-80?) was born in Whitehaven. He was probably apprenticed to Joseph Hinde and was practising as a painter from an address in Roper Street when his son Wilson (1760-1824) was born. While the boy was still young Strickland Lowry moved to Dublin and then to Shropshire, Staffordshire and Worcestershire where he established a considerable reputation. He furnished some illustrations for Phillip's *History and Antiquities of Shrewsbury*, 1779.

For a time Wilson Lowry was apprenticed to a house painter at Worcester. At the age of seventeen he was in London and was admitted into the schools of the Royal Academy. He established a high reputation as an engraver and died in London, after a prolonged illness, in 1824 leaving a son and a daughter who followed the same profession.

Contemporary with Strickland Lowry, and living in a back house in the same street, was Henry Nutter, a wood carver who found employment in the local shipyards. A report of the launching of a 180-ton brigantine, the *Scipio*, in 1790, contains a reference to the figure-head by Henry Nutter which is allowed to be 'a piece of excellent workmanship'. His son Ellis (1746-1809), followed him in his trade as a carver and as he also painted the figure-heads his younger brother, Henry (1758-1808), picked up from him the use of oil paint. Henry failed to find an outlet for his energy in Whitehaven and in 1778 he moved to Carlisle where he set up as a house painter and turned to portraiture. Although successful as a painter he died in poverty on account of his intemperate habits. His wife carried on the business assisted by his sons, William (1779-1815) who was baptised at Holy Trinity Church, Whitehaven, 28 July 1779, and Matthew Ellis (1797-1862) who was born at Carlisle. The latter became a considerable force in the art life of Carlisle. He was the first secretary of the newly constructed Academy of Fine Arts in that city. His son William Henry Nutter (1821-72) was also an accomplished watercolour painter. Another son of Henry Nutter, the carver, William (1753-1802) became an artist in London.

At the moment we do not know who taught Robert Salmon (1775-1844) the art of marine painting. Robert Saloman (he later in life shortened his name to Salmon) was born in King Street, Whitehaven, where his father was in business as a silversmith. From an early age he began painting and became particularly interested in marine subjects. The local shipyards were busy and every master marinier wanted a portrait of his vessel to hang up at home. The Whitehaven Museum possesses an interesting watercolour of the barque *Boyne*, 196 tons, painted by William Jackson of Liverpool in 1794, and had on exhibition on loan another watercolour, unsigned, of the ship *Hartley*, 243 tons, built by James Shepherd in 1795 and captured on a voyage to the West Indies the following year. This latter has some of the characteristics of Salmon's work. By 1800 Salmon had moved to London and in 1802 exhibited one painting of Whitehaven harbour at the Royal Academy. In 1806 he moved to Liverpool where he worked for five years, painting on average about twenty pictures each year. Here he recorded the scene along the Mersey. Between 1811 and 1822 he based himself on Greenock and produced over 250 paintings evoking the romantic picturesqueness of the area.

In 1822 he returned to Liverpool where he painted a further eighty works in the course of the next three years. Actually between 1800 and 1828 Salmon's travels between Scotland and England were extensive. In addition to his paintings of the Mersey and the Clyde his work includes scenes on the Firth of Forth, the mouth of the Tyne and Durham, the Channel coast around Dover and Cornwall.

Although his pictures sold well, the 1820s were a time of depression in England, so he decided to emigrate to America. On the eve of his departure he changed his name from Saloman to Salmon. He settled in Boston in 1828 where he became a scene painter for a local theatre, before setting up a studio which drew a large number of clients. In 1840 he was still actively painting although his doctor advised him not to paint small pictures as his eyesight was failing. All the time he was in the United States he painted reminiscent views of Britain and, feeling a little homesick, he returned to England in 1842. The place and date of his death are uncertain but it is believed he died in 1844.

From records he left it is known that he painted over a thousand pictures of which only about a quarter have been traced. A study of his work by John Wilmerding was published in 1971. Two of his early ship studies are in the Whitehaven Museum.

A few years older than Robert Salmon was John Mounsey (1767-1820) two specimens of whose work came to light in 1978.

By profession Mounsey was a house and sign painter and the bold and rather naive style of his work typifies the painted inn signs of the period.

Painting by Robert Salmon of the ship *David Shaw*, 343 tons. Launched by Wilson, Walker and Co., 1805.

A Ship in Foreign Waters — John Mounsey, 1818.

He was baptised at St Nicholas Church 31 January 1767, the second of eight children of John and Mabel Mounsey, of Chapel Street. His father was a carpenter. There is a headstone to his memory in the St James' Churchyard which indicates that his wife, Eleanor, died 1 November 1799, at the early age of 31 years, and that their three

children all died young. He had a workshop in the Market Place and died on 1 March 1820.

As with Salmon, we have no details at the moment of his apprenticeship.

The paintings of which we have details are:

A large landscape view of Venice with people in the left foreground, painted on filmsy canvas.

A large, 36" x 28" canvas depicting an unnamed ship at anchor in a bay, somewhere in foreign waters, initialled JM and dated 1818, in the lower right corner. After the deaths of his wife and children it is believed he travelled abroad with one of his nephews who was a ship's captain with Brocklebanks, and thus we can be fairly sure that this picture is of an actual place and not just a figment of his imagination. The clue to determining the location is the distinctive colonnaded building on the right of the picture.

A younger contemporary of Salmon was John Clementson (1780-1841). No known example of his work has survived locally but it is evident that he had a considerable reputation among his fellow townspeople. An anonymous contributor to the *Cumberland Pacquet* in 1890, reminiscing about personalities of half a century earlier, writes: 'I have already mentioned Oliver Hodgson, who was a noted painted when I was a boy. I believe that he served his apprenticeship with old Mr Clementson, in Strand Street, a gentleman whose name is almost forgotten today, but as an employer and lover of art he was most successful in producing from his numerous pupils some exceedingly clever workmen.'

John Clementson was baptised at St James' Church on 21 January 1780, the son of Thomas Clementson, tobacconist. The Clementsons were tobacconists in Whitehaven for several generations. In the 1840s they were also shipowners. He died on 30 November 1841 when on a visit to Workington.

Contemporary with John Clementson was Henry Collins (1782-1824) the high quality of whose work is known to us by four canvases which have been traced within recent years. The best known of these is his painting of Brocklebank's *Princess Charlotte*, 515 tons, the largest ship built at Whitehaven up to that time. The picture was executed in 1816 and is now in Liverpool. His death is recorded in the *Whitehaven Gazette* of 16 August 1824: 'On Monday evening last at the house of his mother-in-law Mrs Hamilton at Parton where he was on a visit Mr Henry Collins of this town aged 42: very much respected by a numerous acquaintance. He was a man of very superior taste in his profession, and although inferior to the celebrated Salomon, was considered the first marine painter in the North of England'.

John Bousfield (1793-1856) was a landscape and portrait painter. The contributor to the *Cumberland Pacquet* of 1890 quoted above comments: 'the most celebrated person of the time was Mr John Bousfilde, whose portraits of Whitehaven worthies adorn many a wall and home today. This was before the days of photography, when the wonderful perfection of this art, as manipulated by such gentlemen as Mr Lovell, Mr Bellman, Mr McDonald and others was not known. Mr Bousfilde worked as a journeyman painter in the halcyon days of summer, when work was plentiful, and occupied his spare time in works to order, in the execution of which he had his own time and always made a good job; life likenesses of our leading gentry and their families, also noted hunters, horses, dogs, or cats, were the subjects at once fit for his skilful brush and mind. I have before me one of his paintings, which has evidently been executed to the order of the late Mr Daniel Bird, who was, like the Messrs Jeffersons, of Rothersyke and Springfield, Mr E. G. Jones and the world-known Sir Thomas Brocklebank of today, most enthusiastic lovers of the leash. It is dated 1842 and represents faithfully the likenesses of two noted greyhounds, *Solway* and *Bess*, with a most magnificently executed background and foliage . . . But perhaps as a decorator Mr Bousfilde had no rival; his paintings in the chancels of Trinity and St James' Church are

Painting by Joseph Heard of the
John Scott, 225 tons. Launched by
Whiteside and Scott, 24 July 1835.

works which proved him to be a thorough genius. He was a man of a
quiet, inoffensive disposition and remarkably meek and modest in his
manner, so much so that he never pushed himself in the least before the
public, yet at the same time he excelled in everything he undertook.'

He died at his home in Scotch Street on 21 October 1856.

Joseph Heard (1780-1859) was the son of an Egremont saddler. He
received tuition in the art of painting at Whitehaven where he worked as
a marine painter until 1834 when he moved to Liverpool. He took up
residence at 11 Norfolk Street. In 1835 he is listed as a marine and
portrait painter sharing premises with his younger brother Isaac (1804-)
at 53 Pitt Street. From 1857 until his death on 10 November 1859, he
was at 60 Upper Pitt Street.

There are eight of his paintings in the Whitehaven Museum, several in
the National Maritime Museum at Greenwich, in the Liverpool Museums
and one at Carlisle Art Gallery. He showed a special talent for depicting
water in motion.

The Oliver Ussinon Hodgson (1810-78) mentioned above was baptised
at St Nicholas, Whitehaven, 18 May 1810. His father, Richard Hodgson,
had a shoemaker's business on King Street, but by 1829 had moved to
19 George Street. Oliver Hodgson was apprenticed to John Clementson,
at Strand Street. He took over Thomas Fearon's business premises in
Gregg's Lane in March 1840 and continued there until his death on
23 August 1878. He resided at 19 Wellington Row.

He is represented in the Whitehaven Museum by three paintings: the
brig *Favourite*, 171 tons, painted in 1832; Parton from the sea; and a
picture of the National School, James Pit and Wellington Row.

From time to time portrait and miniature painters came to Whitehaven in search of business. One of these was Tobias Young in 1785, but
it is not clear how long he stayed. Denis Brownell Murphy (d. 1842), a
patriot and strong sympathiser with the cause of United Ireland, came to
Whitehaven for professional reasons in 1798. Four years later he moved
to Newcastle upon Tyne and in 1803 to London. His ability as a miniature
painter caught the attention of Princess Charlotte and in 1810 he was
appointed painter in ordinary to her royal highness. At the command of

the princess he made miniatures of many of the Restoration beauties in the royal collection at Windsor. The princess died before the series was completed and her husband declined to pay Murphy for them. They were however published in 1833 as a series of engravings under the title 'The Beauties of the Court of King Charles the Second' with text by his daughter, Mrs Anna Brownell Jameson.

Another visitor was Charles Jenour (fl. 1825-50) who came here in 1843 and painted portraits of Mr and Mrs George Gibson, of Lingydale, now in the Whitehaven Museum.

James Corson is listed in a local directory for 1847 as a miniature painter, with an address at 40 New Street, but nothing else is known about him.

Another early nineteenth century painter concerning whom we could do with more information is John Alsop (fl. 1827-47), a portrait and miniature artist who advertised drawing and painting lessons in 1827. Day scholars could get three lessons per week for 15/- (75p); evening scholars could get theirs for 10/6d (52½p); while for lessons in their own homes the fee went up to one guinea (£1.05). He offered portraits on canvas and miniatures on ivory at reasonable terms. He was also prepared to copy paintings either on a reduced or enlarged scale.

In 1847 he was operating from 26 Queen Street. At that time William Leigh Alsop was also working from that address as a painter and paperhanger. He had commenced in business in 1839 when the local press commented on a sign he had executed for the Whittington and his Cat on Lowther Street. He painted a copy of Guido's Crucifixion which in 1841 he presented as an altar-piece to the Roman Catholic Chapel in Duke Street.

William Gaythorp (1806-41) was the son of John Gaythorp, a Whitehaven bookseller, who had his home and business premises at 80 King Street. He exhibited regularly at the Carlisle Academy of Arts between 1823 and 1833, first as Master Gaythorp and later as W. Gaythorp. He ran a drawing school at 80 King Street from 1829 onwards and is represented in the Whitehaven Museum by a pen and ink sketch of Whitehaven Castle. He was buried at St Nicholas, 30 April 1841.

John Rook (1807-72) was a landscape artist with a studio in a court at 26a Tangier Street in 1847, by 1864 he was operating from 54 Duke Street. He was for twenty-seven years drawing master at St Bees School. His best known work is a drawing of the opening of Harras Moor race course in 1852 which was engraved.

His son, William H. Rook, was a grocer with an interest in watercolour painting. Several examples of his work are to be found in the area in private collections.

Robert Bell Gunning (1830-1907) was a native of Dumfries who came to Whitehaven about 1867 and set up a studio where he taught drawing and painting and practised portrait and landscape painting in oils and crayons. He died while on a visit to Dumfries on 14 April 1907, but was interred at Whitehaven.

He has been described as 'Kind, gentle, genial, humorous, simple and unobtrusively upright without the least suspicion of pragmatic unction'. His studio latterly was on the corner of Lowther Street and Church Street.

Richard Herd (1835-1910) was born at Sedbergh and came to Whitehaven as a young man to take up a post as chief clerk to Mr J. McKelvie, solicitor, with whom he worked for many years.

About 1870 he became Registrar of Marriages, a post he held until he left Whitehaven in 1900.

He is listed in a directory for 1864 as a solicitor's clerk residing at 17 Albert Terrace.

In 1873 he appears as Registrar of Marriages with an address at 33 Roper Street.

In 1883 he is listed as 'artist and Registrar of Marriages, Brookfield Villa, Victoria Road'.

In 1900 he moved to Huddersfield where he died on 17 February 1910.

His obituary in the *Whitehaven News* says that 'He was an artist of rare ability and produced many splendid examples of landscape and marine painting. He enjoyed a wide reputation as a teacher and turned out many excellent pupils. He was of a quiet and unassuming disposition.'

There is a landscape of the St Bees Valley by him in the Whitehaven Museum collection.

Also active in Whitehaven at the same time as Mr Gunning and Mr Herd was George Nelson (1822-1905). He was born at Wigton in 1822 and came to Whitehaven as a youth. He served his apprenticeship as a sailor, rose from mate to captain, beginning in the coastwise trade and ending in foreign traffic. About 1860 he started ship-broking at Whitehaven. Nelson and Sons became agents for the steamers plying between the Isle of Man and Whitehaven until these sailings ceased during the First World War.

Captain Nelson, in his latter years, did not take a very active part in the business but devoted himself to painting, particularly marine painting for which he showed considerable aptitude, his long nautical experience standing him in good stead. He died 14 June 1905. There are several examples of his work in the Whitehaven Museum.

Captain Nelson's son, George, was apprenticed to Mr T. L. Banks, the most outstanding architect in Whitehaven in the latter half of the nineteenth century. In 1891 he went to the Liverpool School of Art where he stayed for three years. Later he studied at the Slade School of Art, London. He was art master at St Bees School, 1906-18, and became a member of the Lake District Society of Artists. He had paintings hung in the Royal Institute and Liverpool Art Gallery.

His main interest was in landscape painting in watercolour. He collaborated with Mr J. D. Kenworthy in arranging art exhibitions at Whitehaven.

He died 8 March 1921.

The most outstanding artistic personality in Whitehaven at the end of the nineteenth century and through the first half of the twentieth was John Dalzell Kenworthy (1858-1954). He was born at Whitehaven on 5 November 1858, the third son of Mr G. W. Kenworthy, a soap and tallow manufacturer.

He had much more than a local reputation. An Associate of the Royal Cambrian Academy he had a place in its exhibitions over many years as well as in those of the Royal Academy and the municipal galleries at Liverpool, Manchester and Leeds.

A skilled craftsman in oils and watercolours his work is well known in Scotland and in France. In both of these countries he had travelled extensively. He crossed the Atlantic twenty-two times. To the people of West Cumberland however, he is known chiefly as a portrait painter, and to study the work he executed over more than half a century is to survey the personalities who have taken a leading part in local affairs over that period.

He painted the portraits of several Mayors of Whitehaven and other Cumbrian boroughs and a particularly good one of Pte Abraham Acton which is now in the Whitehaven Museum along with a self portrait. In all his paintings and sketches total several hundreds.

Always eager to help young artists he was the President of the Whitehaven Art Club which twice honoured him by arranging exhibitions of his work in the Whitehaven Library, one to mark his ninetieth birthday which was opened by his friend Mrs H. W. Walker of Wasdale Hall, herself a fine artist.

He died on 4 March 1954.

A person who exerted a considerable influence upon young people in the second quarter of the present century was Alfred Chamberlain (1888-). He was trained at the Royal College of Art where he was taught by the distinguished calligrapher Edward Johnson and by W. R. Lethaby and Gerald Moira.

Self portrait by J. D. Kenworthy.

Painting by Bernard Henry
McWilliams of the ship *Dunboyne*,
1,355 tons. Launched by the
Whitehaven Shipbuilding Company,
28 February 1888.

After some part-time teaching he became art master at the Whitehaven Grammar School in 1919 and taught there until his retirement some thirty years later.

He is a portrait painter and sculptor, a metal-worker and enamellist, but became best known for his illuminated work.

A selection of his illuminated work was exhibited at the Scott Gallery at Lancaster University in 1918.

Also working at this period was Bernard Henry McWilliams (1889-1969), foreman painter with the Whitehaven Corporation who, although he has left only a small body of work, is interesting because of what he did. He was fascinated by the nineteenth century marine painters, particularly Joseph Heard.

Two of his oil paintings are in the Whitehaven Museum collection: the *Dunboyne,* launched at Whitehaven, which he remembered seeing as a young man, and the *Friar's Crag,* one of the Kennaugh fleet.

Another person working at the same time or a little earlier than Mr McWilliams was Robert Combe (1878-1947). In his younger days he worked for Bryant and May for whom he did some publicity material. He came back to Whitehaven about 1910 and established the Paramount Photographic Studio on King Street. Towards the end of World War I (from 1917 onwards) he served with the Royal Flying Corps as a photographer. After the war he worked with the C.M.S. and gave private drawing lessons. His reputation rests on his work as a watercolour painter, although he executed a number of portraits.

The most potent influence on art in Whitehaven in the immediate post-World War II period was Frank Waddington (1897-1952).

A native of Blackburn he studied at the Technical College School of Art there where he was for a while a part-time teacher. Later he studied under Albert Woods, A.R.C.A., and William Walcot, R.E., F.R.I.B.A., R.B.A., a brilliant artist with a world-wide fame as an etcher.

Mr Waddington exhibited architectural watercolours at the Royal Academy for many years, having first shown them there in 1927. His pictures have also been exhibited in many other galleries including the Royal Scottish Academy, Edinburgh, the Walker Art Gallery, Liverpool and the City Art Gallery, Manchester. One-man exhibitions of his work were held in the art galleries at Blackpool, Blackburn and Preston.

He came to Whitehaven to follow his profession as an architect and lived first at Beckermet, later at Linethwaite. His watercolours were reproduced in many art magazines and journals.

He was one of the founders of the Whitehaven Art Club to which he acted as tutor. An exhibition of his work was held in the Whitehaven Library in 1951.

Chapter 22

The Hospital Service

In 1783 James Hogarth (1725-96), a local linen manufacturer and philanthropist, gave 107 Queen Street to Dr Joshua Dixon (1745-1825) for use as a Dispensary. The Dispensary did useful work in the alleviation of disease until 1829 when Mr Thomas Hartley's house in Howgill Street was purchased for use as an Infirmary which received its first patients on 1 May 1830. Among the early benefactors of the Infirmary were Mr John Pennyfeather, gardener to the Earl of Lonsdale, and Dr John Hamilton. Dr Hamilton was one of the early members of the first Medical Committee in 1783.

Mrs Stock was the first Matron. She was followed in February 1832 by Mrs Jane Holliday who was Matron for thirty-three years.

Two additional wards, named the Harrison Ward and Steele Ward, were built at the expense of Baroness de Sternberg, a daughter of Dr Hamilton, and opened in 1857. She died in 1859 and in her will left £5,000 for the building of two more wards for fever cases and £1,000 for the establishment of a 'Samaritan Fund'. A very fine and detailed account of the Infirmary was written by Dr G. J. Muriel and published in 1915. It was revised by T. E. Woodhouse and G. G. Carter in 1924.

In 1902 it was felt that a reorganisation of the institution was necessary in the light of current medical developments, but the cost of bringing an old building up-to-date made progress slow. When the Earl of Lonsdale decided in 1924 to sell Whitehaven Castle it was bought anonymously by Mr H. W. Walker and donated to the town along with £20,000 towards the cost of alterations to replace the Infirmary which was purchased by the Whitehaven Education Committee for use as a Central Selective School.

The Whitehaven and West Cumberland Hospital was still a voluntary institution maintained by subscriptions, donations, charity events, workmen's contributions, patients' payments, etc. It provided a minimum of seventy-two beds and a nursing and domestic staff of thirty-seven as

▽ Dr John Hamilton (1739-1814).

▷ Whitehaven Infirmary.

This stone was laid by
E. F. Collingwood Esq., C.B.E.
chairman of the
Newcastle Regional Hospital Board
on the 4th day of October
1957

E. F. Collingwood, C.B.E., Chairman Newcastle Regional Hospital Board, lays foundation stone of the West Cumberland Hospital, 4 October 1957.

compared with a maximum of fifty-nine beds and staff of twenty-nine at the Infirmary. In the period between the wars its budget was modest. In 1935 the total expenditure was £10,589 19s 8d, made up as follows:

Maintenance	£1,732	2	10
Surgery and Dispensary	1,565	1	1
Domestic	1,998	4	11
Salaries and Wages	3,865	3	9
Establishment	347	13	8
Miscellaneous	310	7	10
Administration	681	9	4
Rates and Taxes	89	16	3

In that year 1,727 in-patients were cared for of which 1,304 were surgical cases, 202 medical and 221 obstetrical.

The National Health Service Act, 1946, which came into force on 5 July 1948, brought a dramatic change. The Hospital came under the control of the West Cumberland Hospital Management Committee. This body was responsible for six hospitals in West Cumberland with 281 beds. In addition the Committee had the use of the Hospital Block of eighty-eight beds for the elderly at Meadow View House administered by the Cumberland County Council. Very considerable strides were made in the appointment of consultants, increases in nursing staff, improvement of facilities and general reconstruction of premises.

Despite that it was felt that there was a lack of reasonable hospital accommodation in West Cumberland and consideration was given to the building of a general district hospital of just under 500 beds at Homewood, Hensingham. An architect was appointed in 1951 but funds did not allow active planning to commence until 1955. In that year Homewood mansion was converted to form a chest unit of forty-one beds and early in 1956 a preliminary contract was entered into under which roads, sewers and other main services for the site were provided.

The building of Stage II of the new hospital began in June 1957, the foundation stone being laid by Mr (later Sir) E. F. Collingwood, C.B.E.,

Chairman of the Newcastle Regional Hospital Board on 4 October 1957. This stage was completed in November 1959 and the first patients were admitted just before Christmas 1959. It comprised, in addition to the boiler house, laundry and works area, a psychiatric department of sixteen beds with out-patient facilities, two geriatric wards each of thirty beds and a cubicle block of twenty-four beds which was used as a medical ward. At the same time a first part of the nurses' home was provided together with a block of flats and flatlets for senior nursing staff and some houses for medical staff.

The Main Stage, Stage III, was started in May 1961, the contract completion date being October 1964. The original contract did not include either the orthopaedic wing or the maternity hospital, but subsequently Ministry authority to build these two units was obtained and negotiated additions to the contract were entered into, the two units being brought into use in advance of the main block, the orthopaedic wing in September 1963 and the Maternity Hospital in February 1964. Other major additions approved by the Ministry and completed within the original contract period, subject to a slight extension of time because of exceptional weather conditions, include an addition to the psychiatric department to bring the number of beds to thirty and to improve the facilities for treating day patients, an assembly hall for the use of the staff and an extension to the nurse training school to transform it into a teaching centre for all grades of staff, and in particular, for post graduate medical education.

It was one of the first completely new District General Hospitals to be

Aerial view of the West Cumberland Hospital.

built in England and Wales following the creation of the National Health Service.

The main contractors were Messrs John Laing Construction Ltd, of Carlisle. The building which cost £4½m was officially opened by Her Majesty Queen Elizabeth the Queen Mother on 21 October 1964.

In 1965 the services at Meadow View and Hollins were closed and in 1966 Whitehaven Hospital was developed as a geriatric unit of just under 100 beds including a new Day Hospital.

In 1967 the West Cumberland Hospital was used for teaching medical students and four years later the post-graduate medical centre was extended. In 1969 a school for enrolled nursing training was opened.

Until 1974 the health service in England and Wales had been organised in three separate parts. It was realised that these were interdependent although up till that date each part was organised within different geographical boundaries, separately financed with the development of each planned independently.

After a great deal of consultation a reorganisation of the National Health Service was agreed and established by the National Health Service Reorganisation Act, 1973. The Act came into effect on 1 April 1974, the same day that the Local Government Act, 1972, became operational.

The effect of the Act was to bring together the three formerly separate services — family doctor, hospital service and local authority health service.

The management or control was at three different levels — Area, Region and Secretary of State. England was divided into ninety areas grouped into fourteen regions. Some areas were found to be too large for effective local planning and organisation and have been sub-divided into districts.

The Cumbria Area Health Authority serves the newly created Cumbria local government area and operates through area offices at Carlisle, Workington and Whitehaven.

An indication of the progress achieved by the West Cumberland Hospital Management Committee in twenty-five years is best shown by the following table:

	1948-49	1973-74
Beds available	397	688
In-patients discharged in a year	5,506	12,146
Number of births in hospital	1,023	1,833
Average length of stay, acute cases	15.8 days	10.3 days
Patients dealt with per bed per annum	17.4	17.6
New out-patients	13,757	18,285
Out-patient attendances	33,180	73,948
Accident and emergency attendances	14,973	49,213
X-rays per annum	13,251	348,469
(The method of measurement was changed in 1973)		
Pathology requests per annum	4,866	101,893
Physiotherapy treatments	29,900	67,540
Number of consultant medical staff	6	34
Number of nurses	120	646
Number of paramedical staff	14	72
Number of other staff	167	558
Revenue expenditure	£54,000	£2,286,653
Total capital expenditure		£5,402,235

▷ Her Majesty Queen Elizabeth the Queen Mother at the official opening of the West Cumberland Hospital, 21 October 1964.

THIS HOSPITAL WAS OPENED
BY
HER MAJESTY
QUEEN ELIZABETH THE QUEEN MOTHER
ON THE 7th OCTOBER 1964

Chapter 23   Booksellers and Printers

Johan Gutenberg perfected the idea of printing from movable type about 1450. A little over a quarter of a century later William Caxton set up a printing press at Westminster and in 1477 printed his first book: *Dictes and Sayenges of the Phylosophers*.

It was not until 1735 that the art of printing came to Whitehaven via Cork, Waterford and Kendal.

Thomas Cotton, Whitehaven's first printer, was probably a native of Cork, although his early life is shrouded in mystery. He and Andrew Welsh are featured as the co-printers of a folio sheet entitled: *The Free-holders' Answer to the Pretender's Declaration* which was issued in 1715. A copy of this document was preserved in the Earl of Crawford's library at Haigh Hall, near Wigan.

He disappeared from sight until 1729 when he emerged as a bookseller and printer. Thomas Sherlock (1681-1761), Bishop of London, wrote *The Tryal of the Witnesses of the Resurrection of Jesus* which was published in 1729 in Dublin by S. Powell. It carries an advertisement for a work entitled *The State of the Protestants in Ireland under King James's Government*. Subscriptions for this latter work were to be taken, among others, by 'Mr Thomas Cotton, in Waterford'. It was in that same year that he started a news-sheet called *The Waterford Flying Post*. It was foolscap in size and printed on coarse paper. A copy dated Thursday, 21 August 1729, came to light in 1814. It had no serial number and no price. The *Dublin Freeman's Journal*, commenting on the find says: 'The mechanical part of the printing is very inferior . . . It shows no trace of original editorship. The advertisements are six in number and their appearance is somewhat whimsical. The latest London news is August 9th, twelve days old.'

Two years later he was in Kendal where he established the *Kendal Courant*. In 1735 he came to Whitehaven where he set up his press in an old building with an outside staircase, now demolished, near the United Reformed Church. Here he published his third newspaper, *The White-haven Weekly Courant, containing the most material advices both Foreign and Domestic*.

It measured sixteen inches by twelve inches, had four pages with three columns to a page. It had no local news and a minimum of shipping information. Cotton died in Whitehaven and was buried in Holy Trinity Church grounds on 7 July 1743. Four of his children predeceased him.

The fate of Cotton's press is not clear. The next printer was William Masheder who in 1752 and 1753 printed the two parts of Abraham Fletcher's *The Universal Measurer*.

Masheder was a schoolmaster, or as he preferred to describe himself, a *philomath*. He was the author of a navigational textbook, *The Navigator's Companion: or, Mariner's compendious pocket book*, published in 1754. In 1757 he published *The Youth's Companion, or, A collection of Essays, Moral and Entertaining*. He seems to have prospered, in the 1762 Census he is described as a 'gentleman'.

He was succeeded in business by W. Shepherd who in 1764 printed an edition of John Locke's *Elements of Natural Philosophy*, an undated edition of the *British Apiary, or, Complete Beemaster* by James Petrie, of Whitehaven, and, in 1768, a sermon by John Bell of Bridekirk. Shepherd also established a connection with the Isle of Man which gave him the distinction of being the first printer on that island.

Masthead of *Cumberland Pacquet*, 1808.

Thomas Wilson (1663-1755), bishop of Sodor and Man, arranged for a translation into Manx of the Gospel according to St Matthew to be printed in London. His successor, Mark Hildesley (1698-1772), arranged for a translation of the Gospels and the Acts of the Apostles to be printed in London in 1763, but the second part of the New Testament — the Epistles to Revelation — was printed at Ramsey in 1767 by Shepherd.

An interesting group involved in printing at the end of the eighteenth century was that of John Dunn (1735-1817), his family and his brother-in-law, Alexander Coutts.

In October 1776, Coutts started the *Cumberland Chronicle and Whitehaven Public Advertiser* in opposition to John Ware's *Cumberland Pacquet*, but he failed to secure a wide enough circulation and his periodical folded up in July 1779. He had a brother William, also a printer, who died in 1803.

Coutts died in 1794, the business passing to his nephew Brownrigg Nicholson Dunn. The most important book published by Brownrigg and Ann Dunn was: *The Literary life of William Brownrigg, M.D., F.R.S., to which are added an account of the coalmines near Whitehaven, and observations on the means of preventing epidemic fevers, by Joshua Dixon, M.D.,* 1801.

Brownrigg Dunn died at Woolwich at the early age of thirty-five but John Dunn lived until 1817, dying at his house in Howgill Street at the age of eighty-two.

Contemporary with the Dunns was Allason Foster (d. 1816) who printed a number of books including two on navigation; but the pair who dominated local printing for half a century were John Ware and his son John who made their debut in 1771 with the publication of Wardhaugh Thompson's *The Accountant's Orcale, or, Key to Science, a treatise of common arithmetic.* Their most outstanding task at this time was, however, the printing of the Bible in Manx for Bishop Hildesley.

Shepherd was the Bishop's first choice, but he died of consumption in 1769. The first volume (Genesis to Esther) was printed in two batches, each of 1,000 copies, the first in 1771 and the second in 1772. The second volume, 2,000 copies, (Job to Malachi) appeared in 1773. The manuscript of this volume narrowly escaped destruction in a shipwreck when it was being conveyed to Whitehaven. 'The Rev. Kelly, who had charge of the precious document, saved it by holding it above the water throughout five hours during which he was exposed to the fury of the elements on the rock where the ship had struck.'

The work was completed in 1775 with the publication of 2,000 copies of the third volume containing the New Testament. All these were quarto volumes. In the same year the Wares printed forty one-volume quarto pulpit Bibles. In 1777 they produced octavo and quarto large-paper editions of the *Book of Common Prayer* in Manx; both in the same typeface as the Bible.

The great achievement of the Wares was the establishment of the *Cumberland Pacquet* in 1774 which was published without interruption until 1915.

John Ware, junior, was one of the leading figures in the establishment of the Whitehaven Subscription Library in 1797. The elder Ware died in 1791 and his son carried on the business until his own death in April

1820 when it was acquired by Robert Gibson who had originally been an apprentice with the younger Ware.

The last of the eighteenth century printers were the brothers Joseph and Francis Briscoe. Joseph was the publisher of the *Cumberland Magazine, or Whitehaven Monthly Miscellany* which appeared during the years 1778 to 1781. The periodical contained a little English history, a political summary, biographical sketches and a number of essays, but no local information. He also published some chap-books. In 1783 Joseph Briscoe moved to the Isle of Man leaving the Whitehaven business to his brother. Of the works printed by Francis Briscoe only one extremely interesting item has survived: *The Surprizing Adventures of John Roach, Mariner, of Whitehaven, containing a genuine account of his cruel Treatment during a long captivity amongst savage Indians, and imprisonment by the Spaniards, in South America, with his miraculous Preservation and Deliverance by divine Providence; and happy Return to the Place of his nativity, after being thirteen years amongst his inhuman Enemies*, 1783. A second edition was published by Briscoe in 1784 and an edition was published in Dumfries. Roach, died in the work-house in Workington in 1819 at the age of seventy-eight.

The Wares operated from 26 King Street and Gibson carried on at the same address. In addition to maintaining the *Pacquet* as the bulwark of the Lowther interests Gibson printed a number of books. He retired in 1857 and the business passed to Robert Foster. For a short time between 1878 and 1882 Foster managed both the *Whitehaven News* and the *Cumberland Pacquet* from 26 King Street. He parted company with the *Pacquet* in 1882 when it came under the management of John Washbourne. From that date until 1897 when the old Public Offices were demolished to make way for the Post Office, the *Pacquet* was published at 69 Lowther Street. From then until its demise in 1915 it was published by William Halton at 30 Tangier Street.

The *Whitehaven Gazette* was started in 1819 in opposition to the *Pacquet* but it was bought up by Gibson in 1826 and annihilated. Its printer was James Steel (1796-1851) who went to edit the *Kendal Chronicle* until 1828 and from there to the *Carlisle Journal*.

No.13 Lowther Street has been a printer's and bookseller's shop for more than 130 years. In 1713 Mr James Lowther sold the plot of land on which Nos.9-13 were built to Thomas Lutwidge. The houses remained Lutwidge property until 1808. No.13 was bought by John and Henry Birley. It was a dwelling house until 1831 when William Donnison took it over as a printing works and started the *Whitehaven Herald*. The *Herald* was taken over by Robert Abraham in 1834 and by George Irwin in 1837. In 1854 it passed to William Smith who in 1864 moved to 4 King Street where he continued to publish the *Herald* until it was amalgamated with the *Whitehaven Guardian* in 1879.

He was followed at 13 Lowther Street by John Welsh and Samuel Armstrong as printers and stationers. Welsh had been in business in 1843.

Armstrong sold out in 1868 and on Welsh's death in 1884, his widow sold the property to W. H. Moss. Until the end of the century the business was known as Welsh-Moss, but in 1900 W. H. Moss acquired No.12 — a house that had at one time been the town residence of Admiral Skeffington Lutwidge — and expanded into that, the business becoming W. H. Moss and Sons Ltd. In 1968 Moss's sold out to C. N. Print Ltd. The lease on the property ran out in 1977 when it was vacated. It will form part of Dixon's store which will be expanded to cover Nos.7 to 17.

The mid-nineteenth century was a period of fierce competition in both the printing and newspaper fields. The *Cumberland Pacquet* and the *Whitehaven Herald* faced opposition from William Alsop's *Whitehaven News* which started in 1852 as a monthly and became a weekly in 1855 when Thomas Boustead and Robert Banks started the *Whitehaven Messenger*.

Alsop managed the *Whitehaven News* from 43 Roper Street until 1878 when Robert Foster took over the *News* and published it from the

Halton's Printing Works and Cumberland Pacquet Office, 30 Tangier Street.

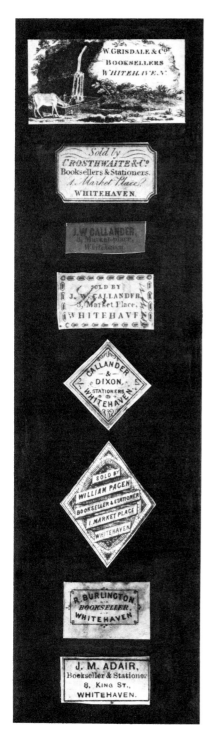

Nineteenth century local booksellers' labels. *Publisher's collection.*

Pacquet office at 26 King Street. Alsop almost immediately brought out *The Cumberland Weekly News and Farmers' Chronicle* which was subsequently sold and, later, *The Whitehaven Guardian* and *The Whitehaven Herald*. He then became manager of a publication called *The West Cumberland Post*, and for a while, he served *The Cumberland Pacquet*. He ultimately gave up newspapers and went to York where he was a traveller for the printing firm of Waterlow and Sons Ltd. He died at Uxbridge in 1905 at the age of seventy-six.

For three years Robert Foster was sole proprietor of the *Whitehaven News*. In 1881 the paper was registered as a private limited company under the Companies Act. The first four directors were William McGowan, William Burnyeat, Robert Jefferson and Robert Foster.

William McGowan was a director of the *News* for forty-nine years and latterly chairman of the Board. He was succeeded by his only son James in July 1918 and the McGowan family were closely associated with the management of the paper until 1962 when it was acquired by Cumberland Newspapers Ltd. It continued to be printed at Whitehaven until 1969 when the printing was transferred to Carlisle.

From 1855 until 1859 Thomas Boustead and Robert Banks published *The Whitehaven Messenger* first from 18 Lowther Street and later from 40 New Street. On the demise of the *Messenger* they started *The Whitehaven Times* which ceased publication about 1864.

There were a number of booksellers who also did some printing. The most distinguished of these is Callander and Dixon's, established in 1827 by James William Callander (1792-1872) at 3 Market Place. He was later joined by John Dixon. On the death of Mr Callander the business was taken over by James Robertson and three generations of the Robertson family have presided over its development of the business. In the nineteenth century and the first half of the twentieth a considerable amount of printing was done, but now the business is restricted to bookselling and stationery. Mr E. S. Robertson opened a second shop at 21a Church Street in June 1960. The Market Place premises were sold in 1977 and in 1978 Mr Robertson sold the Church Street shop to Messrs Mawson and McClure.

In 1808 John Crosthwaite established a bookshop at 1 Market Place where he also did some printing. The shop remained in the Crosthwaite family until 1868 when it was taken over by William Pagen (1844-94) and William Gill who had served their time at Crosthwaite's. The partnership lasted nine years. They were the proprietors of the short-lived *Whitehaven Guardian* and when it closed down Mr Gill dissolved the partnership and Mr Pagen carried on on his own until 1894.

About the same time William Wilson opened a bookshop and printing works at 45 King Street which were taken over in 1858 by John M'Leven Adair. Shortly afterwards he moved to 20 King Street where the family maintained a bookshop, printing and stationery business until the end of the century when they acquired and rebuilt 8 King Street which was known as 'The Book'. John Hindson Douglas, the grandson of the founder, died in 1969 when the premises were sold and incorporated in Blundell's store.

The book trade in Whitehaven has largely been in the hands of individuals. The London-based firm of W. H. Smith and Son Ltd is the only multiple to have a retail outlet locally. The railway bookstalls which made them famous were first opened in 1848 but it was not until about 1901 that one was opened on Bransty Station. A few years later 79 King Street was leased and they have been a landmark on upper King Street for over three quarters of a century. On 23 October 1978 they moved across to larger premises at 10/11 King Street which will give them better opportunities for display.

Whitehaven is fortunate in having more bookshops than many larger towns.

In 1973 Adrian Cribb acquired premises on College Street, previously the offices of the late J. G. Tyson, solicitor, which he turned into an

attractive bookshop with an entrance from Church Street. He has since improved his service still further by adapting the basement to display a wide range of children's books.

In 1978 bookselling was given a new outlet in Whitehaven in the form of a second-hand bookshop opened in Roper Street by Michael Moon. He purchased and renovated that part of the former printing works of the *Whitehaven News* on which the Theatre Royal had previously stood.

Mr Moon, who started his career as an antiquarian and second-hand bookseller at Cleator Moor in 1970, purchased the former Co-operative Store at Beckermet in 1972 and there built up a service which has an international reputation with a stock of over 70,000 volumes.

In addition to bookselling he has branched out into publishing and has been responsible for the printing of some twenty books of local interest. Some are reprints of standard works that have been out of print for some time. Modern historical research owes a great deal to him for making these resources more readily available.

Apart from Smith Brothers (Whitehaven) Ltd, whose printing is of a specialised nature, Whitehaven now has only one printing firm, George Todd and Son.

George Todd (1885-1964), the founder, served his apprenticeship as a compositor with a Whitehaven printing firm and then went to work with a Carlisle printing company. He travelled home each weekend to Parton. Tiring of this he decided to set up on his own. In 1912 he hired a small room in an old brewery where he set up a printing press which he had purchased second-hand for £10.

Initially he worked part-time as an insurance agent until such time as his business grew. For greater convenience he moved to premises in Strand Street, now part of the Beehive. By dint of hard work business increased and he gathered together a small but loyal staff. The economic recession of the 1930s affected his business, but as the general situation improved so did the printing trade. He moved further down the street and occupied the ground floor of 40 Strand Street. Later he acquired the upper floors.

His son Cyril came into the business in 1936. In 1946 they acquired their first automatic printing machine. Mr Todd died in 1964 at the age of seventy-nine. Three years later, in July 1967, Cyril Todd moved into new premises on Marlborough Street. The move represented a £20,000 project and resulted in the firm having one of the most modern commercial and colour printing works with full platemaking facilities in the north west. Since 1967 a further £30,000 has been spent on additional plant.

The main emphasis is on the printing of books and pamphlets for clients who range from Lanarkshire and the Lothians in the north to Northamptonshire and Warwickshire in the south.

Interior of Todd's printing works, Marlborough Street.

Appendix I – VIII

Appendix I

WHITEHAVEN HARBOUR COMMISSIONERS

EXPORTS (Tons)

	1956	1957	1958	1959	1960	1961	1962	1963	1964	1965
Coal Cargoes	284,094	263,113	254,385	223,862	194,947	173,663	155,464	158,650	120,197	116,307
Bunkers	6,917	5,547	4,343	3,462	2,319	2,592	1,461	1,183	1,463	218
Total Coal	291,011	268,660	258,728	227,324	197,266	176,255	156,925	160,833	121,660	116,525
Detergents	18,533	18,818	2,231	663	408		87		695	5,508
Phosphates	133		20	389	60		241			
Sulphuric Acid						3,635				
Sundries	34	5	196	30				986		66
Total Exports	309,711	287,483	261,175	228,406	197,734	179,890	157,253	160,819	121,355	122,099
Total Imports	47,591	81,580	99,427	109,100	115,322	117,375	156,156	194,409	229,495	246,906
Total Imports/Exports	357,302	369,063	360,602	337,506	313,056	297,265	313,409	355,228	350,850	369,005

	1966	1967	1968	1969	1970	1971	1972	1973	1974	1975	1976
Coal Cargoes	82,871	87,404	90,431	77,482	109,939	155,374	125,573	132,021	70,516	86,831	72,401
Bunkers	213	213	201	224	222	169	146	137	107	144	163
Total Coal	83,084	87,617	90,632	77,706	110,161	155,543	125,719	132,158	70,623	86,975	72,564
Coke		310									
Detergents	20,262	19,932	18,073	13,992	11,081	9,788	9,595	6,358			
Cement					2,928		1,700				
Cement Clinker					40,799	48,540					
Irradiated Fuel Tanks					1,856	1,377	1,081		286		
Sulphuric Acid		1,731	4,033	502			917	10,636	4,177		
Uranium Trioxide					50			225			
Sundries	213	213	201	224	222	228					
Total Exports	103,346	109,590	112,738	92,200	166,875	215,476	139,012	149,377	75,086	86,975	72,564
Total Imports	284,649	297,600	350,837	362,942	422,472	382,000	404,099	459,349	489,063	384,272	490,022
Total Imports/Exports	387,995	407,190	463,575	455,142	589,347	597,476	543,111	608,726	564,149	471,247	562,586

WHITEHAVEN HARBOUR COMMISSIONERS

IMPORTS (Tons)

	1956	1957	1958	1959	1960	1961	1962	1963	1964	1965
Aluminium Ingots			1,390	1,651	3,702	4,057	3,625	944	3,294	2,318
Cement	330				1,560					
Oats	801	12,008	12,182	9,544	4,037	4,341	4,492	4,376	2,199	4,199
Potatoes								121	368	
Phosphate Rock	41,863	65,134	82,578	93,596	103,885	106,154	144,977	187,064	218,621	236,148
Sodium Sulphate	2,849	2,707	2,234	2,922	1,110	1,152	1,663	744	369	369
Sulphur									3,805	2,675
Sulphuric Acid										
Timber	1,350	1,672	945	1,387	1,028	1,336	1,081	1,160	839	362
Sundries	398	59	98			335	318			835
Total	47,591	81,580	99,427	109,100	115,322	117,375	156,156	194,409	229,495	246,906

	1966	1967	1968	1969	1970	1971	1972	1973	1974	1975	1976
Alcohol (Fatty)				196	1,660	949	897	878	497		
Alkylates	1,640	1,640							1,750	3,412	1,648
Aluminium Ingots	1,501	1,501	2,435	3,834	401	255					
Detergents (Fat)					520						
Fertiliser				415	497			500			
Irradiated Fuel Tanks				717					301		
Oats	2,170	1,059	2,055	1,708	2,097	1,545	1,174				
Phosphates			1,401		1,360	785					
Phosphate Rock	258,722	280,721	332,333	346,226	379,172	374,660	384,787	448,590	482,277	379,892	488,226
Potatoes			1,024	3,084	604		1,359				
Salt	1,107	3,671				1,258	950	1,093			
Sodium Sulphate	2,980	5,268	4,463		2,107	2,548	1,067				
Sulphur	17,483	2,449	6,219	5,644	33,100		12,653	7,745			
Sulphuric Acid	1,295	1,291	907	514	1,004			543			
Timber				604			1,097			906	
Wood Pulp										62	63
Sundries	835						115		15		85
Total	284,649	297,600	350,837	362,942	422,472	382,000	404,099	459,349	489,063	384,272	490,022

Appendix IIa

COLLIERIES

	HAIG		HARRINGTON No. 10		HARRINGTON No. 11		WALKMILL		WILLIAM	
Year	Manpower	Tonnage	Manpower	Tonnage	Manpower	Tonnage	Manpower	Tonnage	Manpower	Tonnage
1947	1,300		720		113		269		440	
1948	1,300		720		113		269		440	
1949	1,300		720		113		269		440	
1950	1,353		807		124		250		410	
1951	1,385	296,000	785	156,000	120	33,000	245	48,000	380	55,000
1952	1,510	334,000	795	154,000	120	32,000	255	62,000	375	64,000
1953	1,620	348,000	850	166,000	120	28,000	280	81,000	390	76,000
1954	1,585	379,000	855	170,000	125	31,000	275	82,000	365	69,000
1955	1,565	399,000	795	164,000	103	34,000	277	79,000	Closed 1955	
1956	1,766	438,000	932	173,000	102	38,000	283	78,000		
1957	1,788	442,000	967	172,000	113	35,000	276	77,000		
1958	1,802	397,000	923	170,000	101	33,000	277	69,000		
1959	1,777	401,000	907	162,000	93	35,000	281	65,000		
1960	1,701	336,100	841	149,100	90	31,300	232	51,100		
1961	1,570	386,200	598	132,300	84	24,600	Closed 1961			
1962	1,530	360,000	590	140,000	86	28,000				
1963	1,504	366,400	596	105,000	Closed 1963					
1964	1,606	376,900	591	115,500						
1965	1,549	376,436	633	100,579						
1966	1,662	304,500	815	142,686						

Appendix IIb

COLLIERIES

	HAIG		HARRINGTON No. 11	
Year	Manpower	Tonnage	Manpower	Tonnage
1966-67	1,609	322,000	773	109,000
1967-68	1,589	483,000	759	112,000
1968-69	1,487	428,000	458	21,000
1969-70	1,449	372,000		
1970-71	1,385	272,000	Winding ceased at	
1971-72	1,382	291,000	Harrington No. 10 in	
1972-73	1,320	248,000	July 1968 and at	
1973-74	1,271	274,000	Solway, Workington in	
1974-75	1,260	302,000	May 1973.	
1975-76	1,214	349,000		
1976-77	1,158	293,000		

Appendix III

BOROUGH OF WHITEHAVEN RATEABLE VALUES

Year	£	Year	£
1894-95	71,898	1936-37	94,111
1895-96	73,897	1937-38	93,138
1896-97	73,575	1938-39	96,337
1897-98	75,068	1939-40	98,883
1898-99	74,496	1940-41	101,241
1899-1900	73,659	1941-42	102,108
1900-01	75,417	1942-43	102,148
1901-02	77,939	1943-44	102,042
1902-03	76,203	1944-45	102,712
1903-04	77,284	1945-46	102,957
1904-05	77,332	1946-47	104,091
1905-06	74,844	1947-48	105,902
1906-07	75,505	1948-49	111,085
1907-08	76,370	1949-50	111,753
1908-09	76,648	1950-51	117,218
1909-10	76,791	1951-52	125,290
1910-11	76,688	1952-53	130,193
1911-12	74,617	1953-54	135,326
1912-13	74,923	1954-55	139,394
1913-14	75,908	1955-56	227,723
1914-15	76,365	1956-57	216,183
1915-16	76,142	1957-58	220,598
1916-17	78,976	1958-59	247,899
1917-18	79,136	1959-60	253,301
1918-19	78,794	1960-61	269,091
1919-20	78,485	1961-62	274,836
1920-21	78,782	1962-63	864,731
1921-22	76,182	1963-64	895,268
1922-23	78,215	1964-65	983,322
1923-24	80,575	1965-66	986,134
1924-25	79,900	1966-67	1,003,050
1925-26	84,701	1967-68	1,006,767
1926-27	87,576	1968-69	1,071,885
1927-28	85,338	1969-70	1,083,414
1928-29	93,471	1970-71	1,086,983
1929-30	96,550	1971-72	1,095,616
1930-31	81,863	1972-73	1,125,635
1931-32	82,578	1973-74	2,372,583
1932-33	82,936		
1933-34	83,710		
1934-35	91,540	at 1 April	
1935-36	92,767	1974	2,350,598

Appendix IV

WHITEHAVEN POPULATION STATISTICS

* Indicates official census.

Figures up to 1841 are for the Poor Law township.

Figures for 1851, 1861 and 1871 are for the township and for the parliamentary borough.

Figures after 1871 are for the parliamentary borough which included part of Preston Quarter.

† Figures for 1934 onwards are for the extended municipal borough boundary.

All figures after 1891, except for the official census returns are Medical Officer's estimates.

Owing to Local Government re-organisation and Health Service re-organisation population figures for Whitehaven are not available for 1975, 1976 and 1977.

Year	Population	Year	Population
1642	250	1933	21,200
1693	2,222	1934	23,185†
1713	4,000	1935	23,060
1762	9,063	1936	22,970
1801	8,742	1937	22,380
*1811	10,106	1938	22,350
*1821	12,438	1939	22,370
*1831	11,393	1940	22,960
*1841	11,854	1941	23,640
*1851	(14,190) (T.)	1942	22,940
	(18,916) (P.B.)	1943	22,490
*1861	(14,064) (T.)	1944	21,650
	(18,842) (P.B.)	1945	21,650
*1871	(13,030) (T.)	1946	22,390
	(18,183) (P.B.)	1947	22,580
*1881	19,717	1948	23,380
*1891	19,003	1949	23,690
1892	17,800	1950	24,340
1893	18,000	*1951	24,620
1894	19,000	1952	24,630
1895	19,000	1953	24,940
1896	19,000	1954	25,240
1897	19,300	1955	25,290
1898	19,300	1956	25,730
1899	19,300	1957	25,960
1900	19,320	1958	26,150
*1901	19,324	1959	26,250
1902	19,320	*1960	27,450
1903	19,320	1961	27,566
1904	19,320	1962	27,610
1905	19,320	1963	27,600
1906	19,320	1964	27,500
1907	19,320	1965	27,290
1908	19,320	1966	27,130
1909	19,320	1967	27,050
1910	19,320	1968	26,960
*1911	19,050	1969	26,760
1912	19,100	1970	26,460
1913	19,200	*1971	26,724
1914	19,300	1972	26,460
1915	19,300	1973	26,380
1916	18,040	1974	26,260
1917	17,892		
1918	17,693		

Year	Population	Year	Live births
1919	19,450	1965	485
1920	19,171	1966	470
*1921	19,810	1967	430
1922	19,810	1968	425
1923	20,050	1969	465
1924	20,310	1970	390
1925	20,690	1971	470
1926	20,970	1972	379
1927	21,020	1973	427
1929	21,190	1974	436
1929	20,980	1975	392
1930	20,980	1976	383
*1931	21,270	1977	381
1932	21,400		

Appendix V

MAYORS OF WHITEHAVEN SINCE INCORPORATION IN 1894

Rt. Hon. Hugh Cecil, Earl of Lonsdale
1894-95, 1895-96
John Pattinson
1896-97, 1897-98
John Raven Musgrave
1898-99, 1899-1900
John Davis
1900-01, 1901-02
Joseph Isaac Fisher
1902-03, 1903-04
George Clare Bennett
1904-05, 1905-06
Wilson Hastwell
1906-07, 1907-08
Joseph Braithwaite
1908-09, 1909-10, 1910-11
John Gaythorpe Oldfield
1911-12, 1912-13
Herbert Wilson Walker
1913-14, 1914-15
John Raven Musgrave
1915-16, 1916-17, 1917-18, 1918-19
George Palmer
1919-20, 1920-21
William Hood Wandless
1921-22, 1922-23
Evan Henry Evans
1923-24, 1924-25
Samuel Turner
1925-26, 1926-27
Caroline Helder
1927-28, 1928-29
Thompson Reed
1929-30, 1930-31
William Rowe
1931-32, 1932-33
William Stephenson
1933-34, 1934-35
Frederick S. J. Borland
1935-36, 1936-37
Walter Wear
1937-38, 1938-39
James Baird Smith
1939-40, 1940-41
Frances Harvey
1941-42, 1942-43
Henry Harrison
1943-44, 1944-45
John Gill
1945-46, 1946-47
John McSherry
1947-48, 1948-May 1949

John McAllister
1949-50
Joseph Blamire
1950-51
William Edward Knipe
1951-52
William John Pritchard
1952-53
John Walsh
1953-54
William John Denvir
1953-54
George Hanlon
1955-56
George Q. McCartney
1956-57
Thompson Reed, Jr
1957-58
Isaac Park
1958-59
John Boylan
1959-60
Frederick Baxter
1960-61
John Daniel Davidson
1960-61
Eleanor Colley
1961-62
James McMean
1963-64
Atkinson M. Garraway
1964-65
William Fell
1965-66
John Welch
1966-67
Alan C. Daugherty
1967-68
Henry Smith
1968-69
Francis May Reed
1969-70
Joseph B. McAllister
1970-71
James M. Ruddy
1971-72
James L. Johnston
1972-73
Walter Hurst
1973-74

Appendix VI

As a result of the 1832 electoral Reform Act Whitehaven became a parliamentary constituency. The first election was between a Reform candidate, Isaac Littledale, who resided at 14 Scotch Street, and Matthias Attwood, a Birmingham banker who was the Lowther nominee. The electoral base was not very wide — 438 — and the election poll book shows that 211 votes were cast for Attwood, 173 for Littledale and fifty-four persons did not vote.

It was a fiercely fought contest, as were subsequent elections, but Attwood retained the seat in the Lowther interest until 1847. It remained a Lowther seat for a further half century. He was followed by R. C. Hillyard who was a member for the constituency from 1847 until 1857; George Lyall who sat from 1857 until 1865; George Augustus Frederick Cavendish Bentinck 1865 until his death in 1891, and Sir James Bain 1891 until 1892.

The franchise had been extended in 1867, and by the 1880s the gap between the two parties was narrowing, as the results show:

1885	Electorate	2,617
G. A. F. Cavendish Bentinck (Con.)		1,336
W. C. Gully (Lib.)		1,125
	Majority	211

1886	Electorate	2,700
G. A. F.. Cavendish Bentinck (Con.)		1,216
H. G. Shee (Lib.)		1,110
	Majority	106

Bye-election 1891

Sir James Bain (Con.)		1,338
H. G. Shee (Lib.)		1,105
	Majority	233

The Liberal breakthrough came in 1892:

T. Shepherd Little (Lib.)		1,306
Sir James Bain (Con.)		1,088
	Majority	218

At the next election the pendulum swung back:

1895		
Augustus Helder (Con.)		1,380
T. Shepherd Little (Lib.)		1,114
	Majority	266

1900		
Augustus Helder (Con.)		1,553
William McGowan (Lib.)		876
	Majority	677

The national Liberal revival of 1906 saw one more swing:

W. J. D. Burnyeat (Lib.)		1,507
J. Robertson-Walker (Con.)		1,194
	Majority	313

In that year the Labour Representation Committee won 29 seats in Parliament and became the Labour Party. At the election in January, 1910 the contest became a three-cornered one:

J. Arthur Jackson (Con.)		1,188
W. H. Wandless (Lib.)		852
Andrew Sharpe (Lab.)		825
	Majority	336

In December 1910 it was a straight fight which gave Labour its first but not last representation locally:

Thomas Richardson (L. & S.)		1,414
J. Arthur Jackson (Con.)		1,220
	Majority	194

In 1918 electoral boundaries were altered, and a new Whithaven Division created from an amalgamation of the former Whitehaven and Egremont Divisions:

J. A. Grant (Con.)		10,716
T. Gavan Duffy (Lab.)		9,016
	Majority	1,710

In 1922 all three parties entered the arena with the result:

T. Gavan Duffy (Lab.)		10,935
Sir J. A. Grant (Con.)		8,956
H. K. Campbell (Lib.)		4,029
	Majority	1,979

In 1923 when the electorate was 28,203 it was again a straight fight:

T. Gavan Duffy (Lab.)		12,419
Robert Spear Hudson (Con.)		11,029
	Majority	1,390

In 1924 it was again a straight fight with the outcome reversed:

Robert Spear Hudson (Con.)		13,149
T. Gavan Duffy (Lab.)		11,741
	Majority	1,408

1929	Electorate	34,006
M. Phillips Price (Lab.)		14,034
R. S. Hudson (Con.)		12,582
Prof. H. D. Naylor (Lib.)		3,558
	Majority	1,452

1931	Electorate	34,079
William Nunn (Con.)		16,286
M. Phillips Price (Lab.)		14,255
	Majority	1,652

1935
Frank Anderson (Lab.)
William Nunn (Con.)
Thomas Stephenson (I.L.P.)

Electorate 34,767
14,794
14,442
1,004
Majority 352

1945
Frank Anderson (Lab.)
Wing Com. W. E. Hill (Con.)

18,568
11,821
Majority 6,747

1950
Frank Anderson (Lab.)
William Nunn (Con.)

Electorate 43,751
22,850
15,233
Majority 6,747

1951
Frank Anderson (Lab.)
G. W. Iredell (Con.)

23,190
15,990
Majority 7,200

1955
Frank Anderson (Lab.)
G. W. Iredell (Con.)

Electorate 45,957
22,348
16,154
Majority 6,194

Bye-election: 18 June 1959:

J. B. Symonds (Lab.)
G. W. Iredell (Con.)

21,475
15,151
Majority 6,324

1959 (October)
J. B. Symonds (Lab.)
H. Pedrazza (Con.)

Electorate 48,966
22,783
16,653
Majority 6,130

1964
J. B. Symonds (Lab.)
Brudenell (Con.)

23,267
15,440
Majority 5,874

1966
J. B. Symonds (Lab.)
J. A. Kevill (Con.)

Electorate 46,532
22,726
13,935
Majority 8,791

1970
J. A. Cunningham (Lab.)
W. G. Mackay (Con.)

Electorate 50,674
22,974
16,418
Majority 6,556

1974, 28 February
J. A. Cunningham (Lab.)
P. B. Vose (Con.)

Electorate 50,792
23,229
15,867
Majority 7,362

1974, 10 October
J. A. Cunningham (Lab.)
P. B. Vose (Con.)
M. Gilbert (Lib.)

21,832
11,899
5,563
Majority 9,933

RECENT RESULTS

John A. Cunningham (Lab.) 22,626
John Somers (Con.) 17,171
Edward Akister (Lib.) 2,559
Bill Dixon (Ind.) 790
Majority 5,455
No change.
Electorate 52,787.
Poll 81 per cent.
Lib. and Ind. lost their deposits.
6.3 per cent swing Lab. to Con.

Appendix VII

LIST OF MINE DISASTER VICTIMS 1839-1947

WILLIAM PIT DISASTER – February, 1839
List of victims

	Name	Address	Age
1	Stott, George	New Houses	60
2	Davidson, William	New Houses	41
3	Smith, William	New Houses	22
4	Harrison, Richard	New Houses	43
5	Tordiff, John	New Houses	31
6	Curran, Barney	Tangier Street	24
7	M'Ginnis, Felix	Tangier Street	33
8	Gilmour, Thomas	Tangier Street	60
9	Roney, Hugh	Banks' Lane, George Street	46
10	Firth, John	Charles Street	33
11	Teare, James	Nicholson Alley	18
12	Teare, Robert	Nicholson Alley	12
13	Shields, Richardson	New Houses	16
14	Fisher, John	New Houses	10
15	MacMullen, Willam	New Houses	11
16	Dornan, William	New Houses	14
17	Wheatley, Michael	New Houses	13
18	Dunn, John	New Houses	11
19	Pearson, Christopher	New Houses	14
20	Hoskins, Levi	Banks' Buildings	16
21	Atkinson, William	New Town	14
22	Ross, John	Charles Street	16
23	Clarke, James	Kelsick Lane	14

WILLIAM PIT DISASTER – 11 May 1910
List of victims No. 6 NORTH

	Name	Address	Age
1	Bell, William Chris	Dixon's Square, Ginns	30
2	Benson, William	44 Front Row	51
3	Boyd, George	58 & 59 Front Row	21
4	Branch, Daniel	18 Mid Street, Kells	21
5	Brannon, George	87 Mount Pleasant	49
6	Brannon, John	74 Back Row	22
7	Brannon, Thomas	13 Mount Pleasant	25
8	Brocklebank, Alfred	24 Court 2, George Street	34
9	Butler, Joseph	84 Queen Street	26
10	Butler, Edward	Rose Bank, Hensingham	36
11	Corkhill, Anthony	104 Queen Street	29
12	Farrah, Joseph	27 North Row, Kells	23
13	Garroway, Robert Little	36 Ginns	15
14	Glaister, Jacob	67 Back Row	33
15	Gregg, Alexander	22 Sandhills Lane	36
16	Henderson, William	27 Mid Street, Kells	32
17	Heslop, Chris F.	30 New Street	30

	Name	Address	Age
18	Heslop, John William	1 Cunning's Lane	34
19	Heslop, Joseph	84 Newtown	28
20	Hutchinson, John	27 North Row, Kells	51
21	Kelly, William John	Bragg's Court, Marlborough Street	29
22	Kenmore, Thomas	3 Rosemary Lane	27
23	Lynn, Edward	6 Bragg's Court, Marlborough Street	26
24	McBain, James	16 Mount Pleasant	35
25	McClusky, Henry, sr	6 Dickinson's Court, Church Street	55
26	McClusky, Henry	Reed's Court, Scotch Street	26
27	McClusky, James	Reed's Court, Scotch Street	21
28	McCourt, James	25 Mid Street, Kells	36
29	McCourt, Robert	17 Mid Street, Kells	34
30	McCourt, Thomas	4 Mid Street, Kells	29
31	McCumisky, Michael	3 Front Row	41
32	McGarry, James	18 Castle Row	44
33	McGarry, John	68 Back Row	27
34	McGarry, Thomas	7 Granby Terrace	31
35	McGee, James	7 Dickinson's Court, Queen Street	34
36	McMullen, James	23 Quay Street	44
37	Nicholson, Edward	21 Schoolhouse Lane	34
38	O'Fee, Edward	72 Back Row	35
39	O'Hara, William John	78 Court, Low Church Street	26
40	O'Pray, Henry	7 Back Ginns	20
41	Reed, Thomas	2 Littledale Lane	23
42	Reid, Joseph	8 North Row, Kells	55
43	Riley, James	129 Court 1, Queen Street	31
44	Roney, James	3 Walker's Court, Newtown	46
45	Smith, George	7 Ellison's Place	38
46	Smith, James	7 Ellison's Place	18
47	Smith, Robert	11 Dixon's Square, Ginns	18
48	Southward James	69 Back Row	18
49	Tinnion, Andrew	26 Front Row	29
50	Todhunter, William	16 Gore's Buildings	33
51	Trainor, Arthur	9 West Strand	33
52	Walker, William, sr	2 Castle Row	57
53	Walker, William	2 Castle Row	18
54	Welsh, Isaac	7 Back Row	20
55	Wren, Isaac	25 Front Row	50
56	Wren, John	19 Ginns	37
57	Wren, Thomas	25, Front Row	20

No. 5 NORTH

58	Connor, Patrick	23 West Strand	21
59	Connor, John	6 Nicholson's Lane	43
60	Davy, John	74 Strand Street	20
61	Denver, Edward	33 Newtown	20
62	Fidler, Joseph	1 South Row, Kells	42
63	Finn, Arthur John	60 Peter Street	41
64	Joyce, Thomas	1 Harris Green	33
65	Joyce, John	28 South Row, Kells	35
66	Lucas, John James	54 Back Row	52
67	McAllister, Hugh	5 South Row, Kells	49
68	McAllister, John	63 Ginns	16
69	McAllister, Henry	58 & 59 Front Row	22
70	McCormick, jr	98 Castle Row	15
71	McCumisky, George	18 James Place	36
72	McLaughlin, Alex Duncan	54 Ginns	16

	Name	Address	Age
73	Moore, Henry	2 Senhouse Court, Senhouse Street	45
74	Moore, James	6 Dixon's Place, Michael Street	31
75	Mossop, Joseph	89 Dukes Street	22
76	Mullings, John	51 Lowther Row	23
77	O'Connor, James	1 Winter's Buildings, Ginns	25
78	O'Pray, William	5 Front Row	35
79	Robertson, William Henry	21 Plumblands Lane	25
80	Toner, Edward	61 High Queen Street	18
81	Unidentified, No. 53		
82	Unidentified, No. 62		
83	Walker, William	5 Howgill Street	32
84	Wear, Robert	44 Lowther Row	21
85	Welsh, Matthew	7 Back Row	17

No. 3 NORTH

	Name	Address	Age
86	Anderson, John	74 Ginns	23
87	Benson, William	19 Court, Sandhills Lane	33
88	Cooper, Richard	23 Brackenthwaite	22
89	Dunn, William John	81 & 82 Castle Row	21
90	Elliott, William	22 Gore's Buildings	39
91	Ferryman, James	10 Mid Street, Kells	17
92	Fisher, Mark	10a Howgill Street	36
93	Garroway, John	3 Williamson Lane, Tangier Street	32
94	Garroway, Alex	7 Gore's Buildings	37
95	Glave, Henry	88 Castle Row	35
96	Greenan, Peter	32 Quay Street	34
97	Harrison, Henry	39 Front Row	39
98	Harrison, John	56 Back Row	41
99	Irving, James	43 & 44 Castle Row	21
100	Johnstone, Robert	24 Back Row	41
101	Kennedy, James	62 Grey Street, Workington	27
102	Lewthwaite, Dan	55 Main Street, Hensingham	27
103	Lucas, John Dalton	39 Lowther Row	34
104	McAllister, Thomas	63 Ginns	44
105	McAllister, James	63 Ginns	17
106	McAllister, Edward	108 Castle Row	23
107	McAllister, John	7 Quinn's Square, Preston Street	21
108	McCourt, Thomas	61 Castle Row	29
109	McQuillam, Joseph	40 Back Row	34
110	Mitchell, William	5 Barker's Court, Tangier Street	25
111	O'Neill, Thomas	Low Church Street	38
112	O'Hara, Thomas	19 Mid Street, Kells	16
113	Reed, Joseph	4 Birkett's Court, Irish Street	25
114	Reed, Joseph	4 Marlborough Street	26
115	Reed, John	28 Chapel Street	47
116	Ritson, George Matthew	32 Ginns	47
117	Ritson, George Matthew	32 Ginns	15
118	Rogan, Henry	27 Back Row	16
119	Stephenson, Fred	20 George Street	32
120	Stephenson, Joseph	2 Barker's Court, Tangier Street	32
121	Taggart, John B.	4 Arrowthwaite	39
122	Taggart, James McKenzie	18a Schoolhouse Lane	28
123	Taylor, James	32 Newtown	31
124	Unidentified, No. 72		
125	Usher, Jonathan	3 Peet's Place	33
126	Vaughan, John James	7 Quinn's Terrace, Charles Street	23

Name	Address	Age
127 Walker, Ralph	81 & 82 Castle Row	44
128 Wilson, William	96 & 97 Castle Row	21
129 Armstrong, John	61 Newtown	
130 Armstrong, George	7 High Row, Hensingham	
131 Cowie, Benjamin	24 Ginns	28
132 Cooper, Robert	69 Newtown	
133 McCormick, James	98 Castle Row	58
134 Mullholland, William	45 Back Row	
135 Walker, Joseph Henry	41 Lowther Row, Ginns	
136 Wright, John	Irish Street	

Wellington Pit Disaster, 11 May 1910;
collective picture of victims.

HAIG PIT DISASTER – 11 July 1922
List of Victims

	Name	Address
1	Thomas Parker Telford	7 Low Harras Moor
2	Robert Routledge McCreadie	4 Thwaiteville
3	Robert Denwood	13 Quay Street
4	Joseph Moore	22 Thwaiteville
5	Albert Powe	Low Harras Moor
6	James Graves	Goosebutts, Hensingham
7	Moses Huddleston Tyson	3 Thwaiteville
8	Thomas Corlett	Birley Court, Duke Street
9	John Kirkpatrick	1 Hills Place, Church Street
10	Gordan McCreadie	4 Thwaiteville
11	William Hope	10 Schoolhouse Lane
12	John Moore	10 Bransty Road
13	George McCreadie	4 Thwaiteville
14	Robert McDowell	High Hensingham
15	Thomas Moore	3 Garden Villas, Hensingham
16	Thomas Gilhooly	40 Keekle Terrace, Hensingham
17	Leonard Ixon Hellon	3 Thwaiteville
18	Bernard Murphey	56 Bowthorn Road, Cleator Moor
19	Sylvester McAvoy	29 Thwaiteville
20	Thomas Haig	2 Cooks Court, Scotch Street
21	Albert Shepherd	135 Main Street, Parton
22	William Weightman	16 Thwaiteville
23	Samuel Coulter	Main Street, Hensingham
24	George Stephenson Parkinson	Low Harras Moor
25	William Carter	30 Thwaiteville
26	Thomas McDowell	Streeton's Terrace, Hensingham
27	Jackson Sparks	4 Williamsons Lane, Hensingham
28	John Pattinson	13 Williamsons Lane, Hensingham
29	William John Sparks	4 Williamsons Lane, Hensingham
30	Thomas Robinson	53 Main Street, Hensingham
31	John Carson Brewster	17 Lonsdale Place, Whitehaven
32	John Bennett	28 Arrowthwaite
33	Thomas Henry Cooper	28 Auction Yard, Newtown
34	Henry Golding	2 Ravenhill
35	Richard Denver	2 Low Road, Whitehaven
36	Issac Osborne	Crookdale, Brayton
37	Douglas James Michael Fell	Holy Trinity Vicarage, Whitehaven
38	John Casson	Low Harras Moor
39	George Watson	5 Brookbank, Hensingham

HAIG PIT DISASTER – 13 December 1927
List of Victims

	Name	Address
1	Knox, James	1 Mountain View, Prospect
2	Fitzsimmons, James	1 Back Ginns
3	Bradley, William	5 Mitchell's Court, Irish Street
4	Horrocks, Harold	1 Todhunter's Buildings, Queen Street

HAIG PIT DISASTER – 12 February 1928
List of Victims

	Name	Address
1	Steel, Robert	Whelpside

	Name	Address
2	Loudon, William	Earls Road
3	Burdess, Peter	(attached to the Newcastle centre)
4	Fell, Robert	3 Mountain View, Prospect
5	Hanlon, Henry C.	Brayton Road, Bransty
6	Tyson, John	West View, Bransty
7	Walker, Tom	1 Rydal Avenue, Seacliffe
8	Hodson, George	37 Solway Road, Arrowthwaite
9	Rothery, James	43 Front Row, New Houses
10	Wilkinson, Frank	1 Ladypit Cottages
11	Cresswell, Jesse	Brickworks House, Low Road
12	McKenzie, Hugh	8 Sandhills Lane
13	Graham, William	24 Church Street

HAIG PIT DISASTER – 29 January 1931
List of Victims

	Name	Address
1	Holliday, John	26 Main Street, Parton
2	Wilkinson, William	4 Plumblands Lane
3	Gainford, Joseph Henry	28 Hilltop Road, Arrowthwaite
4	Parkin, Robert	68 High Scotch Street
5	Kelly, Joseph	The Bungalow, Low Road
6	Storey, Matthew	16 George Street
7	Slack, John Edward	53 Ennerdale Terrace
8	Hewitson, Robert	86 Buttermere Avenue
9	Richardson, James	Union Buildings, Whitehaven
10	Richardson, John	Union Buildings, Whitehaven
11	Cowan, William	6 Countess Terrace, Bransty
12	Parker, George sr	Middle Row, New Houses
13	Parker, George jr	Middle Row, New Houses
14	Telford, John	Middle Row, New Houses
15	Cockbain, Edward	8 Ennerdale Terrace, Kells
16	Hocking, William	High Harras Moor
17	Rogan, Joseph	Thwaiteville, Kells
18	Rogan, John Thomas	Thwaiteville, Kells
19	Knox, James	31 Old Arrowthwaite
20	Armstrong, Fred	91 Buttermere Avenue (native of Plumbland, Aspatria)
21	Bailey, John jr	9 York Road, Arrowthwaite
22	Vincent, Robert	Hill Top Road, Kells
23	Hayton, Richard	20 Front Row, New Houses
24	Groggins, Robert	26 Mount Pleasant
25	Ruddy, John	65 Hill Top Road, Arrowthwaite
26	Quirk, Thomas	8 Littledale Lane, Whitehaven
27	Smith, Joseph	East Row, Kells

WILLIAM PIT DISASTER – 3 June 1941
List of Victims

	Name	Address	Age
1	Barbour, Sydney	25 Queen Street	21
2	Burney, John P.	Bentinck Row, The Ginns	20
3	Curwen, Jonathan	North Row, Kells	57
4	George, James	49 Fell View Avenue	18
5	Harker, William E.	Countess Terrace, Bransty	20

	Name	Address	Age
6	*McGrievy, Robert	50 Valley View Road	19
7	*Martin, Charles	South View Road, Bransty	45
8	Moore, Cornelius	34 Scotch Street	40
9	Perry, William	South View Road, Bransty	50
10	Wells, James	9 Charles Street	

*Died following admittance to hospital

WILLIAM PIT DISASTER – 15th August 1947
List of Victims

	Name	Address	Age
1	Agnew, Andrew	17 Todhunter's Buildings, Queen Street	36
2	Allan, Thomas	26 Buttermere Avenue	33
3	Allan, Harry T.	45 Hill Top Road	39
4	Allan, John	5 Buttermere Avenue	59
5	Anderson, John	28 Buttermere Avenue	50
6	Atkinson, James	4 Gameriggs Road	45
7	Atkinson, Richard	Ladypit Cottages	28
8	Barker, Henry	4 Ehen Road, Cleator Moor	34
9	Barwise, James R.	5 Low Harras Moor	49
10	Bowes, James M.	5 Garfield Place, Parton	34
11	Brannon, Thomas	55 Haig Avenue	57
12	Brannon, Joseph	21 Greenbank Avenue	45
13	Bridges, Jacob E.	85 Grasmere Avenue	37
14	Byers, Hartley	15 James Street, Frizington	35
15	Calvin, Herbert	67 Peter Street	40
16	Campbell, James	81 Woodhouse Road	40
17	Carr, Harold J.	9 Jane Street, Frizington	22
18·	Cartmell, Richard	59 Valley View Road	25
19	Clark, William	15 The Square, Parton	46
20	Clifford, James	72 Frizington Road, Frizington	26
21	Conkey, Robert	29 Smithfield, Egremont	43
22	Crofts, William H.	111 Queen Street	45
23	Devlin, Samuel	9 Union Buildings, Low Road	27
24	Diamond, Joseph G.	8 Grasmere Avenue	33
25	Dixon, Thomas G.	25 Yeathouse Road, Frizington	55
26	Doran, John H.	8 Low Harras Moor	50
27	Farrer, Wilfred	66 Windermere Road	34
28	Fisher, William	12 Gore's Buildings, Scotch Street	39
29	Fox, Thomas	29 Bowness Road	24
30	Fox, Joseph	11 Woodhouse Road	35
31	Garner, John H.	41 Frizington Road, Frizington	37
32	Gibbons, James	60 Seven Acres, Parton	47
33	Gibson, Henry	17 Foundry Road, Parton	36
34	Glaister, Edward	14 Windermere Road	40
35	Glosson, Robert N.	67 Windermere Road	39
36	Grearson, Richard E.	173 Main Street, Parton	36
37	Grearson, William F.	96 Main Street, Parton	36
38	Hewer, Joseph W.	18a Seven Acres, Parton	40
39	Hewer, Ronald W.	110 Main Street, Parton	38
40	Hughes, Ronald	Hospital House, Bransty	20
41	Hutchinson, George	7 James Pit	40
42	Johnson, William	43 Trumpet Terrace, Cleator	27
43	Johnson, George	38 Lakeland Avenue	41
44	Lambert, James W.	1 Plumblands Lane	35
45	Lancaster, Thomas	33 Basket Road	27
46	Lee, William H.	29 Aldby Street, Cleator Moor	27
47	Leeson, James	10 Dyke Street, Frizington	48
48	Lyons, Dennis	4 Lakeland Avenue	31

	Name	Address	Age
49	Maddison, John H.	72 Fell View Avenue	22
50	Marshall, Joseph B.	70 George Street	48
51	Martin, William	3 Wellington Row	22
52	McAllister, Edward	Sun Inn, Parton	24
53	McAllister, Isaac	15 Bentinck's Row	54
54	McMullen, James	16a Sandhills Lane	27
55	McMullen, William T.	20a Roper Street	22
56	McSherry, Vincent	2 Crummock Avenue	37
57	Milburn, John	94 Grasmere Avenue	40
58	Moore, John E.	3 John Square, Peter Street	37
59	Moore, Joseph	64 Seven Acres, Parton	46
60	Moore, James	96b George Street	63
61	Mowat, John R.	3 Lowther Street	26
62	Murdock, Francis	11 Todhunter's Buildings, Queen Street	38
63	Murray, James	22 Crummock Avenue	36
64	Murray, William	5 Ladypit Terrace	39
65	Murtagh, Lawrence H. P.	73 Buttermere Avenue	41
66	Murtagh, Patrick	Old Woodhouse	28
67	Musson, William R.	Rose & Thistle, West Strand	22
68	Musson, Richard	22 Briscoe Crescent, Parton	36
69	Nelson, Thomas	Summergrove Cottages, Hensingham	36
70	Nicholson, William	1 Temple Terrace, Catherine Street	33
71	Norman, Joseph	1 The Close, Bransty	41
72	O'Fee, Sydney	62 Windermere Road	34
73	Paragreen, John A.	9 Bransty Road	30
74	Pickering, William L.	28 Haig Avenue	24
75	Pilkington, John	6 Longmire's Court, Queen Street	32
76	Pilkington, William	60 Windermere Road	66
77	Pilkington, William	21 Woodhouse Road	51
78	Pilkington, Thomas	60 Windermere Road	27
79	Porthouse, George	16 North Road	54
80	Quirk, John	23 Victoria Road	30
81	Raby, Adam	Fleswick Avenue	45
82	Ray, Edward R.	1 Front Row, Northside, Workington	31
83	Renwick, John R.	12 Gameriggs Road	39
84	Richardson, Thomas	150 Queen Street	40
85	Rigg, James	12 Marlborough Street	28
86	Robbs, John	6 Brayton Road	56
87	Saulters, Albert E.	12 Meadow View, Castle Croft, Egremont	40
88	Seward, Leonard	7 Pasture Road, Rowrah	36
89	Shackley, Thomas E.	76 Low Church Street	40
90	Shaw, Mark J.	40 North Road	45
91	Shilton, Henry	23 Main Street, Parton	44
92	Smith, Thomas B.	2 Torrentine's Buildings, Tangier Street	62
93	Smith, Thomas T.	7 South Row, Kells	38
94	Smith, Harold	17 George Street	41
95	Turner, Thomas		46
96	Tweddle, Albert	6 Fleswick Avenue	31
97	Walby, William A.	The Lodge, Ewenrigg Hall, Maryport	46
98	Walker, Ralph	16 Valley View Road	34
99	Williamson, William	14 Hilton Terrace	27
100	Wilson, George H.	Douglas Burn, Market Place	29
101	Wilson, Matthew	27 South View Road	46
102	Wilson, Joseph	72 Valley View Road	38
103	Woodend, Thomas	11 South View Road	64
104	Wylie, Walter	36 Fell View Road	26

Appendix VIII

WHITEHAVEN AND THE WASHINGTONS

Throughout the eighteenth century Whitehaven had very strong connections with Virginia and Maryland. One of the most interesting of these connections concerns a marriage that nearly changed the course of world history. George Gale, a member of the important Gale family, was a merchant trading with the colonies of Virginia and Maryland. In 1699 he met and married a widow named Mildred Washington. She had three children by her first marriage, John, Augustine and Mildred. She and the family came to Whitehaven, the boys being sent to Appleby School for their education.

Mildred Gale died following the birth of a daughter in January 1700. She, the daughter and a negro servant who came with them from Virginia, were all buried in the grounds of St Nicholas Church. Mildred Gale's will was contested by executors of her her first husband's estate and the boys were sent back to Virginia.

Augustine married and eventually became the father of George Washington, first President of the United States. It is interesting to reflect on what might have happened if Mildred Gale's will had not been contested and he had been brought up as an English merchant's son.

It is interesting to note that the registers of St Nicholas Church contain a number of entries concerning a branch of the Washington family resident in Whitehaven. Robert Washington settled at Bransty and had a dye-works on the site now occupied by the bus station. Of five children born to him and his wife, Eleanor, while resident in Whitehaven four died young, Robert died in 1742 and was succeeded in business by Lawrence Washington, who was probably a son, although his baptism is not recorded locally. Lawrence died in 1766 and his wife, Grace, in 1781.

One interesting entry refers to Thomas Washington, *a stranger*, who died 31 October 1744. The connection between this family and the Washingtons of Wharton in Lancashire or the American Washingtons has never been solved.

Where to look for more information

To the student who wishes to go more deeply into the history of Whitehaven there are three main sources of information:

1 *Manuscripts and theses.* Of the former the most important are the Lowther archives, now at the Record Office, Carlisle, although some are available on microfilm at the Whitehaven Library; the Whitehaven shipping registers, now at the Customs Office, Workington; and the minutes books of the Whitehaven Town and Harbour Trustees, in Whitehaven Library.

Of the latter the most important are a London University Ph.D. thesis by Oliver Wood, 'The development of the coal, iron and shipbuilding industries of West Cumberland, 1750-1914', 1952; and a Leeds University thesis by James E. Williams, 'The growth and decline of the port of Whitehaven', published in the *West Cumberland Times*, 1951.

2 The next important source is the files of local papers, especially *The Cumberland Pacquet*, 1774-1915; *The Whitehaven Gazette*, 1819-1826; *The Whitehaven Herald*, 1831-74; *The Whitehaven Guardian*, 1875-77; *The Whitehaven News*, 1852 to date; *The Northern Counties Gazette*, 1876-86; *The Whitehaven Advertiser*, 1882-1920;

3 Finally, there are printed sources of which the following are the most important:

Abercrombie, Patrick. *Cumbrian regional planning scheme.* 1932.
Barnett, Winston and Winskell, Cyril. *A study in conservation.* 1977.
Bulmer, T. and Co. *History, topography and directory of Cumberland.* 1901.
Bulmer, T. and Co. *History, topography and directory of West Cumberland.* 1883.
Burlington, Joseph. *Whitehaven Congregational Church, Scotch Street, 1874-1924.* 1924.
Caine, Caesar. *A history of the churches of the Rural Deanery of Whitehaven.* 1916.
Carvel, John L. *The Coltness Iron Company: a study in private enterprise.* Privately printed. 1948.
A century of West Cumberland history (extracts from the *Cumberland Pacquet*, 1774-1780). n.d.
Commissioner for the Special Areas. Reports of the Commissioner for the Special Areas (England and Wales). 1935-1938.
Crossland, J. Brian. *Looking at Whitehaven.* 1971.
Cumberland and Westmorland Antiquarian and Archaeological Society: *Transactions, Old Series,* Volume 1-16, 1875-1900, *New Series,* Volume 1, 1901 to date.
Cumberland Development Council Ltd. *Cumberland: the story of industrial progress in the development area of West Cumberland.* 1957.
Daysh, G. H. J. *West Cumberland (with Alston): a survey of industrial facilities.* 1938.
Daysh, G. H. J. *Cumberland with special reference to the West Cumberland development area.* 1951.

Defoe, Daniel. *A tour through England and Wales, 1724.* Reprinted 1928.

De Koven, Mrs Reginald. *The life and letters of John Paul Jones.* 2 Volumes. 1930.

Denton, John. *An account of the most considerable estates and families in the county of Cumberland,* 1610. Reprinted 1887.

Dixon, Joshua. *The literary life of William Brownrigg, M.D., F.R.S., to which are added an account of the coal mines near Whitehaven and observations on the means of preventing epidemic fevers.* 1801.

Ferguson, Richard S. *A history of Cumberland.* 1890.

Field, F. J. *An armorial for Cumberland.* 1937.

Fuel and Power, Ministry of *Whitehaven 'William' Colliery, Cumberland: final report on the causes of, and circumstances attending, the explosion which occurred at Whitehaven 'William' Colliery, Cumberland, on 15 August 1947;* by A. M. Bryan. 1948.

Health, General Board of. *Report to the General Board of Health on a preliminary enquiry into the sewerage, drainage and supply of water, and the sanitary conditions of the inhabitants of the town of Whitehaven,* by Robert Rawlingson. 1849.

Geological Survey. *The geology of the Whitehaven and Workington district, explanations of sheet 22;* by T. Eastwood, E. E. L. Dixon, S. E. Hollingworth and Bernard Smith. 1931.

Gibson, John Frederic. *Brocklebanks 1770-1950.* 2 Volumes. 1953.

Gradon, W. McGowan. *Furness Railway, its rise and development 1846-1923.* 1946.

Hay, Daniel. *St Begh's, 1868-1968: centenary celebrations and visit of Apostolic Delegate, 14-16 September 1968.* 1968.

Historical Manuscripts Commission: *Thirteenth report, appendix, part VII: the manuscripts of the Earl of Lonsdale.* 1893.

Home Office. *Explosion and underground fire at the Wellington Pit, Whitehaven Colliery: report on the causes and circumstances attending and explosion and underground fire which occurred at the Wellington Pit, Whitehaven Colliery, on 11 May 1910;* by R. A. S. Redmayne and Samuel Pope. 1911.

Hughes, Edward. *North country life in the eighteenth century.* Volume II *Cumberland and Westmorland, 1700-1830.* 1965.

Hutchinson, William. *The history of the county of Cumberland.* 2 Volumes. 1794.

Jackson, William. *Papers and Pedigrees mainly relating to Cumberland and Westmorland.* 2 Volumes. 1892.

Jefferson, Samuel. *The history and antiquities of Allerdale-above-Derwent, in the county of Cumberland.* 1842.

Jewkes, John and Winterbottom, Allan. *An industrial survey of Cumberland and Furness: a study of the social implications of economic dislocation.* 1933.

Jollie, F. and Sons. *Jollie's Cumberland guide and directory.* 1811.

Jones, Clement. *Pioneer shipowners.* Volume II. 1938.

Joy, David. *Cumbrian coast railways.* 1968.

Kelly' Directory of Cumberland: 1873, 1894, 1897, 1910, 1914, 1921, 1925, 1934, 1938.

Knight, E. M. *Men leaving mining: West Cumberland 1966-67. Report to the Ministry of Labour.* 1968.

Labour, Ministry of. *Reports of investigations into the industrial conditions in certain areas of: 1 — West Cumberland and Haltwhistle, 2 — Durham and Tyneside, 3 — South Wales and Monmouthshire, 4 — Scotland.* 1934.

Lancaster, J. Y. and Wattleworth, D. R. *The iron and steel industry of West Cumberland.* 1977.

Lawrence-Dow, Elizabeth and Hay, Daniel. *Whitehaven to Washington.* 1974.

Lewis, William. *Diary of the Reverend Thomas Larkham, M.A., vicar of Tavistock,* with an appendix. 1871.

Linton, John, *A handbook of the Whitehaven and Furness railway.* 1852.

Lonsdale, Henry. *The worthies of Cumberland.* 6 Volumes.

Lorenz, Lincoln. *John Paul Jones. Fighter for Freedom.* 1943.

Mannex, P. and Co. *History and directory of Furness and West Cumberland.* 1882.

Mannix and Whellan. *History, gazetteer and directory of Cumberland.** 1847.

Marsh, H. W. 1823-1940. *Howgill Street Methodist Circuit, Whitehaven.* Souvenir plan on the occasion of the amalgamation with Lowther Street Circuit, 1 September 1940. 1940.

Marshall, John D. and Davies-Shiel, M. *The Lake District at work.* 1971.

Marshall, John D. and Davies-Shiel, M. *The industrial archaeology of the Lake Counties.* 1969. Reprinted with extensive revisions 1977.

Mines Department. *Explosion at Haig pit, Whitehaven, on Tuesday, 5 December, 1922: Inquest and Mines Department Inquiry, before D. J. Mason and a jury and Thomas Mottram. Minutes of proceedings (held) at . . . Whitehaven . . . October 1922.* 6 Volumes.

Mines Department. *Report on the causes of and circumstances attending the explosion which occurred at Haig Pit, Whitehaven Collieries, Cumberland, on 5 September 1922;* by Thomas Mottram. 1923.

Mines Department. *Report on the causes of and the circumstances attending the explosion which occurred at Haig Pit, Whitehaven Colliery, on 29 January 1931;* by Sir Henry Walker. 1931.

Mines Department. *Explosion at the William Pit, Whitehaven Collieries, Cumberland: report on the causes of and circumstances attending the explosion which occurred at the William Pit, Whitehaven Collieries, on 3 June 1941;* by F. H. Wynne. 1942.

Moon, Michael and Sylvia. *Bygone Whitehaven.* 1973. Volume Two, 1976.

Muriel, G. J. *A short history of the Whitehaven and West Cumberland Infirmary, 1783-1924;* revised by T. E. Woodhouse and G. G. Carter. 1924.

Napper, Errington, Collerton, Barnett. *Whitehaven: a new structure for a Restoration town.* 1971.

Nicholson, Joseph and Burn, Richard. *The history and antiquities of the counties of Westmorland and Cumberland.* 2 Volumes.* 1777.

Nightingale, B. *The Ejected of 1662 in Cumberland and Westmorland.* 2 Volumes. 1911.

Northern Economic Planning Council. *Regional ports survey.* 1969.

Parson, William and White, William. *History, directory and gazetteer of the counties of Cumberland and Westmorland.* 1829. Reprinted 1976.

Pears, Eileen. *Monkwray School centenary, 187601976.* 1976.

Peile and Nicholson. *A directory of Whitehaven. 1864.*

Poll Book of the election of a representative in Parliament for the Borough of Whitehaven. 1832.

The Register of the Priory of St Bees; edited by the Revd J. B. Wilson. 1915.

Rolt, L. T. C. *Mariners' market: Burnyeat Limited: growth over a century.* Privately printed. 1961.

Sawyers, William. *A list of Cumberland shipping, corrected to February 1840.* Reprinted 1975.

The Scallop Shell (St. James' Church Magazine), Volumes I-VIII, 1936-1943. (Contains valuable series of articles by Mr William Watson.)

Sewell, Donald P. *History notes on St James' Church, Whitehaven.* 1972.

Simmons, Jack. *The Maryport and Carlisle railway.* 1947.

Sutherland, Douglas. *The yellow earl: the life of Hugh Lowther, Fifth Earl of Lonsdale, 1857-1944.* 1965.

Tonkin, J. H. *Lowther Street Methodist Church, Whitehaven: a centenary brochure, 1877-1977.* 1977.

The Victorian history of the counties of England: Cumberland. 2 Volumes.* 1901-1906.

---

* Denotes that a modern reprint is available.

Whellan, William, Ed. *The history and topography of the counties of Cumberland and Westmorland.* 1860.

Whitehaven and District Festival of Britain Committee: *Souvenir programme of events: from May to December.* 1951.

Whitehaven Coporation. *Annual report of the Medical Officer of Health for the years 1894-95 onwards.*

Whitehaven Corporation. *Minutes of Council and committees, 1894-95 to 1973-74.*

Whitehaven Corporation. *The Municipal insigna: its history and origin.* Compiled by Daniel Hay. 1961.

Whitehaven Corporation. *Presentation of the honorary freedom of the borough to Alderman William Stephenson, J.P., C.C., and Alderman Francis Harvey, 19 March 1952.* 1952.

Whitehaven Corporation. *Presentation of the freedom of the borough to the Right Hon. The Viscount Nuffield, G.B.E., O.B.E., F.R.S., and the Right Hon. the lord Adams, O.B.E., J.P., M.A., C.A., Thursday, 9 April 1953.* 1953.

Whitehaven Corporation. *Presentation of the honorary freedom of the borough to Frank Schon, Esq., and Frederick Marzillier, Esq., Thursday, 23 March 1961.* 1961.

Whitehaven Corporation. *Whitehaven, 1894-1954.* Compiled by Daniel Hay. 1954.

Whitehaven Review: the quarterly bulletin of the Whitehaven Public Library. 1947-1949.

Whitehaven Scientific Association. *Annual Journal,* No. 1-15. 1898-99 to 1912-13.

Willans, T. S. *The English coasting trade, 1600-1750.* 1938.

Williams, J. R. *The Whitehaven News, 1852-1952, an outline of history.* 1952.

Williams, L. A. *Road transport in Cumbria in the nineteenth century.* 1975.

Index

Illustrations numbered in italics

Acton, Pte Abraham, V.C. 88, *88*
Acton, Memorial to 88, *88*
Adair, John M'Leven 187
Adams, John Jackson, First Baron, of Ennerdale 128, 167-9, *167*
Aerial view of Whitehaven *by Roger Savage, Frontispiece*
Albright and Wilson Ltd 135-40
Aldermen 84-7
Aldermen, Honorary 90
Alsop, John 176
Alsop, William 186
Alsop, William Leigh 176
American War of Independence 28, 33, 65, 68
Anderson, Frank, M.P. 128
Annals of the Four Masters 11
Anti-slavery notice *163*
Armstrong, Samuel 186
Arrowthwaite, Margaret of 15
  Maurice of 15
  Nigel of 15
  Reginald of 15
Arrowthwaite, manor of 15
Artists 171-8
Assemblies of God 118-119

Bain, Sir James 53
Baines, Peter 137
Banks, Robert 186
Banks, Thomas Lewis 177
Bateman, John 47, 50, 51
Bateman pit 43
Beacon Mills 141, *141*
Bearmouth pit 45
Beaver and Dawley 50
Bentinck, G. A. F. Cavendish, M.P. 71, 103, 105
Blackburn, Thomas 169, 170
Booksellers bookplates *187*
Border Engineering Contractors Ltd 145
Border Regiment, The 87, 88
Borough boundary 86
Bourne, Peter 51,52
Bousfield, John 174
Boustead, Thomas 186
Bowes, William 67
Bransty Arch *43*, *147*
Brethren, *see* Christian Brethren
Briscoe, Francis 186
Briscoe, Joseph 186
Brockbank's fish shop, c. 1840 *61*
Brocklebank, Daniel 65, 67
Brocklebank, John 66
Brocklebank, Thomas 66
Brocklebank, Thomas and John 70,71
Brown, Edith, D.B.E. 164, 165
Brown, Edith, D.B.E. *164, 165*
Brownrigg, William 44, 46, 156, 157
Brunlees, Sir James 76, 77
Bulwark 74, 83

Callander, James William 187
Carlyle, Dr Alexander 24
Chaloner, Thomas 19
  Sir Thomas 20, 39
Chamberlain, Alfred 177, 178
Christ Church 106, 107
  clergy 107
Christian, John 39, 48, 49
Christian Brethren 102, 111
Chronicon Cumbria 13
Civic Hall 99, 101
  H.M. Queen Elizabeth II at the *100*
  Official opening by H.R.H. the Duchess of Kent *100*
Clark, John E. 142
Clementson, John 174
Coach Road council houses under construction *144*
Coal Industry Nationalisation Act 58
Coal mining 16, 39-60
Coalgrove pit 45
Coal seams 40
Coat of arms of borough 85
Coleman, Ann Raney 161, 162
Colliery Mission 28, 108
Collingwood, Sir E. F. 180, *180*
Collins, Henry 174
Coltness Iron Co. Ltd 57
Congregational Church 110
  ministers 110
  order of final service *110*
Copeland Borough Council 89, 90, 99
Copperas works 28, 41, 42
Corson, James 176
Cotton, Thomas 184
Coulthard, William 67
Countess of Huntingdon's Connexion 109, 110
Countess pit 51
Coupland, Barony of 13, 15
Coutts, Alexander 185
Cowen, Thomas 69
Cribb, Adrian 187
Croft pit 46, 51-4
Crosthwaite, John 187
Cumberland Chronicle and Whitehaven Public Advertiser 185
Cumberland Coal Company (Whitehaven) Ltd 57
Cumberland Curled Hair Manufacturing Co. Ltd 141, 143
Cumberland Development Council Ltd 128, 168, 169
Cumberland Magazine, or Whitehaven Monthly Miscellany 186
Cumberland Motor Services Ltd 146, 147
  early buses *146*
Cumberland Newspapers Ltd 187
Cumberland Pacquet 51, 65, 67, 68, 92, 174, 185

Cumberland Pacquet – masthead *185*
  – printing works *186*
Cumbria Area Health Authority 182, 183
The Cupola *91*

Daniel, William, *View of the harbour, 1816 Cover illustration*
Davidson, Councillor John D. *87*
Davy lamp 44
Davy pit 48
Daysh, G. H. J. 169
Defoe, Daniel 29, *29*
De Gara, T. L. 129
Detergents and Chemicals Group 139
Distington Crematorium *146*
Dixon, John 187
Dixon, Dr Joshua 46, 157, 178
  Life of William Brownrigg – title page *46*
  portrait *46*
Dixon (Holdings) Ltd, Peter 143
Donnison, William 186
Duke pit 52, 53, 99
Dunn, Brownrigg 185
Dunn, John 185

Edgard and Sons (London) Ltd, H. 140
Edgard's factory – interior *140*
Education 123, 124
Egremont Tubes Ltd 143
Eilbeck, Robert 70
Electricity supply 95, 96
Election posters *84*
Elections – parliamentary 196-8
Elim Pentecostal Church 119, 120
  ministers 120
Ennerdale, chapel at 102
  manor of 14
Ennerdale Lake 83, 94
Excursion poster *80*

Fagandini, Dr D. A. A. 137
Farrington, Joseph 25, *Fly leaves*
Fish Quay 75
FitzDuncan, William 14, 15
Flatt, The 21, 31, 42
Fleming, Christina 16
  Hugh 16
Fletcher, Abraham 184
Fletcher, Isaac 46, 49
Forts 34, *36*, 36, 38
Foster, Allason 185
Foster, Robert 186
Franklin, Benjamin 34
Freemen of the borough 87-9
Friends, Society of 102, 110, 111
Furness Railway 81

Gale coat of arms *28*
Gale family 27, 28, 41, 43, 82, 83, 102

Gaythorp, William 176
  Whitehaven Castle 31
Gibson, Elizabeth 102
Gibson, Robert 186
Gill, William 187
Gilpin, John Bernard 171
  William 27, 42, 43, 83, 171
Ginns 28, 29, 41, 61, 91, 92
Ginns pit 42
Glasson, William 144
Greenbank colliery 42, 43
Grindal, Edmund, abp. 151, 152, *151*
Guibal fan 52
Gunning, Robert Bell 176

Hadwen, Benjamin 64
Haig pit 50, 54, 57-9, 60, 192, 203, 204
Haig pit *58*
Half Moon Battery 34, 37, 38
Hamilton, Dr John *179*
Harbour Commissioners' coat of arms
  77
Harbour, engraving of, *circa* 1840 *74*
Harbour statistics — exports *190*
  — imports *191*
Hardy, Robert 83
Harper, Matthew 52
Harras, Adam of 15
Harrington 30, 70, 80
Harrington No. 11 59, 192
Harrison and Younghusband 67
Hartley, Thomas 179
Hartley House, Marlborough Street *75*
Health Report, 1863 *97*
Heard, Joseph 175
Henry pit 52, 53
Hensingham 86, 87, 95, 106, 113
Herd, Richard 176
Heslop engine 48, 49, 50, *50, 60*
High Street Presbyterian Church 109
Hill, N. E. L. 142
Hinde, Henry 171
Hinde, Joseph 171
Hodgson, Joseph 158, 159, *158*
  — publications *158*
Hodgson, Oliver Ussinon 175
Hogarth, James 91, 97, 179, *112*
  Philosophy of — broadsheet 112
Hogarth Mission 112
Holden, Fr Gregory — funeral card *114*
Holy Trinity Church 30, 47, 51, 67
  102, *105*
  — clergy *105*
Homewood mansion 180
Hospital service 179-183
Hothwaite 14, 15
House building 98, 99
Howard, John, Street plan, 1790 *32*
Howgill colliery 40-3, 46, 47, 51
Howgill Street theatre — playbill *121*
Howgill surface incline 51
Howgill staith 51
Huddart, William 70
Incorporation of borough 84, 88
Industries, twentieth century 128-50
Infirmary 179
Irish Street Senior School — official
  opening *124*

Jackson, Henry 67
James, Frank 142
James pit 42, 51, 53
Jars, Gabriel 46

Jefferson, J. H. *149*
  Robert 187, *149*
  Robert and Henry 148-50
  advert *148*
John Gaskell Court flats: official
  opening by H.R.H. Princess
  Alexandra *101*
Jollie's Directory 67
Jones, John Paul 33, 36, 37, *33*

Kells Miners' Welfare 97
Kells pit 48, 49, 52, 53
Kelsick, Richard 28
Kennedy, Lumley 66, 70
Kenworthy, John Dalzell 177
  — self-portrait *177*
Kirk, Thomas 67-9
Kirk Mission 109
Kirkbride Engineering Co. Ltd 146
Knockmurton pit 41

Lady pit 48
Lady pit pottery 126
Ladysmith pit 53, 57, 60, 131
Langton, Nicholas 15, 38
Lattera colliery 42
Lawson, John James, First Baron,
  of Beamish 161, *161*
Leslie and Sons, James 143, 144
Litt, William 157, 158
  — poem *157*
Liverpool 23, 29-30, 61, 63
Local government 82-101
Local Government Acts, 1858, 1861 94
Local Government Act, 1972 89, 90, 97
Local Government Board 94
Local government wards 84, 90
Logan, Caird 76
London, shipping 29, 63
Lorenz, Lincoln 34-6
Low Wreah pit 49
Lowca Iron Works 48
Lowry, Strickland 171
  Wilson 171
Lowther coat of arms *20*
Lowther Hall 25
Lowther, Sir Christopher, of
  Whitehaven 20, 21, 23, 27, 36, 39,
  42, 74
  Elizabeth 21
  George 20
  Gerard 20
  Sir Gervase de 20
  Henry, Third Viscount Lonsdale 24-5
  Henry, Third Earl of Lonsdale 26,
  26, 46
  Hugh Cecil, Fifth Earl of Lonsdale
  26, *26*, 85, *83*
  Sir Hugh de 20
  Sir James, later Earl of Lonsdale 24
  25, 31, 44, 91
  Sir James, Seventh Earl of Lonsdale
  26, 85
  Sir James, of Whitehaven 23, 28, 36,
  39, 42-4, 46, 82, 83
  — crypt screen *30*
  — portrait by Richardson *23*
  Sir John, of Lowther 20, 21
  of Whitehaven 20, 21, 23, 27, 30,
  40-2, 64, 82, 91
Lowther, Katherine 21
  Sir Richard 20
  Robert, of Maulds Meaburn 24

St George Henry, Fourth Earl of
  Lonsdale 26, *26*
Sir Thomas de 20
Sir William of Holker 24
Sir William of Swillington, First Earl
  of Lonsdale 20, 25, *25*
  William, Second Earl of Lonsdale 25,
  25, 80, 81
Lowther Street *82*
Lutwidge coat of arms *28*
Lutwidge family 27-9
Lutwidge, Thomas 186
Lyon, G. E. E., Town Clerk *90*
Lyon, Fr Paulinus — celebrating mass
  116

McAllister, John 53, 86
Mace *85*
McGill, Henry 90
McGowan, William 187
Mannix and Whellan 11, 37, 38
Marchon Division 137
Marchon France 137
Marchon Italiana 136-8
Marchon-Paragon Holdings (Pty) Ltd
  139
Marchon Products Ltd 79, 85, 131-4
Marchon works *131*
Marchon works — H.R.H. Princess Mary
  at *133*
  H.R.H. the Duke of Edinburgh at
  134
Mardon Packaging International 143
Markets 17, 27, 40
Martin, R. F. 52
Martindale, Roger 64
Maryland 23
Maryport 30, 63, 65
Maryport and Carlisle Railway 81
Marzillier, Frederick 131, 132
Masheder, William 184
Mayoral chain *85*
Meadow View House 180
Merchants' Quay 75
Meschin, Ranulf 13, 14
Meschin, William 13, 14
Methodist church 111-3
  — ministers 113
Middleton, William 70
Milburn, Thomas 145, 146
Miller, John Fletcher 163, 164
Mining disasters — list of victims 199-206
Mining statistics 192
Moon, Michael 188
  — logogram *188*
Moore, R. W. 46, 51, 84
Moss, W. H. 186
Mounsey, John 172, 174
  Ship in foreign waters 173
Mount Pleasant 29, 61, 91-3, 97
Mulcaster, Henry 52
Multi-storey car park 101
Multon, Thomas de 15, 19
Multon, de — coat of arms *15*
Municipal insignia 85
Murphy, Denis Brownell 175
Museum 96, 172, 175
Museum catalogue *96*
Musgrave, John *84*

National Coal Board 58, 59
National strike 55, 79
Nef, Dr 39
Nelson, George 177

New Houses 29, 61, 91, 93, 97
New Houses *93*
New Quay 75
Newcomen, Thomas 43, 44
Newtown 96
Nicholson and Peile 38
Nicholson, Samuel 67
North Pier 75
    Lighthouse *76*
North pit 52
Nuffield, Lord 57, 87
North Wall 75
Nutter, Henry 172
    Matthew Ellis 172
    William 172
    William Henry 172

Old New Quay 75
Old Quay 75
Old Tongue 75
Oppenheim, Kurt 141

Page, R. Arnot 57
Pagen, William 187
Palmer, William 64, 65
Parker pit 41
Partis pit 40
Parton drifts 51
Parton harbour 42
Parton shipping 30
Pattinson, John 141, *141*
Paul, John *see* Jones, John Paul
Pears, Anthony Benson 160
    John H. 161
Peile, John 38, 51, 70
Petrus Pindarus, Secundus 154, 155
    Poetical Epistle title page *47*
Population statistics 23, 29, 61, 194
Potteries 63, 125-7
Pottery *125-7*
Pow Beck 30, 41, 83
Presbyterian church 27, 109
    – ministers 109
Preston Quarter 84, 86, 92
Priestgill colliery 41
Priestman (Whitehaven) Collieries Ltd
    57
Privateers 25
Public Baths Co. Ltd 96
Public Health Act, 1848 92, *96*
Public Library 96

Quaker Oats Ltd 141
Queen's Dock 74, 76, 77

Railways 80, 81, *81*
Ravenhill pit and wagon-way 41
Rawlinson, Sir Robert 92, 93, 97
    Report title page *92*
Ray, James 36, 152, 153
    Acts of the Rebels, title page *152*
Read, Matthias 23, 30, 41, 171
    *Bird's Eye View of Whitehaven,
    1738 24*
Rennie, Sir John 75, 76
Richard, of Whitehaven, chaplain 16, 102
Richardson, Jonathan, artist *23*
Richardson's pottery 126, 127
Roach, John 155, 156, 186
Robertson, E. S. 187
Robson, J. and W. Ltd 144
Roman Catholic churches 113-8
Rook, John 176
Rook, William H. 176

Rosehill theatre 130
    – interior *130*
Rowe, Martin 138, 140
Royal Society 44, 46

St Andrew's Mirehouse 108
    – clergy 108
St Bees Grammar School 39, 45, 52, 53
St Bees, priors 18, 19
    priory 11, 13, 14, *14*, 39
    cross fragments *12, 13*
St Begh's church 114, 115
    – clergy 115
St Benedict's church, Mirehouse 117,
    117
St Helen's colliery 59
St James' church 30, 51, 102, 105,
    106
    – clergy 106
St John's church, Hensingham 106
St Mary's church, Kells 115, 116
    – interior *116*
St Nicholas church 27, 42, 68, 102,
    103, *103, 104*
    – clergy 105
St Paul, Sisters of 118
St Peter's church, Kells 107
    – clergy 108
Salmon, Robert 172
Salt making 14
Saltom pit 40, 42, 44-6, 51-3, *45*
Salvation Army 119, 120, *120*
Sandwith 12
Sankey award 54
Schon, Frank 131, 132
    knighted 137; Peerage 137, *137*
Scot, Alexander, master of *Mariote* 17
Scott, John 69
Seaton Iron Works 48, 50
Secher, Otto 137
Sekers, Sir Nicholas 129, 130
Sekers Silk Mills *128, 129*
Shepherd, James 67
Shepherd, Joseph 70
    W. 184
Shipbuilding 23, 64-73
Shipping 29, 61, 63, 78
Ships:
    Alexander 66
    Alfred 34
    Alice A. Leigh 71, *72*
    Ant 67
    Banterer, H.M. brig 68
    Baroda 66
    Beckermet 70
    Betsey 33
    Blengfell 71
    Boyne, painting by William Jackson
    65, 172
    Busk 141
    Calder 70
    Candida 71
    Carson 66
    Cassiope 71
    Castor 66, 67
    Clarendon, 68
    Clint 141
    Cookson 65
    Cyrus 66, 67
    Dale 67
    David Shaw 173
    Davina 67
    Dunboyne 71, *178*
    Earl of Lonsdale 68

    Eleanor Dixon 69
    Eliza 66
    Elizabeth Buckham 69, 70
    Englehorn 71
    Favourite 175
    Friendship 33
    Galgate 71
    Gilcrux 71
    Grasmere 71
    Greta 71
    Hartley 65, 172
    Hope 67
    Isabel 71
    John 33, 67
    John o' Gaunt 70
    John Scott 175
    Julius Caesar 69
    King George 33
    Kitty 65
    Lady Gordon 66
    Lord Shaftesbury 71
    Lowther Castle 70
    Marchon Enterprise 79, 135, *136*
    Marchon Trader 135
    Marchon Venturer 136
    Maria 70
    Mariote 17
    Mary 67
    Mary and Betty 65
    Nancy 68
    Neptune 68
    Odin 135
    Patterdale 71
    Phoenix 66
    Pollux 66
    Precedent 66
    Prince Regent 67
    Princess Charlotte 68, 174
    Ranger 34
    Refuge painting by Charles de Lacy 77
    Resolution 28
    Rydalmere 71
    Sarah 70
    Silverhow 71
    Sovereign 66, 68
    Superior 69
    Thirlmere 71, *71*
    Thompson 35
    Two Friends 33
    Urania 68
    Wasdale 71
    Wellington 69
    Whitehaven 67
    Whitehaven, steam tug 77
    Whitehaven Lass 72
    Windermere 71
Sibson, Thomas 64
Siddick colliery 59
Silk mills 129, 130
Six Quarters Band colliery 41
Smirke, Sir Robert 25, 96
Smith, 'Bully' 55
Smith Brothers (Whitehaven) Ltd 188
Smith and Son Ltd, W. H. 187
Smith William 186
Solway anhydrite mine, visit by H.R.H.
    the Duke of Edinburgh *134*
Solway Chemicals Ltd 134
Solway colliery 59
Soup kitchen *56*
South Beach Recreation Area 99, 101
South Cumberland Water Board 94
South East Prospect, 1642 16
Spedding family 27, 41-4, 46, 47

Spedding, James and Co. 66-8
Spedding, steel mill *44*
Steam engines 48
Steel, James 186
Stephenson, George 51, 80, 81
Stitt, William 68
Stone pit 42
Stout and Sons Ltd, J. 146-8
Street Plan 1815 *62*
Strikes 53-5
Stute, Alan 17
    Alexander 17
Sugar Tongue 75
Sumner (Holdings) Ltd, Francis 140
Swift, Jonathan *153*, 153, 154

Tannery *166*
Tenneco Incorporated 140
Theatres 121, 122
    – playbills *121, 122*
Thompson, J. R. 77
Thompson, William, Abp. 159, 160
Tickell, Thomas 43
Tobacco trade 23, 27, 28
Todd and Son, George 188
    Printing works *188*

Town and Harbour Trustees 23, 36-8
    51, 67, 74-7, 82, 83, 85, *91*, 91-6
Town Centre Redevelopment Committee
    99
Town Mission 108
Town Plan 1693, 1710, 1790 *21, 22, 32*
Township boundaries 13, 14
Turnpike Trust 83

United Reformed Church 108

Virginia 23, 27

Wade, John 142
    John C. *89*, 139, 142
    Freeman's scroll *89*
Wagons being loaded at South Harbour
    58
Wales, H.R.H. the Prince of Wales at
    Haig colliery *56*
Walker, Herbert Wilson *56, 165*, 165-7
Walker, Musgrave 68
Walkmill colliery 59
Ware, John 185
Washington family 207
Water Act, 1973 94

Water supply 94
Watson, William 49, 86
Watt, James 48, 49
Wear, Joseph 37
Wellington pit, 1910 *54*
Wellington pit disaster, 1910 – message
    board *55*
    – Rescue team *55*
    photographs of victims *202*
Welsh, John 186
West Cumberland Hospital – Aerial
    view *181*
    E. F. Collingwood, C.B.E.
        lays the foundation stone *180*
    H.M. Queen Elizabeth the Queen
        Mother at Official Opening *183*
Wetheral 13, 15
Wellington pit 45, 46, 51-4, *51, 54,
    55*, 57, 79, 99
West Cumberland Industrial
    Development Co. Ltd 145
West Cumberland Farmers, Trading
    Society Ltd 142
William Pit 59, *59*
Wyburg *19*